drawing trees

Step by Step

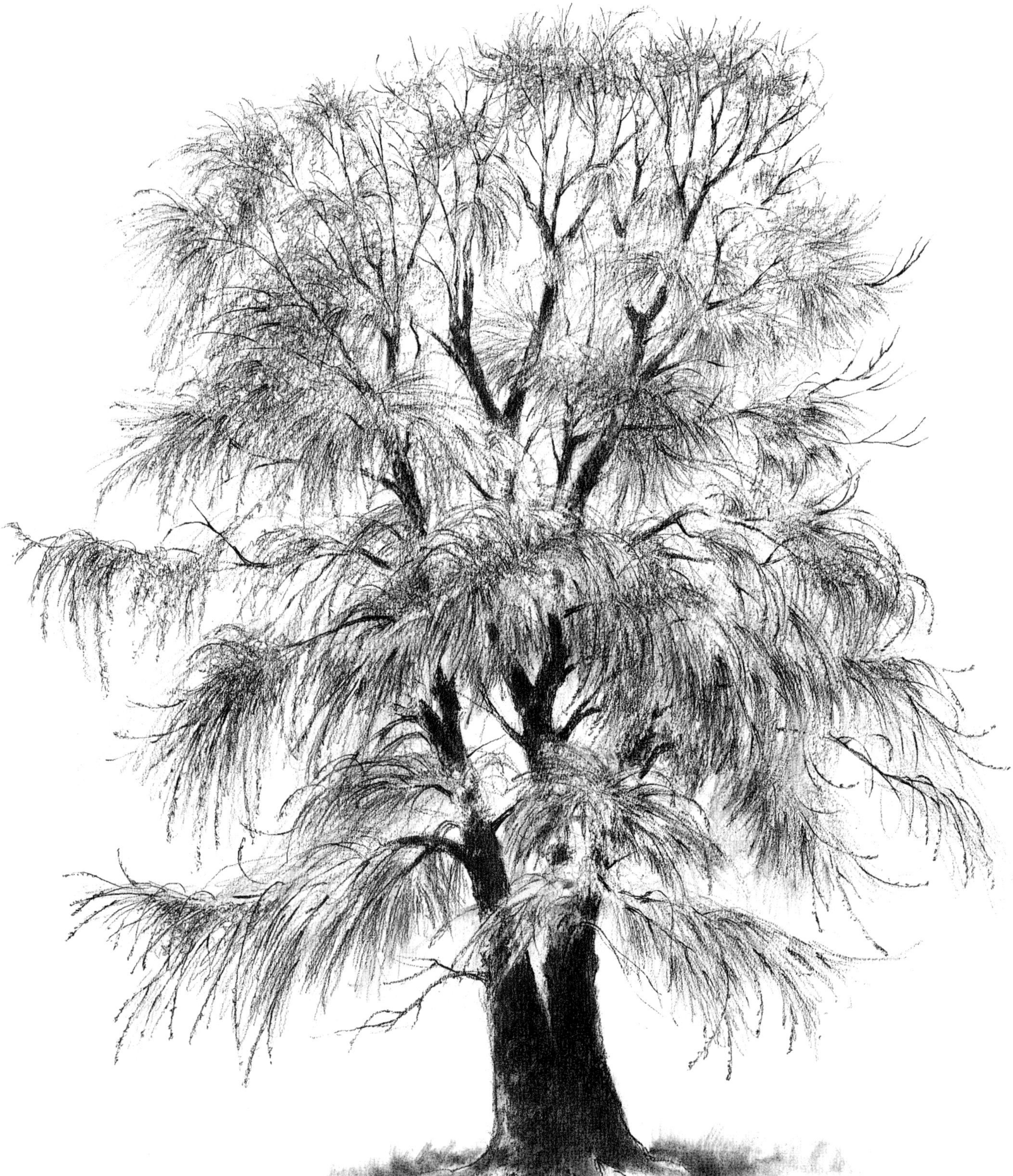

drawing trees

Step by Step

Stanley Maltzman

NORTH LIGHT BOOKS
Cincinnati, Ohio
www.nlbooks.com

ABOUT THE AUTHOR

Stanley Maltzman is a naturalist artist whose affection for working outdoors stems partially from his years in scouting and from living in the Hudson Valley region so rich in art history and scenery. Living in this environment makes it a natural for Maltzman to draw his inspiration from nature, and the drawings in this book attest to his love of this area and a willingness to share his knowledge with all.

Maltzman's drawings have been widely exhibited in museums and galleries around the country, including the American Academy of Arts and Letters, the National Academy of Design, the Elliot Museum and the Carnegie Museum of Natural History.

His strong belief that good painting evolves from the ability to draw well leads to frequent invitations to lecture and conduct his "plein air" seminars and workshops for high school and adult students. Maltzman teaches professionally at the Hudson River Workshops in Greenville, New York. He has been featured in the April 1986 issue of *American Artist* and is listed in *Who's Who in American Art*. Maltzman is a member of the Pastel Society of America and the Hudson Valley Art Association.

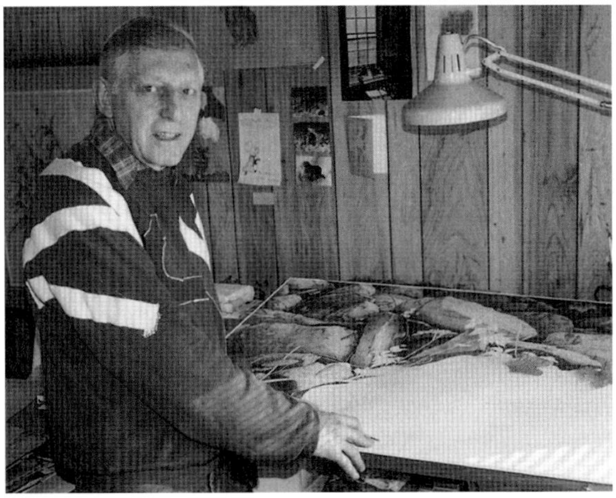

 Published by North Light Books, an imprint of F&W Publications, Inc., 1507 Dana Avenue, Cincinnati, Ohio 45207. (800) 289-0963. First edition.

Other fine North Light Books are available from your local bookstore, art supply store or direct from the publisher.

04 03 02 01 00 5 4 3 2 1

Library of Congress Cataloging-in-Publication Data
Maltzman, Stanley.
Drawing trees step by step. / Stanley Maltzman. - 1st ed.
p. cm.
Includes index.
ISBN 0-58180-015-0 (alk. paper) — ISBN 0-89134-885-9 (pbk. : alk. paper)
1. Trees in art. 2. Drawing — Technique. I. Title. II. Title: Drawing trees.
NC810.M36 1999 99-26559
743'.7-dc21 CIP

Editor Michael Berger
Production editor Amy J. Wolgemuth
Interior designer Leslie Meaux-Druley, Angela Lennert Wilcox
Cover designer Mary Barnes Clark
Production coordinator John Peavler
Interior production artist Joy Morell

DEDICATION

To my friend and patient companion,
my wife Rachel.

ACKNOWLEDGMENTS

Susan M. Story for her keen eye.

Dotsie Cook for her computer expertise.

The Bunzeys for their timesaving help.

The Greenville Library staff
for their friendly assistance.

The wonderful photography of
Jeannine Poulton,
Randy Williams &
Tom Tiech.

And...

The many wonderful people at North Light Books whom I never met, but know they are there. The layout people, the typographer and the production department, who start with piles of paper and end up with another great book — Thank You!

My appreciation to Rachel Wolf for giving me another opportunity to express myself. Most importantly, I'd like to thank my editor, Michael Berger, who brought the ship into port with a smile and a most admirable sense of professionalism.

Many thanks to all.

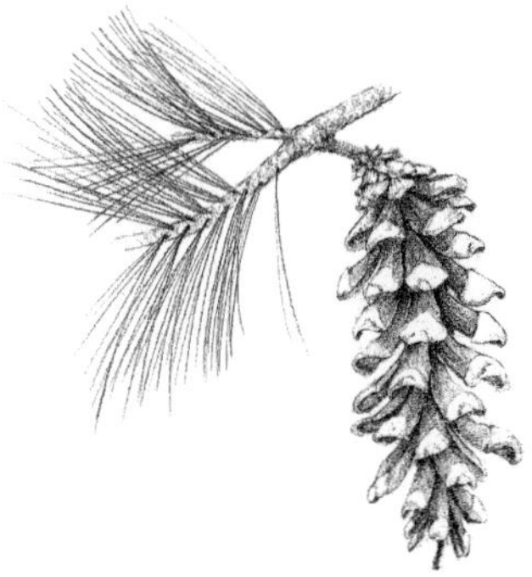

CONTENTS

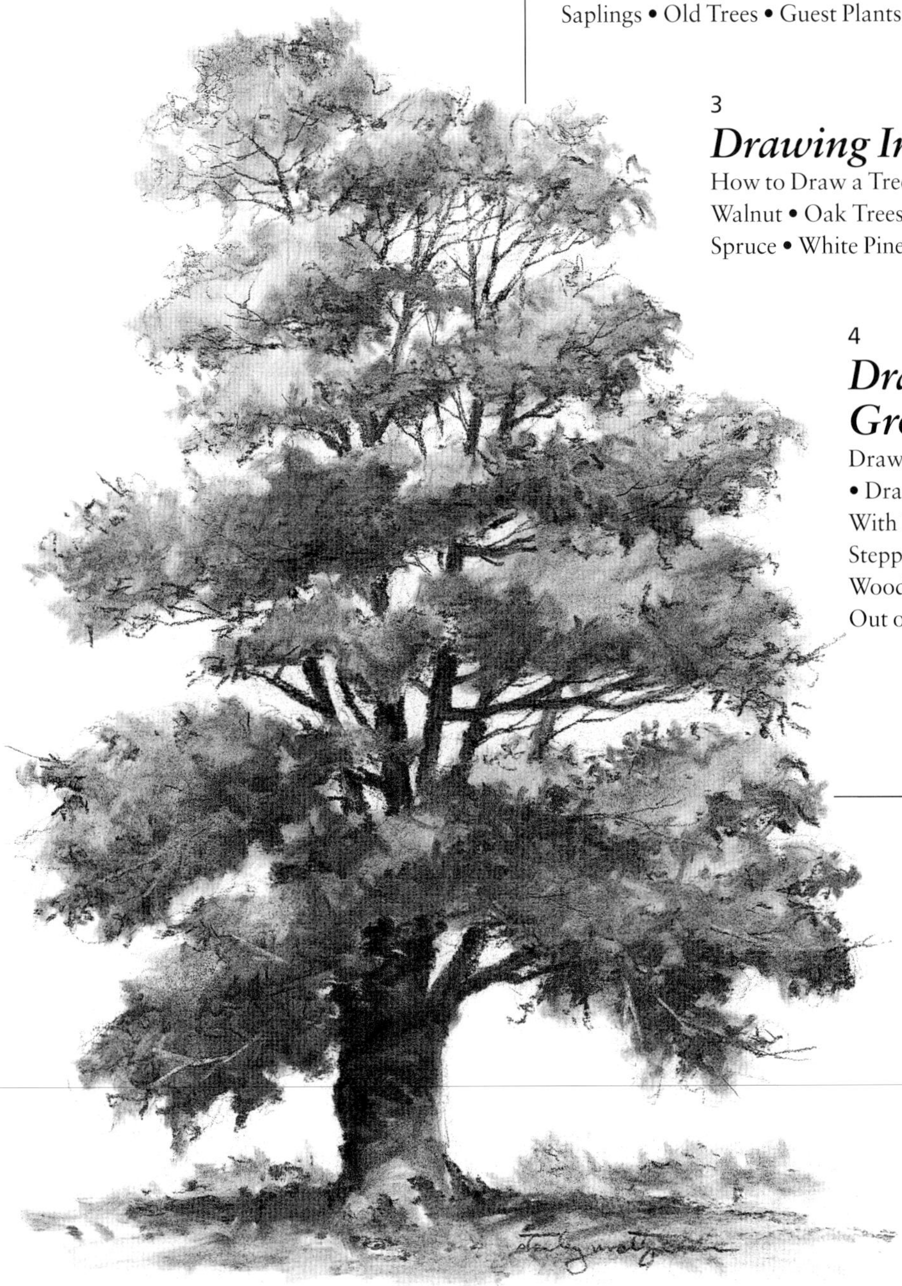

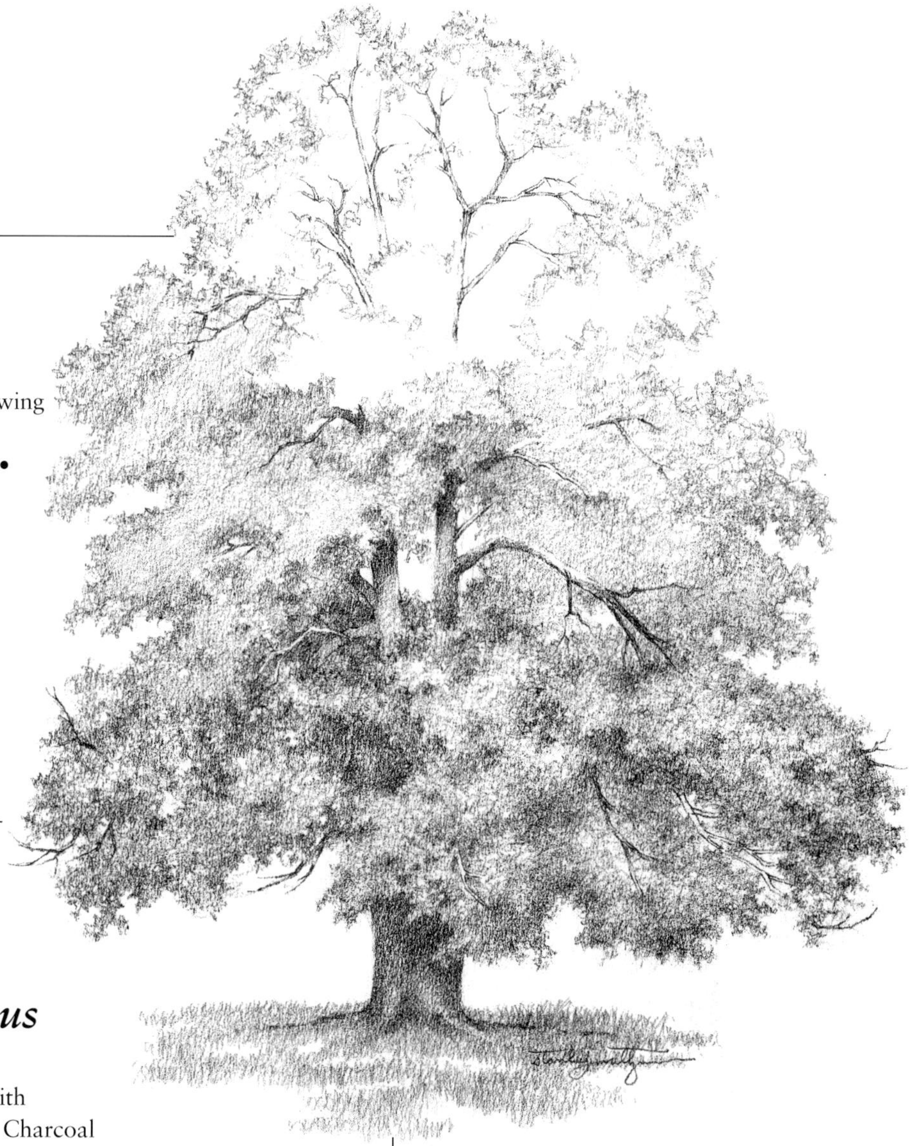

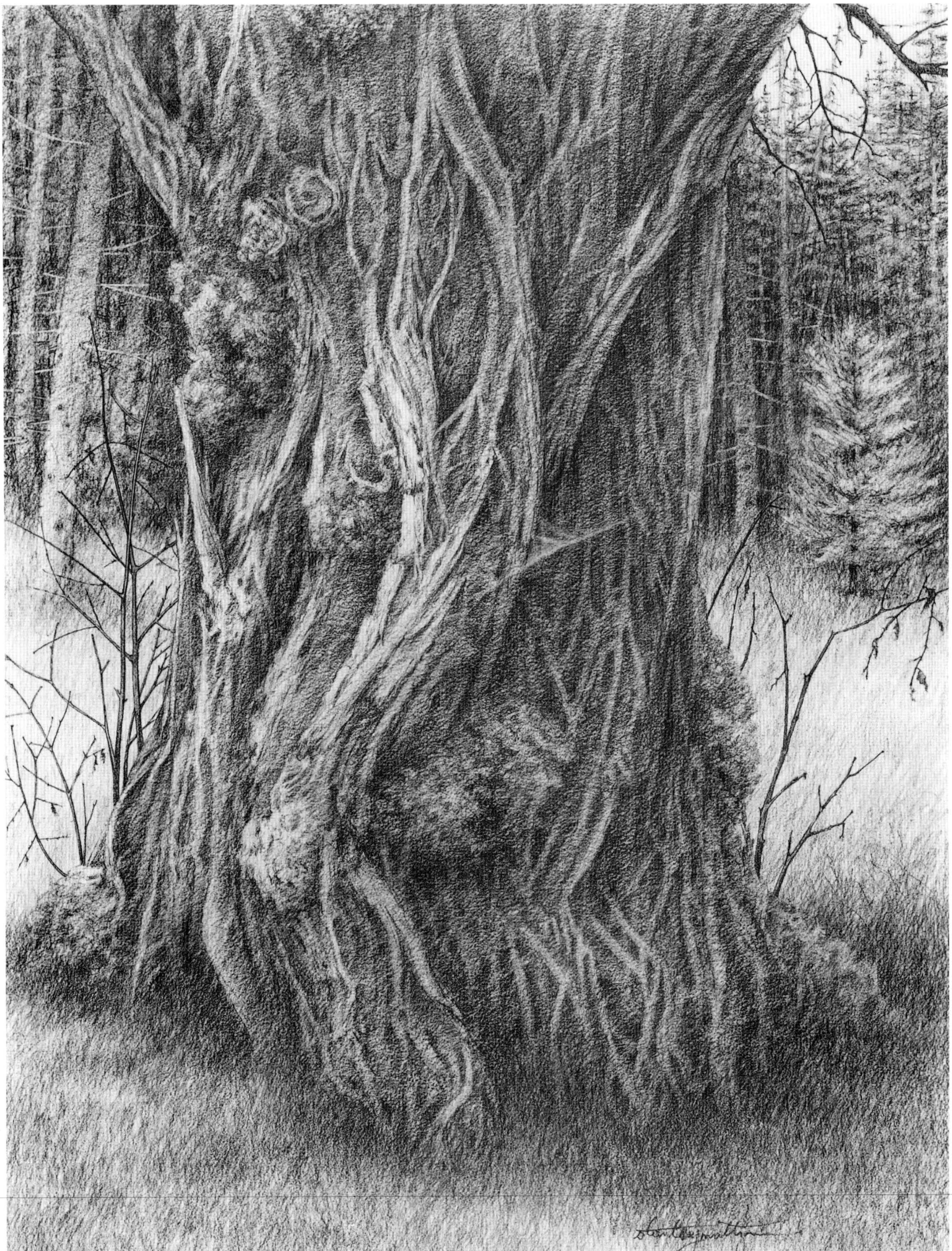

The Patriarch, 19" x 25" (48cm x 64cm), charcoal on handmade Twinrocker paper.

This tree, every green has a song. They have a language of their own. There's a life there. You say there is a chemistry language there. So each green has a song. There are a lot of songs we don't know yet. One man could never get to know all of them.

If you see a tree, it doesn't move. It doesn't talk or walk. You just see it. You just see a tree. That's all. But the trees talk. They have a language of their own.

— Black Elk

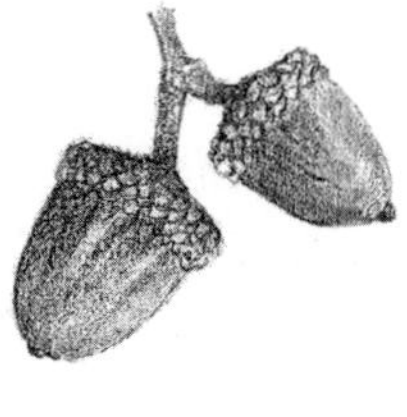

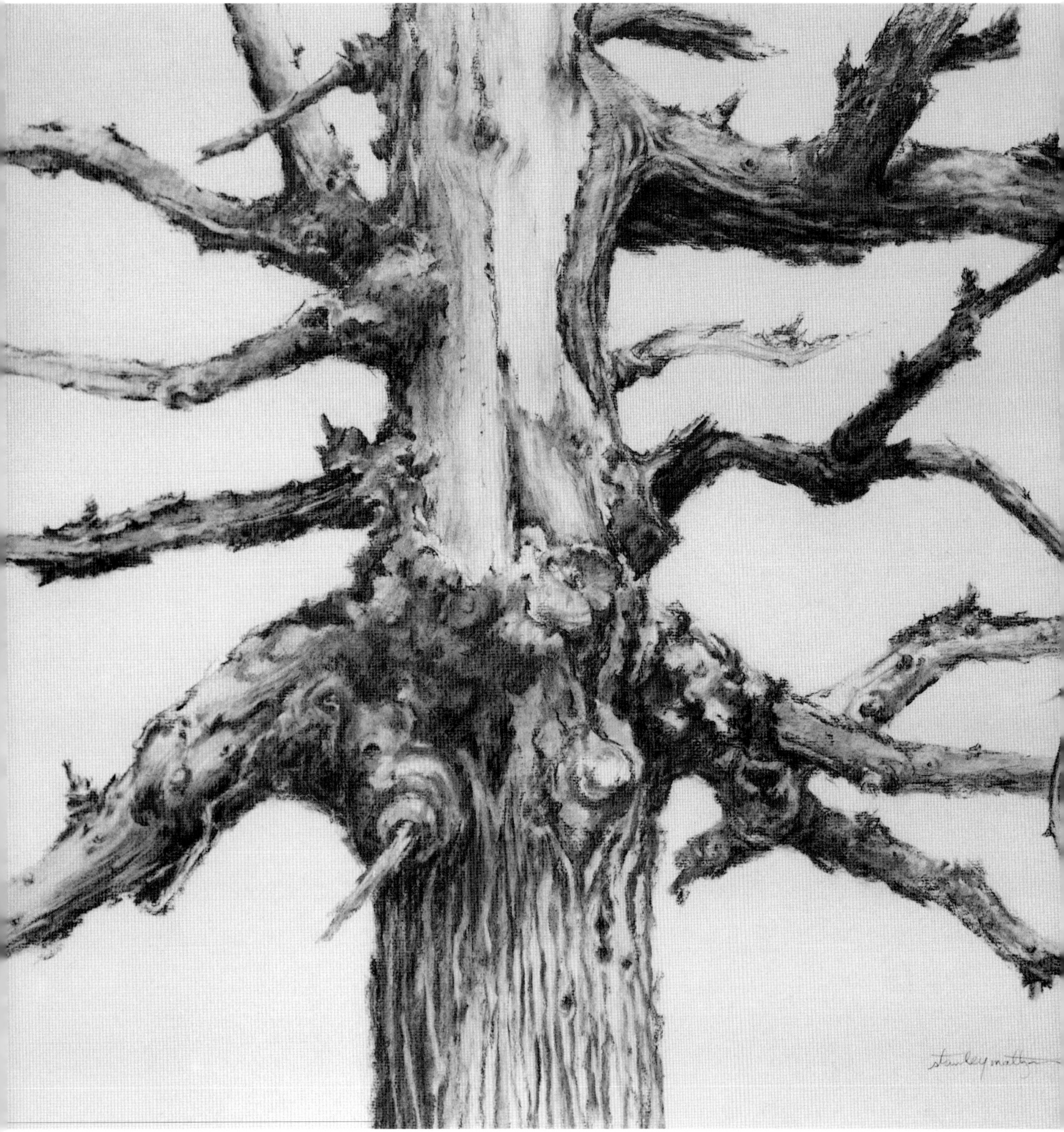

Sumi Warrior, 22" x 30" (56cm x 76cm), vine charcoal on handmade Irish paper.

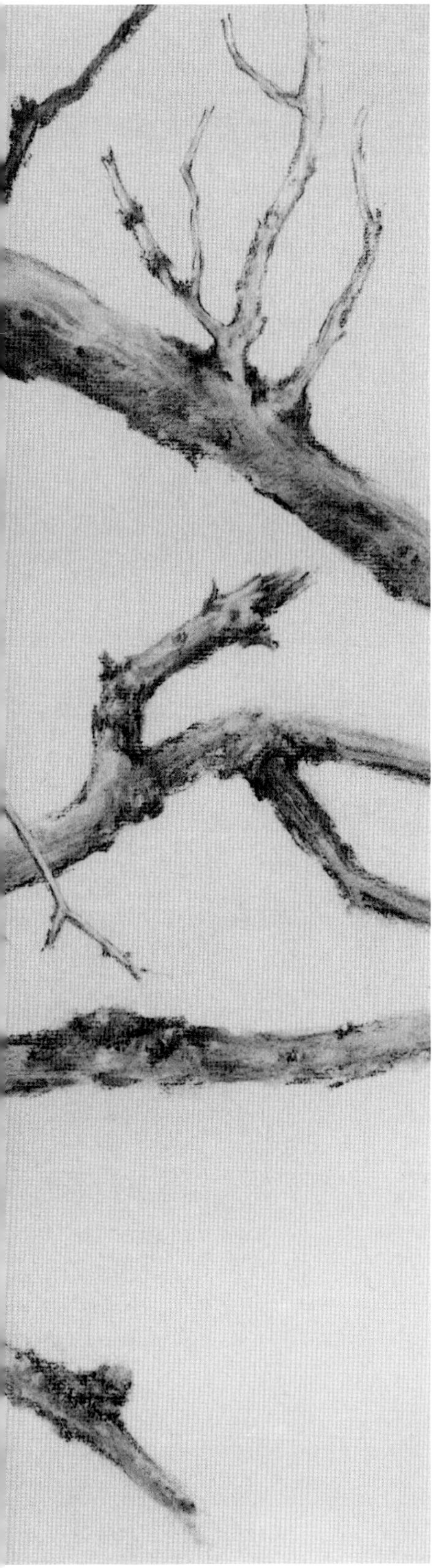

Introduction

Trees are, without a doubt, among my favorite subjects. To understand trees, to be able to adapt them to your work, you must realize that a tree is (or was) a living thing with living characteristics. Trees can suggest all kinds of ideas and designs just waiting to be incorporated into your work. To study and learn about these characteristics will make your artwork more interesting. This is one of the purposes of this book: to make you aware of trees and their potential.

One of the reasons trees are so popular is that they readily lend themselves to telling a story by showing the changing seasons, from the buds and flowers of spring to summer foliage and autumn color. But my favorite season is winter, when the trees have no foliage. It is when a tree's soul is bared that you can study its anatomy.

Have you ever noticed the giant trees in a George Innes landscape, or the shimmering, glowing trees of Charles Burchfield? Their studies of nature enabled them to successfully include trees in their work. This brings us to the main reason for this book: to study, understand and draw trees in their various environments, and to respect and preserve them for the future.

So let's gather our sketching gear, go out into the fields and woods, and meet the "quiet folk."

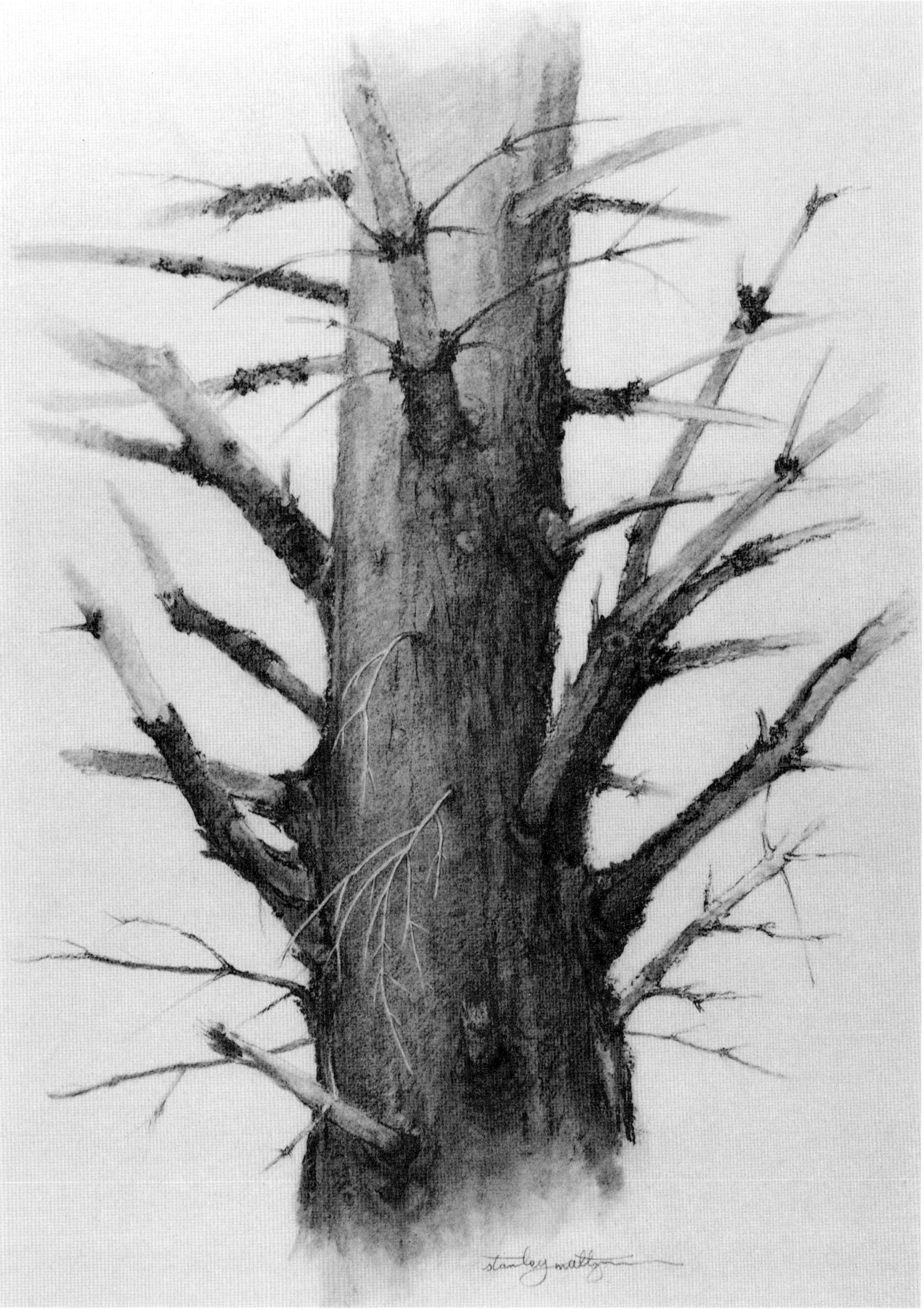

Pine Study, 12 ½" x 19" (32cm x 48cm), charcoal on Twinrocker handmade paper.

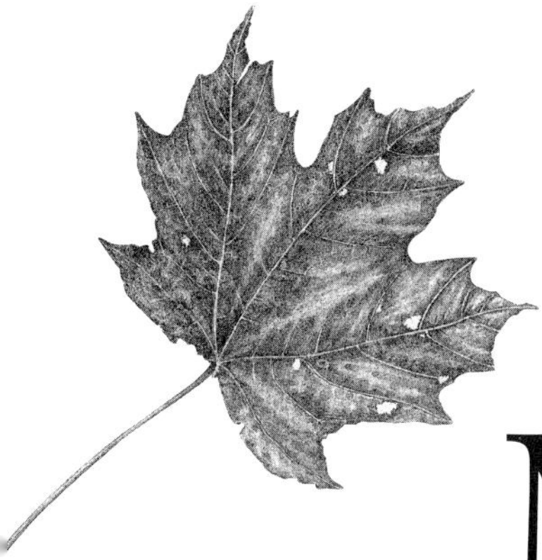

CHAPTER ONE

Getting Started

Making marks on a sheet of paper can be very exciting. The unlimited combinations of various mediums, together with a beautiful piece of handmade paper, can create a whole new world with countless possibilities for you. The following materials are but a small selection of the many supplies available for you to work with. While working, you may discover that you do not like the way a certain pencil reacts to your touch; that's fine — just try another. As you progress, you may find yourself visiting a local art store or thumbing through your favorite mail-order catalogs looking for something new to try. That's the way it should be. Always look for another mountain to climb. There are no hard-and-fast rules, and that is what will make your artwork more interesting and unique!

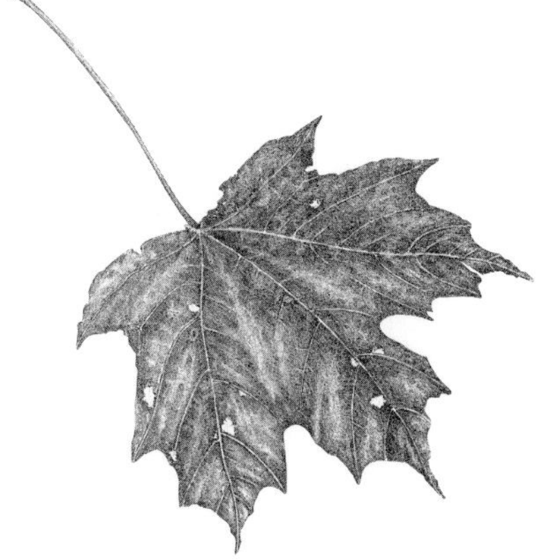

GRAPHITE PENCILS

One of the most familiar and accommodating tools available to the artist is the graphite pencil. It comes in various shapes and sizes, and is readily adapted to working indoors or out. To distinguish between a hard and soft lead, and to aid you in knowing what a particular pencil can do for you, each pencil has a number and letter stamped on it. The letter "H" stands for hard. H, 2H and 4H thru 9H indicates the degree of hardness: the higher the number, the harder the lead and the grayer the mark or value. Soft pencils are designated with a "B." Ranging from HB and 2B thru 9B, the higher the number, the blacker the mark.

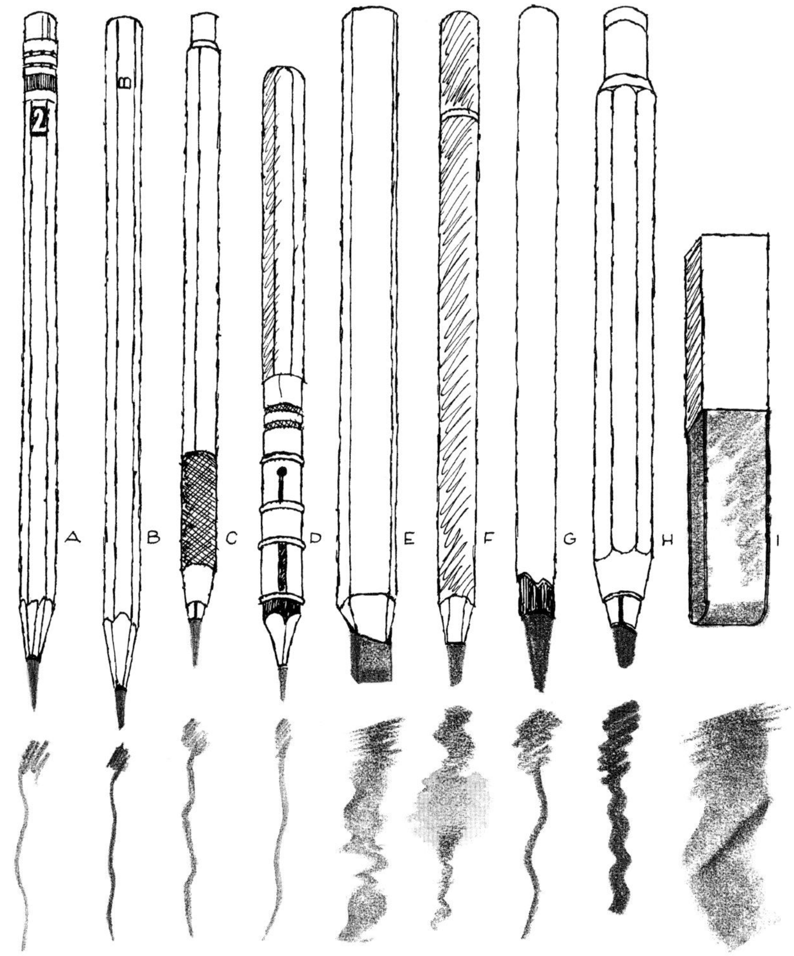

Graphite

This is a partial list of the different forms of graphite you might like to try.

A. Office or school pencil: good for sketching, but is not available in many degrees.

B. Artist's pencil: appears under various logos, but degrees of intensity should be similar from brand to brand.

C. Mechanical pencil: a convenient way to carry multiple degrees of thin leads, enabling you to change as needed.

D. Pencil extender: a versatile tool that lets you get that extra mile out of your favorite pencil.

E. Carpenter's pencil: a wide piece of graphite encased in ⅛-inch-thick wood; wonderful for laying in broad values.

F. Water-soluble pencils: a way for you to add another degree of excitement to your sketches. After drawing with it, go over the graphite with a brush dipped in water. Wherever the water touches the graphite, the water will break it down, creating a wash effect that can be reworked once dry.

G. Woodless pencils: graphite covered with a protective coat. They can be used thick and juicy for outdoor sketching, or can be sharpened to as fine a point as you desire.

H. ¼-inch mechanical pencil: one of my all-time favorites. Lead is available in varying degrees.

I. Graphite sticks: similar to carpenter's pencil, but a little wider and thicker, and not encased in wood. Wonderful for quick tonal indication.

CHARCOAL

Perhaps because it is so pliable, charcoal, in all its many forms, is one of the most enjoyable and exciting mediums to work with. You can blend it, push it around with your fingers or chamois cloth, lay in rich blacks or make beautiful silver grays without much effort. One of my favorites is a ¼-inch charcoal stick that fits into a metal or plastic holder — a wonderful sketching tool. You can also acquire sticks of compressed charcoal with carbon added, which produce greater coverage and richer blacks. There is also natural vine charcoal, which is easy to apply and blend. All forms are worth trying.

FIXING VINE CHARCOAL

A word of caution when spraying fixative over vine charcoal: because of the charcoal's softness, you should stand back at least 2' (61cm) and spray several times until it is fixed to your satisfaction.

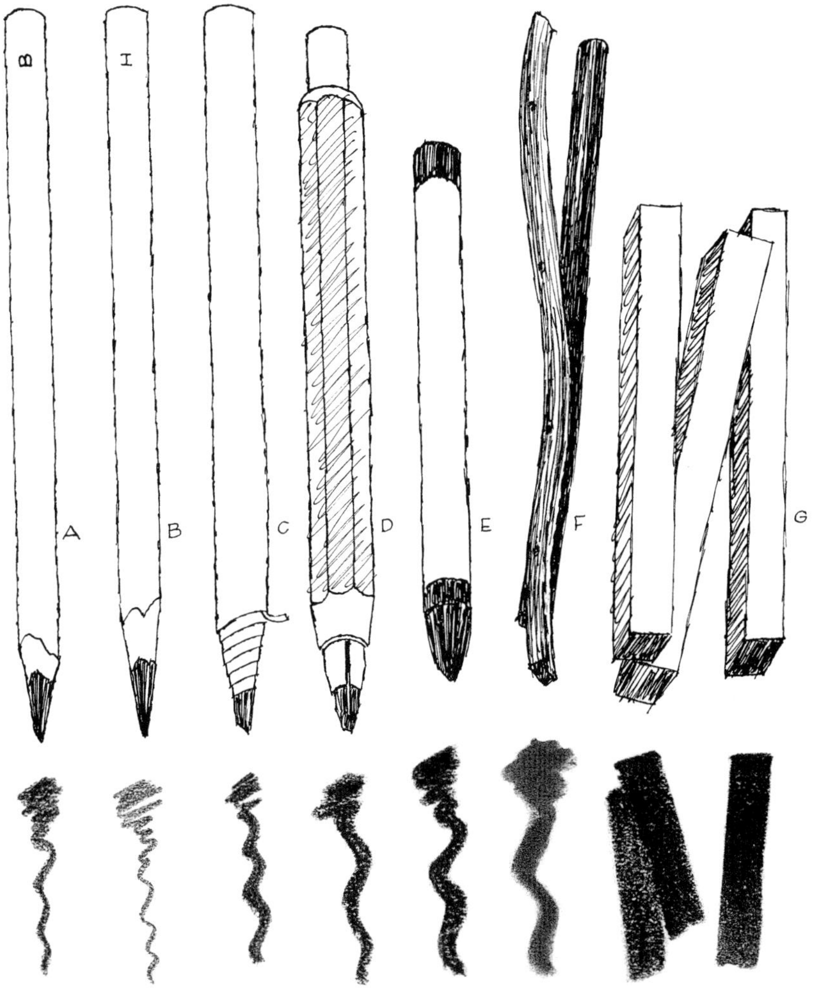

Charcoal
Here are some of the many varieties of charcoal for your drawing pleasure.

A. Soft charcoal pencil: good for sketching or finished work; degrees of softness will vary with manufacturer.
B. Hard charcoal pencil: good for laying in preliminary outlines.
C. Wrapped charcoal pencil: available in four degrees (H, medium, soft and extra soft). The charcoal is exposed by peeling away the paper pencil covering.
D. Charcoal holder: a very convenient method for carrying a sketching tool, as it keeps the charcoal from breaking and helps to keep things clean.
E. Compressed charcoal with carbon: gives wonderful rich blacks.
F. Vine charcoal: an absolute must; produces rich blacks to beautiful grays and also fine linear work.
G. Charcoal sticks: yet another form of compressed charcoal.

SKETCHBOOKS, PADS AND DRAWING BOARDS

An artist has many wonderful pads and sketchbooks to choose from. There are many great brands, such as Canson, Arches, Fabriano and Strathmore, and many different types, like spiral-bound or sewn sketchbooks. Using your sketchbook should become a part of your daily activity. Carry it with you, and fill it with sketches of everything in sight. For drawing pads, you can buy many papers in rolls and then cut them to whatever size you need (an economical way to go).

To make a drawing board, select a piece of ¼" (.64cm) plywood, Masonite or double-weight illustration board. Cut several different sizes so you will have a choice. Leave extra board, at least 2" (5cm) over size. Next tape some newsprint sheets to the board as shown in Figure F. This will provide you with some give beneath your pencil, so that you are not working on a hard surface. You will notice a marked difference if you try to sketch with paper underneath, as compared to drawing directly on top of the board.

Types of Sketchbooks
A. Spiral-bound top
B. Sewn-bound hard cover
C. Spiral-bound center
D. Illustration boards
E. Paper in rolls
F. Drawing board

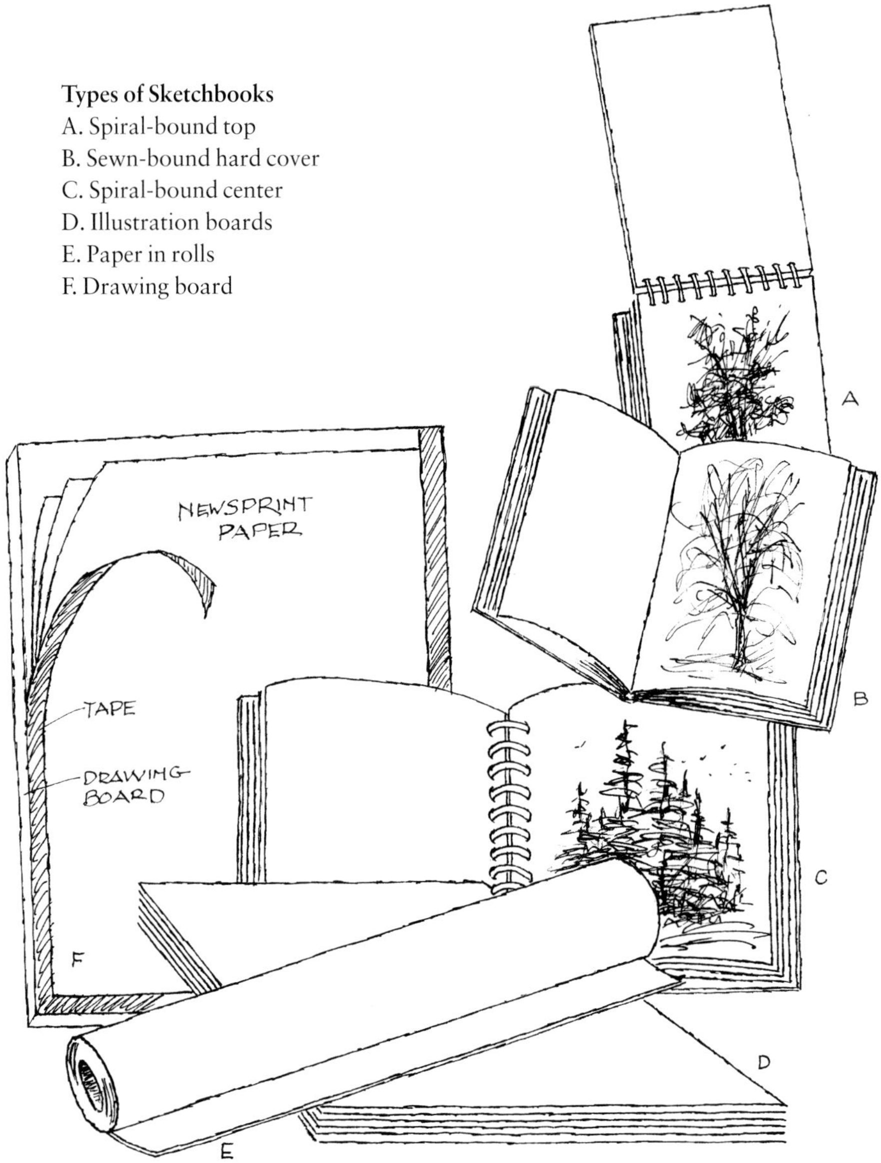

PAPER

One of the real pleasures you'll experience when drawing is discovering all the wonderful papers available to work with. Their different surfaces and colors will help to create various moods in your drawings. And though I won't go into great detail on papermaking, I do want to acquaint you with the various types of paper available.

Handmade Paper

With handmade paper, each sheet is individually created by a craftsman. It is recognizable by its four rough, ragged, deckled edges, so named because the frame around the edge of the mould is called a deckle. When some pulp gets caught between the mould and deckle, it forms a ragged deckled edge. To produce handmade paper, a mould (wooden frame with mesh) is dipped into a bath of pulp, then rocked and shaken to remove excess pulp and water. As the pulp settles against the mesh (usually wire) and the remaining water drains out, the fibers will dry, forming a solid sheet of paper. The thickness or weight of each sheet is determined by how much pulp settles against the mesh, and will vary according to the components of the initial mix (rags, plants, wood or whatever else is in the batch). The paper may also have sizing (or buffering) added, which helps control the acidity and keeps the paper from turning brown. This type of acid-free or archival paper is very important to artists.

Mould-Made Paper

Mould-made paper is made through a refined process where a cylinder mould machine revolves through a batch of fibers in a vat. As the mould turns, fibers adhere to a screen, which in turn places them on a belt that goes through a series of rollers which squeeze out the water. The result is then dried by heated metal cylinders. This method produces two deckled edges and watermarks. Some very fine papers, such as Arches, German Ingres, Rives BFK and Somerset, are made by this process.

Machine-Made Paper

Machine-made paper is produced by a Fourdrinier machine in a process in which the pulp is laid down on a fast-moving belt and run over the surface of steam-heated cylinders. The paper comes out dry and ready to be cut into various sizes. The Fourdrinier machine can also produce deckled edges which simulate handmade sheets. Some fine papers are made this way: Strathmore 400 Drawing, Rising Stonehenge, and Canson Mi-Teintes.

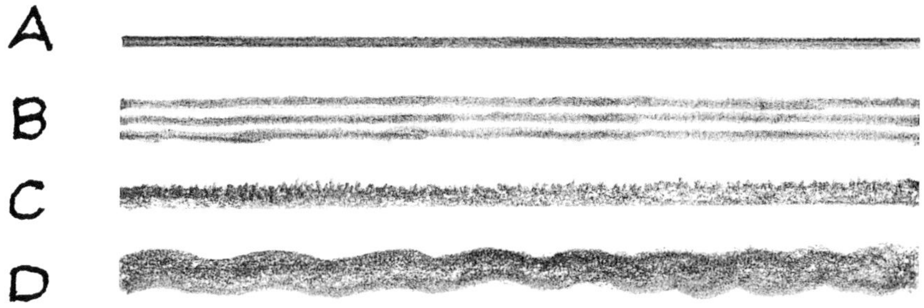

Paper Cross Sections

This diagram illustrates cross sections of the following paper types:

A. Plate finish: a smooth surface, good for detail and pen and ink.
B. Laid paper: has a pattern of lines created while being manufactured; good for reproduction.
C. Vellum or Bristol: has a little tooth; good for fine work and general drawing.
D. Rough paper: has deeper valleys and higher hills (diagram exagerated); works well with softer graphite or charcoal.

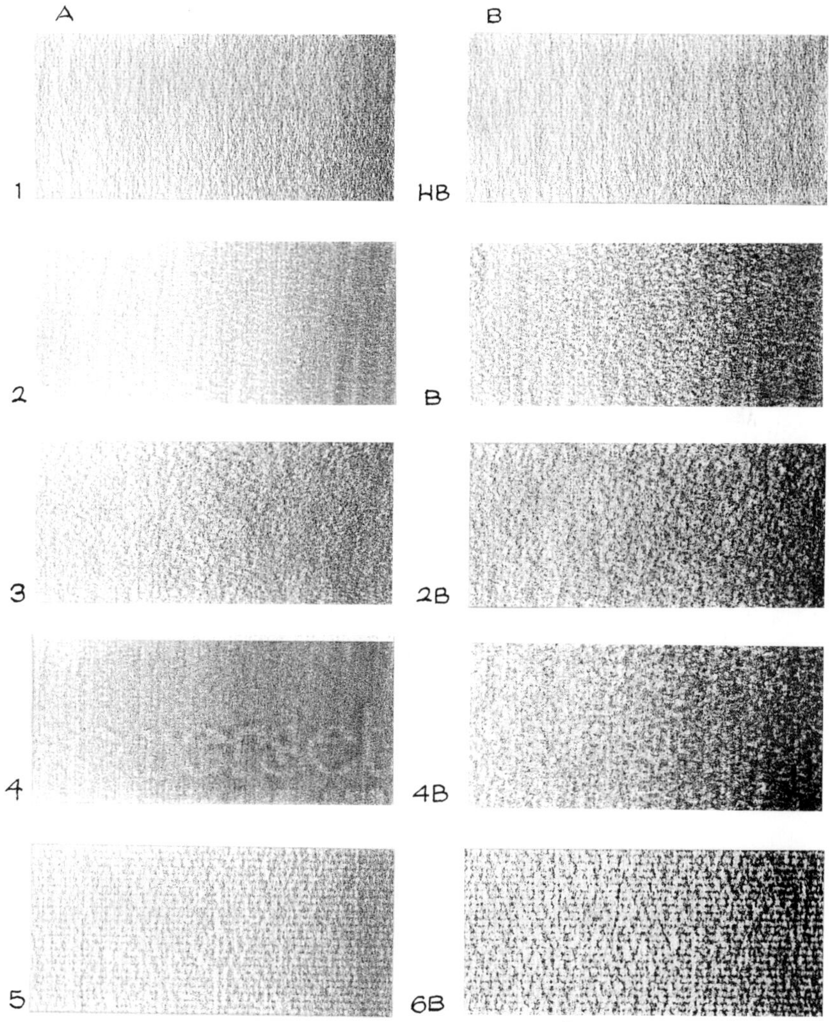

Paper Types

These are some of the papers you might want to experiment with. The papers in both columns are the same, but in column A, I used a graphite pencil, and in column B, a charcoal pencil. Notice the different densities, going from HB (hardest) to 6B (softest), and observe how the various pencils work on the different papers.

1. Strathmore Bristol
2. Museum board
3. Rives BFK
4. Somerset, textured (note watermark)
5. Arches Ingres

OTHER TOOLS

Along with pencils and paper, there are a few other handy items and tools you'll want to have.

Erasers

Though often necessary, erasers are not a must. You do not want to make a mark, erase it, make another, then erase it. The surface of your paper would become so disturbed that it would not take your pencil marks properly. Develop the habit of working lightly so that you can correct your work as you draw and cover your preliminary lines.

An especially handy eraser is the kneaded eraser. It can be squeezed and molded into any shape and be used to lift out tones or to highlight an area. Just press it against the area you want to lighten and lift. Remember to rub the eraser on another old sheet of paper to remove the residue you just lifted. Otherwise you will be putting back what you have just removed!

Sandpaper Block

The sandpaper block is a piece of wood about 7" (18cm) long with a pad of sandpaper sheets stapled to one end of the wood. Its main function is to sharpen your pencils and charcoal sticks after you have exposed the lead or charcoal with a razor or knife.

Stomps and Tortillions

Stomps are usually made from a heavy, felt-like paper rolled into the shape of a cigar with a point on both ends. Tortillions are smaller with only one pointed end. Both are good aids for making toned areas. A chamois or piece of soft tissue can also be used for toning or for correcting a specific area.

Fixative and Tape

Use a sprayable matte finish fixative to protect your work. Spray several light coats, rather than one heavy coat, by holding your arm at least 12" (30cm) away, continuously moving it back and forth while spraying. Spray in a well-ventilated area, preferably away from where you and your friends are working.

It's also good to include a roll of tape in your kit. It has dozens of practical uses, from keeping your paper from flying away to temporarily holding broken equipment together — kind of a catchall.

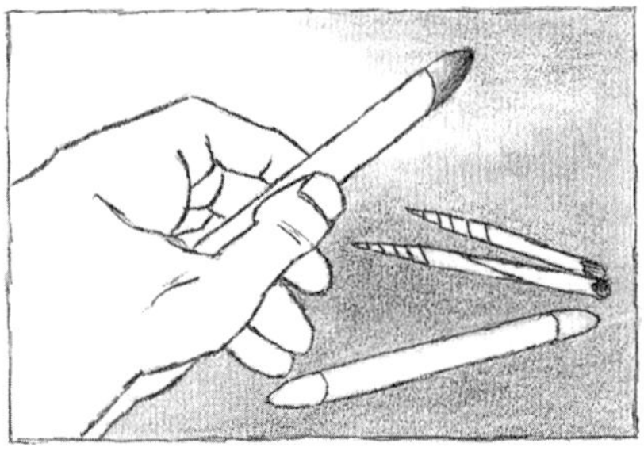

Stomps and Tortillions
These are great tools for creating soft tones and blending in small areas. A clean stomp or tortillion can also be used to remove tone.

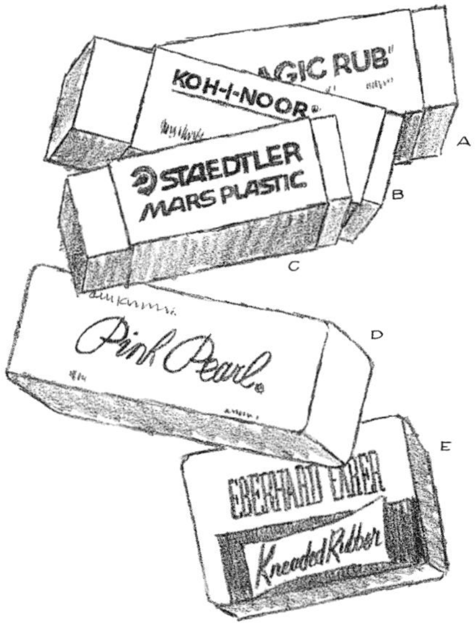

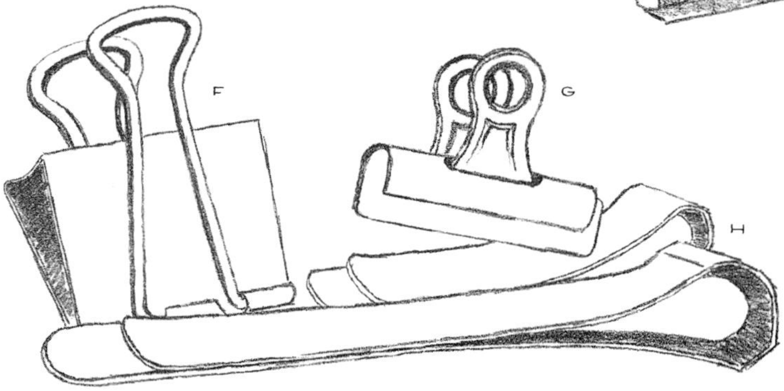

Erasers
There are several kinds of erasers that will serve your purpose, and the clips shown here are handy for holding your work to your board in lieu of tape.

A. Magic Rub: a white eraser that does a competent job.
B. Koh-I-Noor: a yellow plastic eraser for stubborn or inked lines.
C. Staedtler: a white plastic eraser, excellent for pencil and charcoal.
D. Pink Pearl: a soft pink eraser.
E. Kneaded eraser: pliable into any shape; excellent for lifting values or highlighting.
F., G. Two different types of spring clips.
H. Stainless steel Banker's clasps: available at office supply stores; great for holding papers to your board.

SHARPENING YOUR PENCIL

It is important for you to feel comfortable when you are drawing. One of the most important aids in achieving this feeling is having a proper amount of graphite or charcoal exposed on your pencil. Too often a mechanical sharpener puts a point on your pencil, but the point is gone after a couple of strokes on your paper.

The following is a good and safe method for sharpening your pencil with a single-edged razor blade. Never ever use double-edged blades!

Place the blade between your right thumb and forefinger as shown in Figure 1. Place the pencil in your left hand, and with your left thumb push the blade forward into the wood, rotating the pencil while making short shallow cuts (Figure 2). While pushing forward with the left thumb, your right hand turns the blade upward, away from the lead as shown in Figure 3. Continue this procedure until you have the desired amount of lead exposed. Then take your sandpaper block, as in Figure 4, and rotate your pencil gently, sharpening to as fine a point as you desire. If you find that you left your sandpaper block at home, look for a flat rock. It will work nicely.

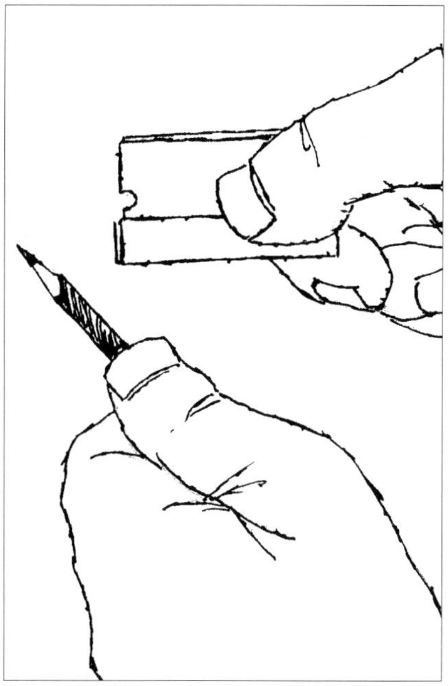

Fig. 1

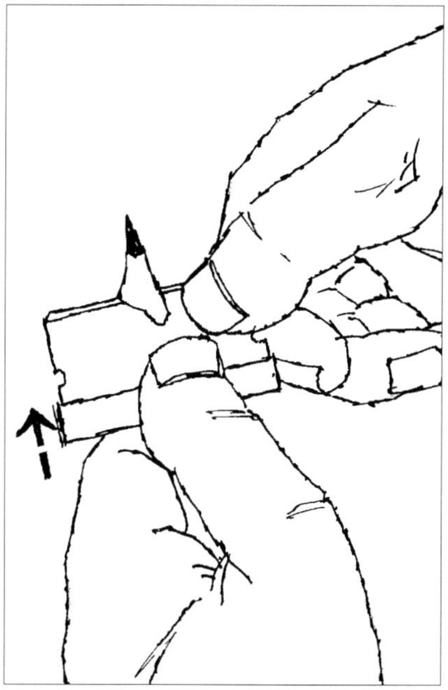

Fig. 2

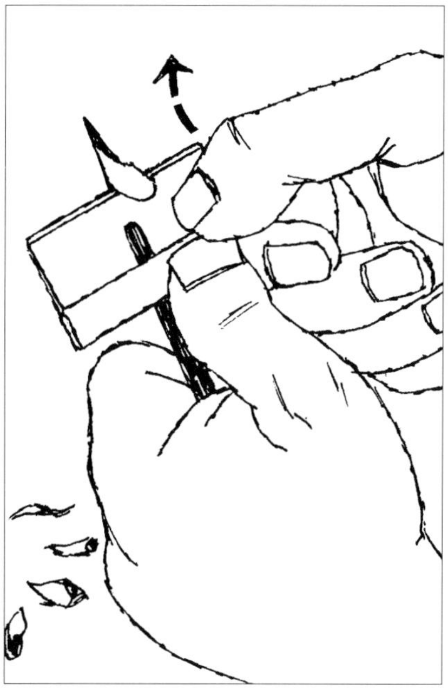

Fig. 3

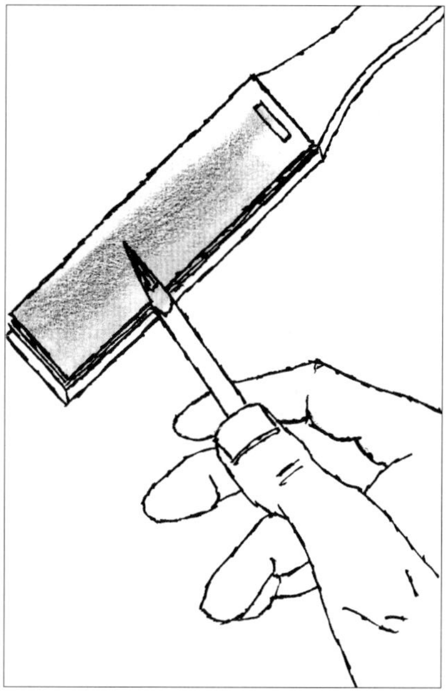

Fig. 4

WORKING OUTSIDE

There is a certain enjoyment and feeling of accomplishment in working outdoors on location. The equipment you bring along helps to achieve that feeling and should be chosen based on where you are going. For example, if you are going to be walking over rough terrain for a distance, you might want to consider a folding easel. Talk with fellow artists to get an idea of what is available. Determine whether the equipment they are using will work for you, and ask why they like it. Remember that the whole idea is to carry your materials in as compact and light a package as possible.

Easels

Among the many easels available, one I use is a French easel, which has a tray for paints, pastels, pencils, or whatever I wish to carry. It folds to about 12" x 16" (30cm x 41cm), however sizes will vary slightly depending on the manufacturer. You can work sitting or standing, or use it as a table if you prefer to work flat. Its canvas carrying bag is very sturdy, has extra pockets, and will hold a 16" x 20" (41cm x 51cm) board and paper very easily.

Quite often I use a folding easel made for me by D. C. Story, a cabinetmaker from Rensselaerville, New York. It folds to a very convenient size that I lay across my folding seat and can easily carry both quite a distance if needed. You can use this easel in a sitting position, as shown, or with the legs extended for standing. The middle board can be tilted to your liking or lie flat.

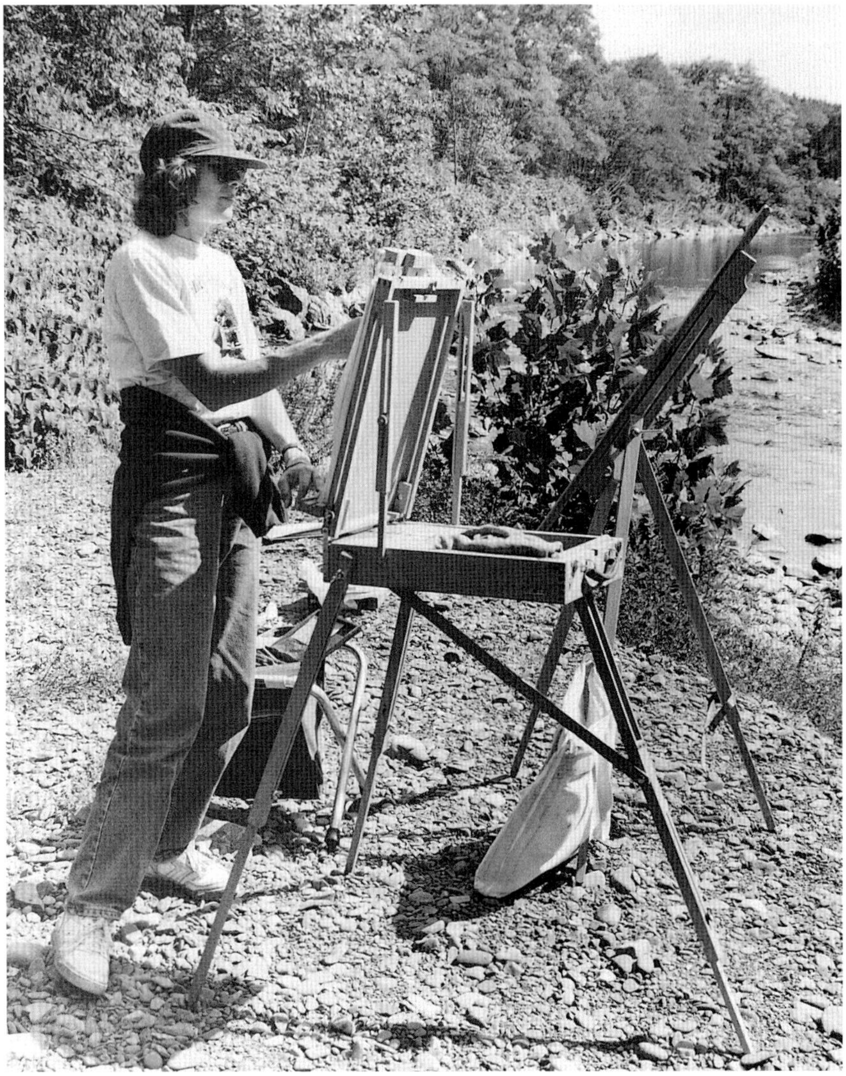

French Easel
This is a French easel with a sturdy folding easel behind it. The top can lay flat if you want a table-like surface, or it can be shortened if you want to sit while working.

> **FIND YOURSELF AN ORCHARD**
>
> Locate an orchard, and ask for permission to sit and sketch some trees. The pruned trees usually make for interesting shapes and studies. Leave the farmer a sketch that you do not need, as this will more than likely make you welcome again. Be neat, leaving the area as you found it.

Umbrella

An umbrella is a wonderful piece of equipment to have if you must be out in the sun, as it will enable you to shade your work — a big asset. I strongly advise you not to skimp on this piece of equipment. Check carefully to make sure that it will be serviceable for a good while. The umbrella should attach to your easel with a C-clamp and can be tilted by using a gooseneck. Again, it is important that your materials be as compact and easy to carry as possible.

Seats

Seats should be sturdy. Look for one with pockets — the more pockets, the merrier. You will always find something to fit in these extra pockets, such as a lunch, an extra sweater, and so on. Seats are also available as backpacks, but again do some investigating to get the best one for your needs.

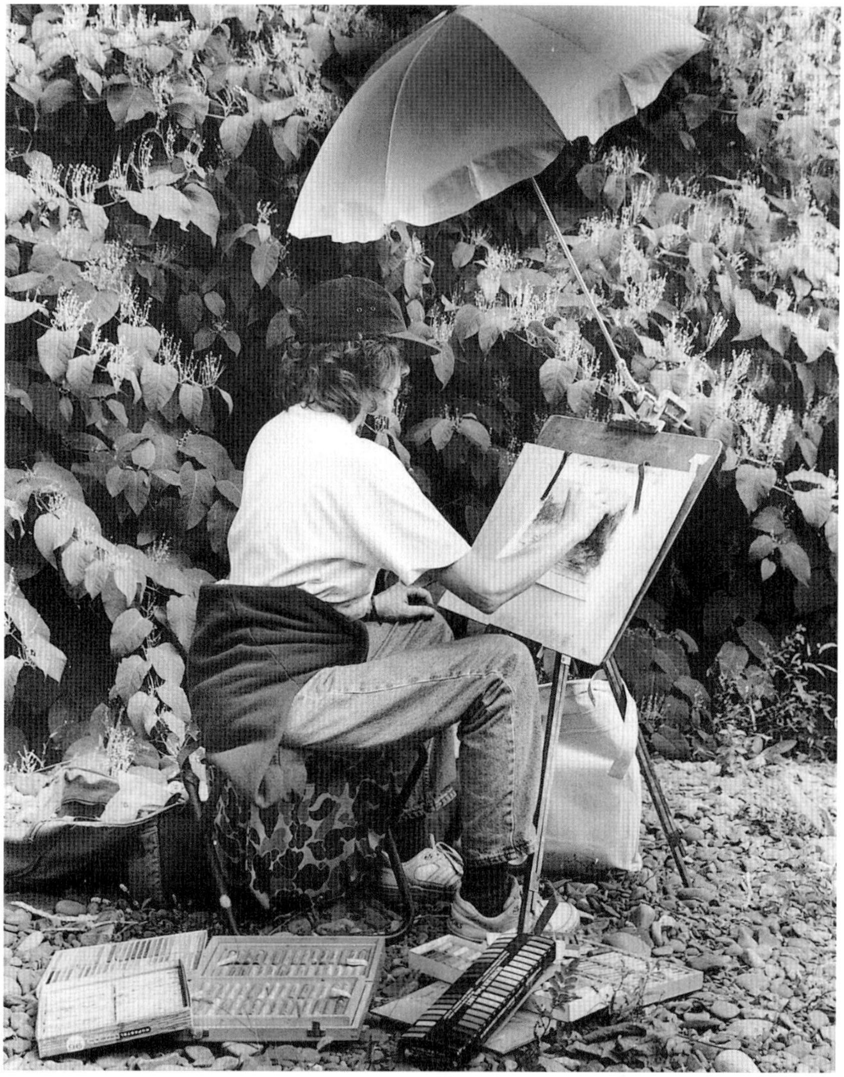

Folding Easel
The folding easel is lightweight and folds to a convenient carrying size. The whole idea is to carry your materials in as light a package as possible. An umbrella and seat, as shown here, also make useful additions to your outdoor gear.

HOLDING YOUR PENCIL PROPERLY

You will find that when you work outdoors, you will be more comfortable if you hold your pencil as shown to the right. This position might feel a little strange at first, but with a few tries you will find that it enables you to work longer without tiring your arm. It will also offer more freedom and dexterity as you move your pencil around your drawing.

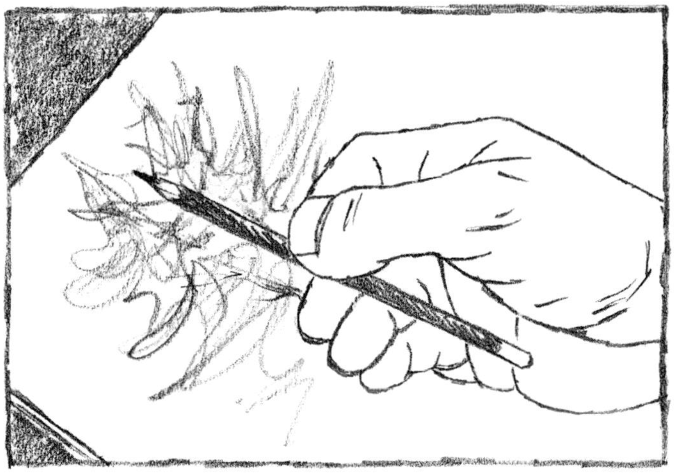

Holding Your Pencil for Sketching
Hold your pencil like this when sketching outdoors. This position will give you more freedom, enabling you to move your whole arm.

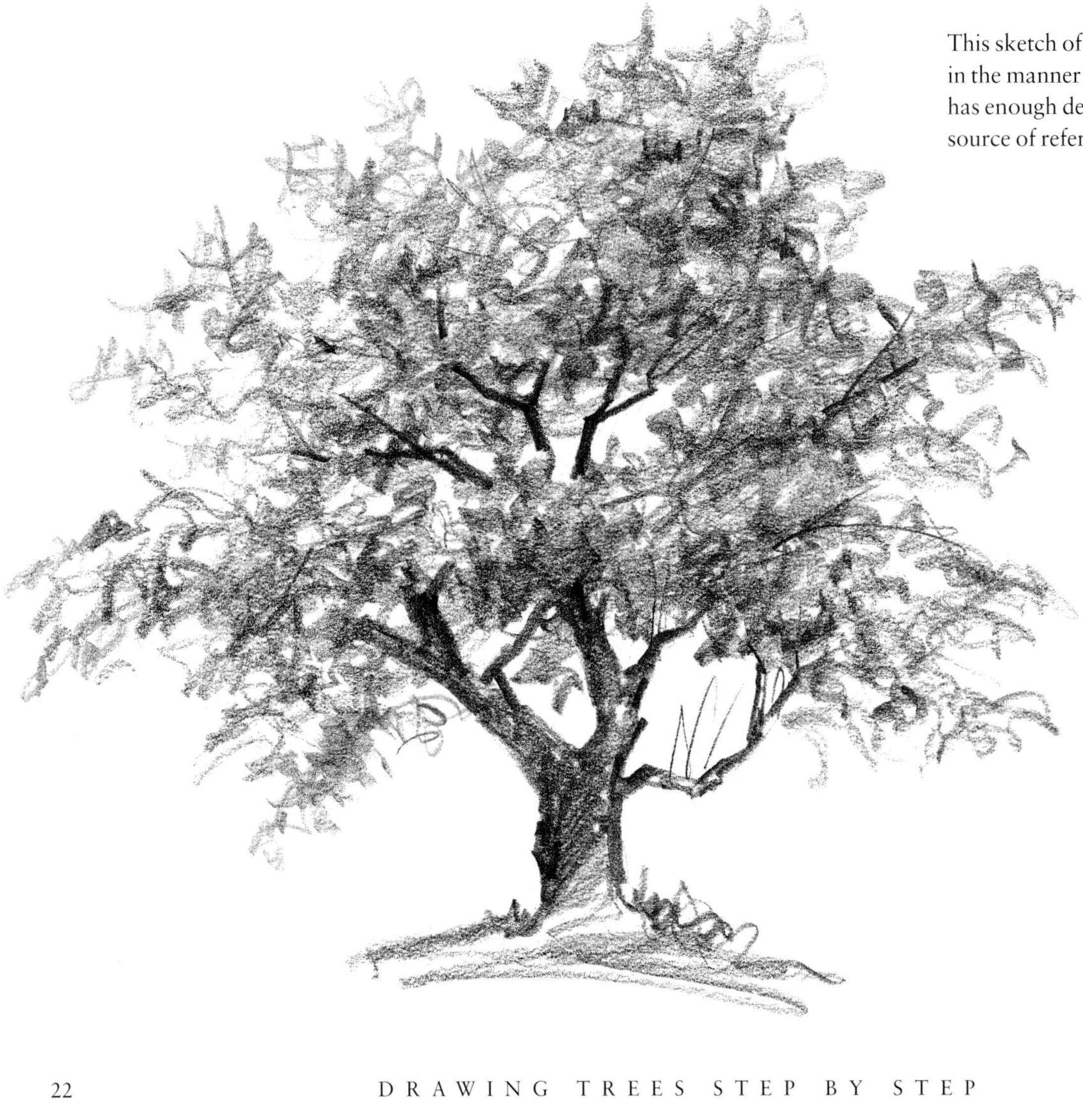

This sketch of a fruit tree was done in the manner shown in Fig. A. It has enough detail to become a source of reference for future needs.

When making a more detailed piece of work, hold your pencil as shown here rather than as shown on the previous page. This grip will give you more control over your pencil. Since it allows your hand to rest directly on top of your drawing, you may want to place a piece of scrap paper under your hand to avoid smudging your work. Also, remember that the sharper the point, the more control you will have over your pencil.

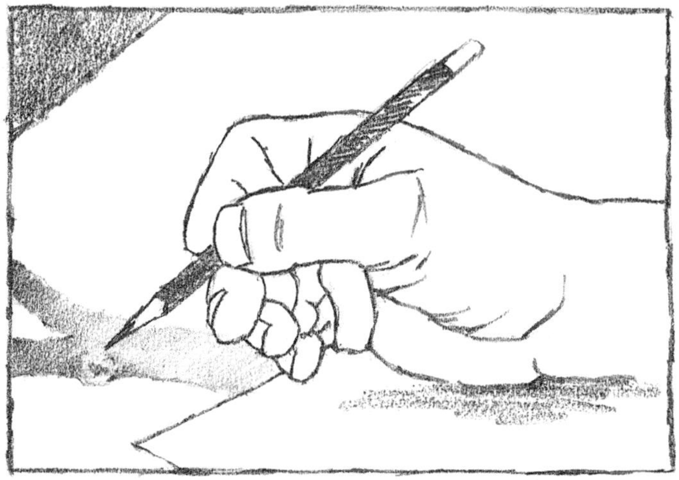

Holding Your Pencil for Detailed Work
Hold your pencil in this manner while creating detailed drawings and small works.

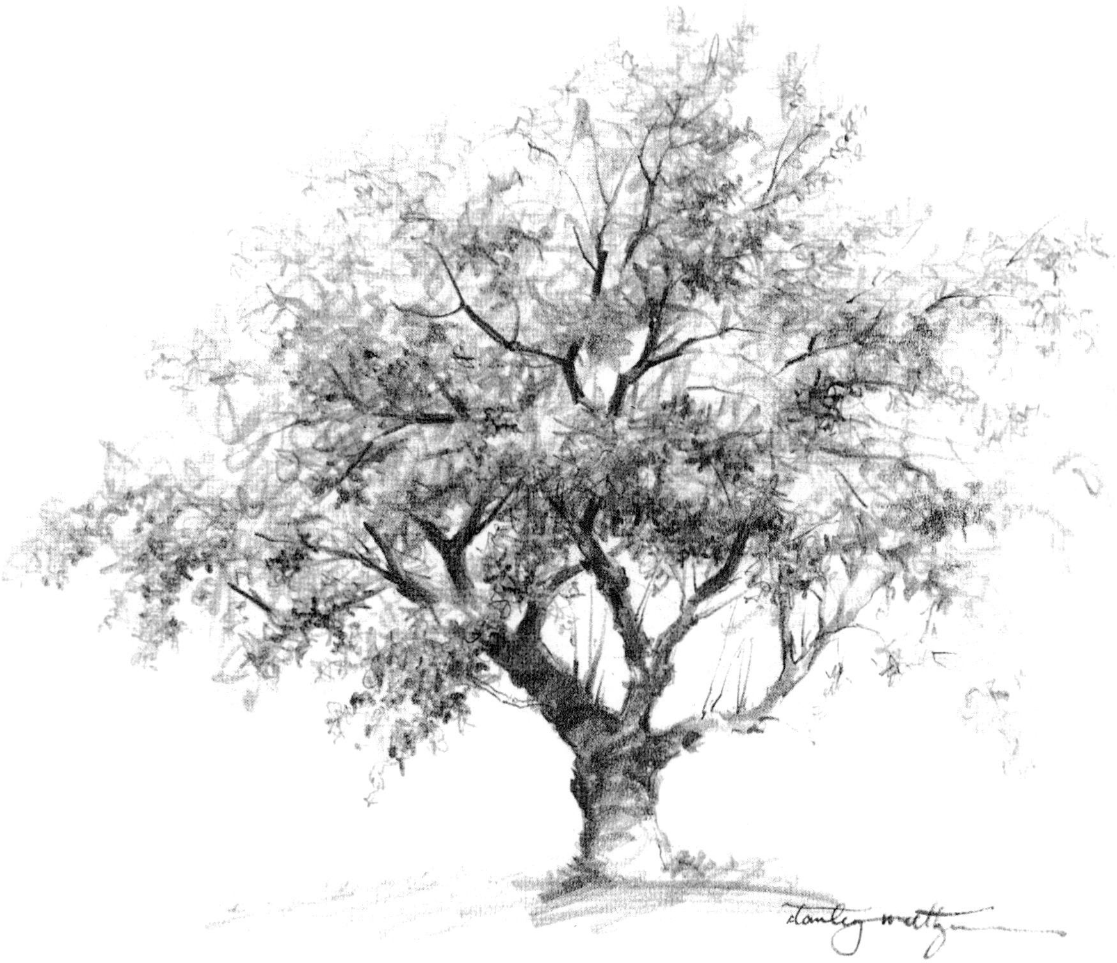

This drawing is of the same fruit tree as on the opposite page, but with more detail. After sketching it, change to holding the pencil for detailed work, which will enable you to have more control while adding the finishing touches.

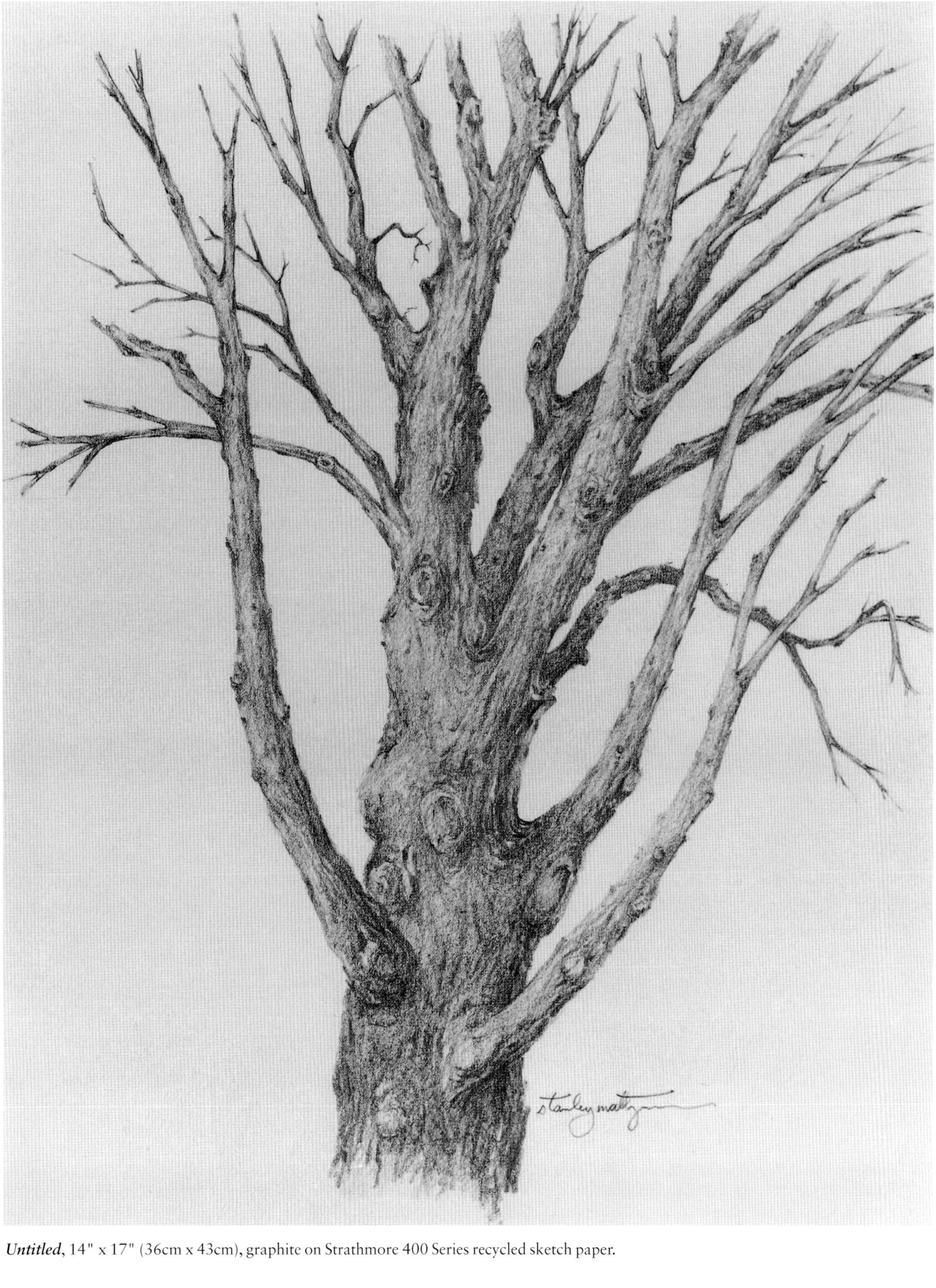

Untitled, 14" x 17" (36cm x 43cm), graphite on Strathmore 400 Series recycled sketch paper.

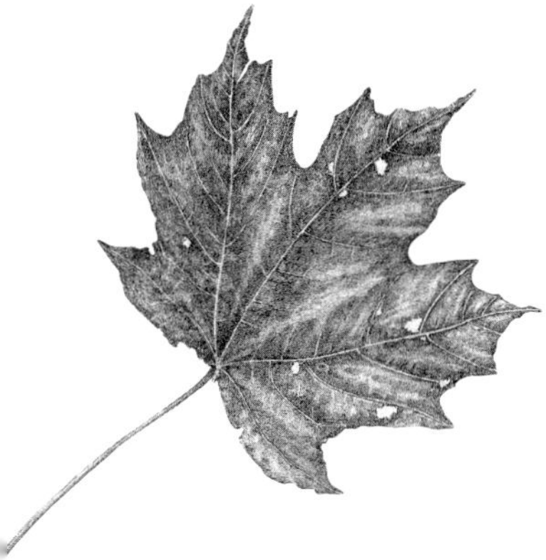

CHAPTER TWO

How Trees Grow

As you study trees, you can't help but marvel at what a wonderful feat of engineering you are looking at. Certain species, such as oaks, pines and redwoods, reach unbelievable heights. All that weight above and still they sway gracefully in the breeze.

When you have considered which tree you want to draw, think of a telescope, each section a little smaller, fitting into the other, so that when opened to full length you have a balanced, tapered shape. This comparison to a telescope will help you remember how a tree grows, from bough to branch to twig.

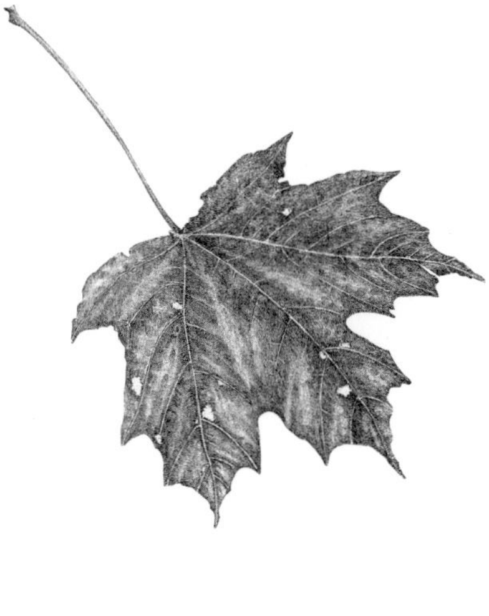

CREATE A BALANCED FORM

There is, of course, much more to a tree growing. For the present, that is not our concern. If you would like to get more technical information about growing trees, I strongly recommend your local state conservation office or the library, which should have many fine books on the subject. For now, your goal is to draw a tree that looks as if it belongs in your picture.

The illustration below shows part of a trunk, and growing from the trunk is a bough which should be smaller in girth than the trunk from which it grows. Extending from the bough are branches, then twigs. Each one is smaller, creating a balance that enables the tree to withstand much punishment from both time and the weather.

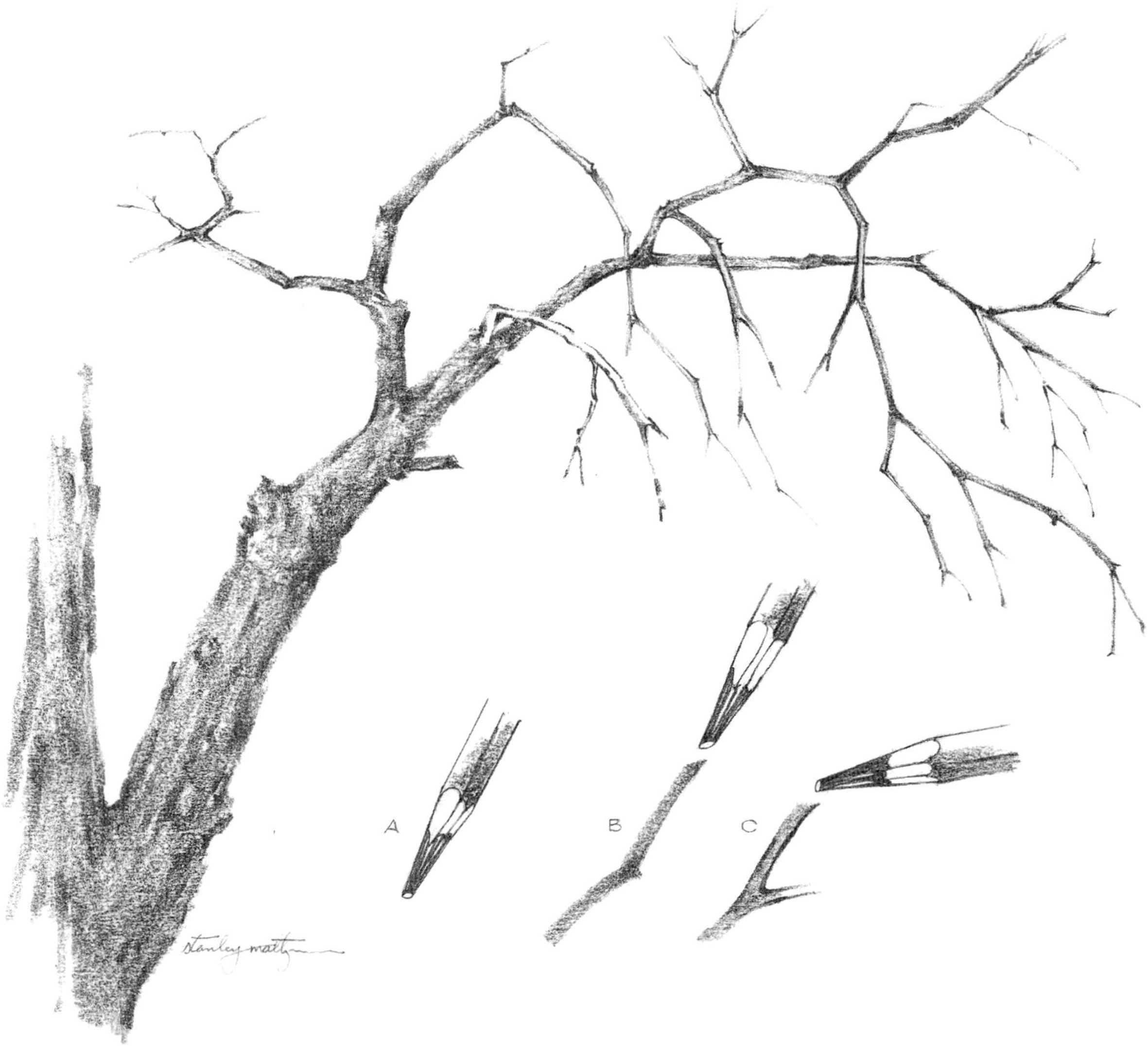

Change Your Pencil Pressure

This drawing was completed with a 6B graphite pencil on a piece of Rives BFK paper by increasing and decreasing the pressure of the pencil. To master this technique, sharpen your pencil (soft lead) and create an angle, instead of a point, as shown in diagram A.

Leaning on the flat side of the pencil, begin to draw your branches and twigs to fit your drawing as indicated in diagram B. When you first sharpen your pencil, concentrate on the finer details. As the lead wears, focus on the thicker branches. Repeat until your drawing is finished.

To give the branches, twigs or whatever the appropriate emphasis, turn your pencil so that you are using the edge of the lead, as shown in diagram C, instead of the flat part. This edge will enable you to make as sharp and clean a line as you need. A little practice on some scrap paper will help you capture the spirit of this technique.

CONTOUR DRAWING

A contour drawing is merely the outline (or contour) of an object. Contour drawings are an excellent way for you to overcome a problem you might have capturing a likeness of something in particular. By directing your concentration on the outline, you'll be able to more easily picture and understand the shape and form of your subject. This intense study will help you to see many details that you never noticed before, which will contribute to making a better picture.

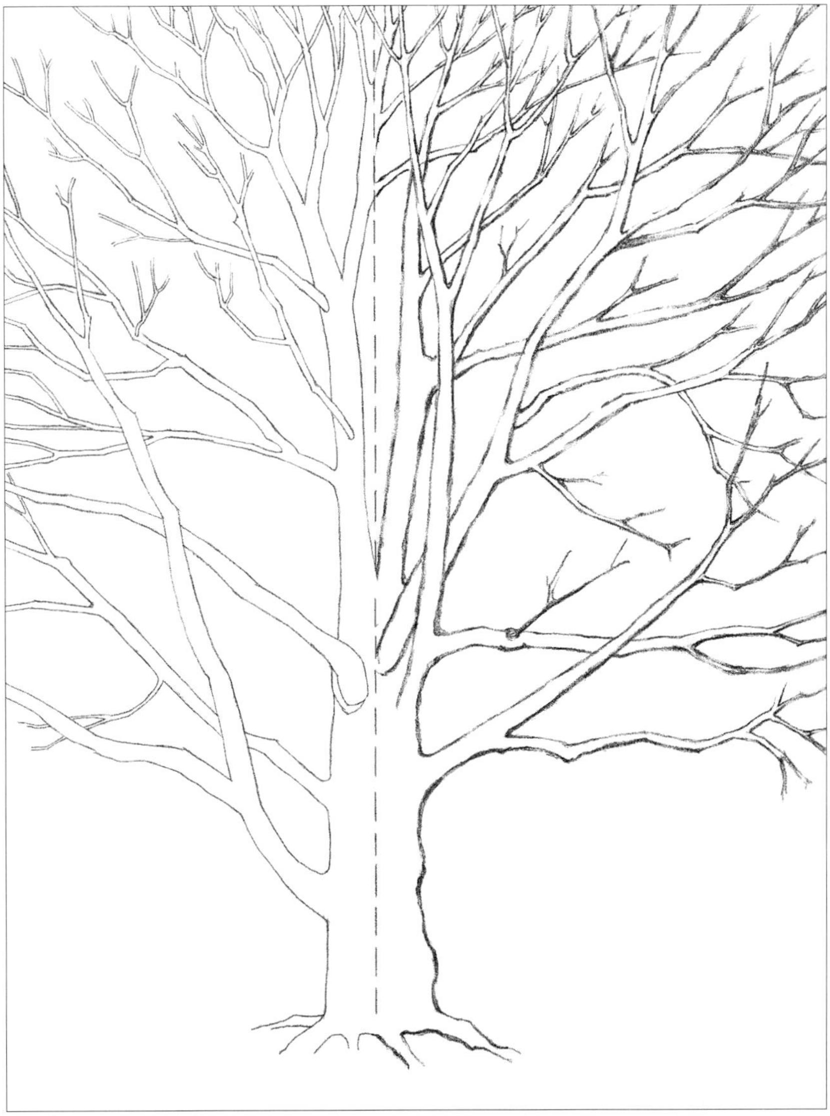

Vary Your Line Thickness
In this illustration is a contour drawing of a tree. The tree is divided in half by a dotted line. The left half was drawn with a HB graphite pencil, keeping the same line thickness throughout. Though an interesting composition, the constant line can become boring. To make a line as in the drawing to the right, use a 2B or 4B pencil. As you draw, vary the pressure, easing up for a thinner line and bearing down for a thicker or heavier one. By doing this, you can create light and shade with just a line. Notice how much more interesting the right side becomes by varying the line.

TRUNKS AND ROOTS

It is important that your tree gives the impression that it is growing out of the ground. There is nothing more disappointing than a great looking tree floating above the ground because someone did not take the trouble to do a little research. When you sketch outdoors, take a little time to make some studies of trees, trunks, roots, branches, and so on. You will find the experience rewarding, and you will be building a wonderful source of reference material.

In this drawing, the trunk was executed with the point of a 6B pencil sanded down, as previously demonstrated. This is an old tree; young trees have smooth bark. You will observe that mature trees offer an abundance of details that can be incorporated into your drawings.They have growths, broken limbs, holes, lichen and much more, all there for you to observe and record.

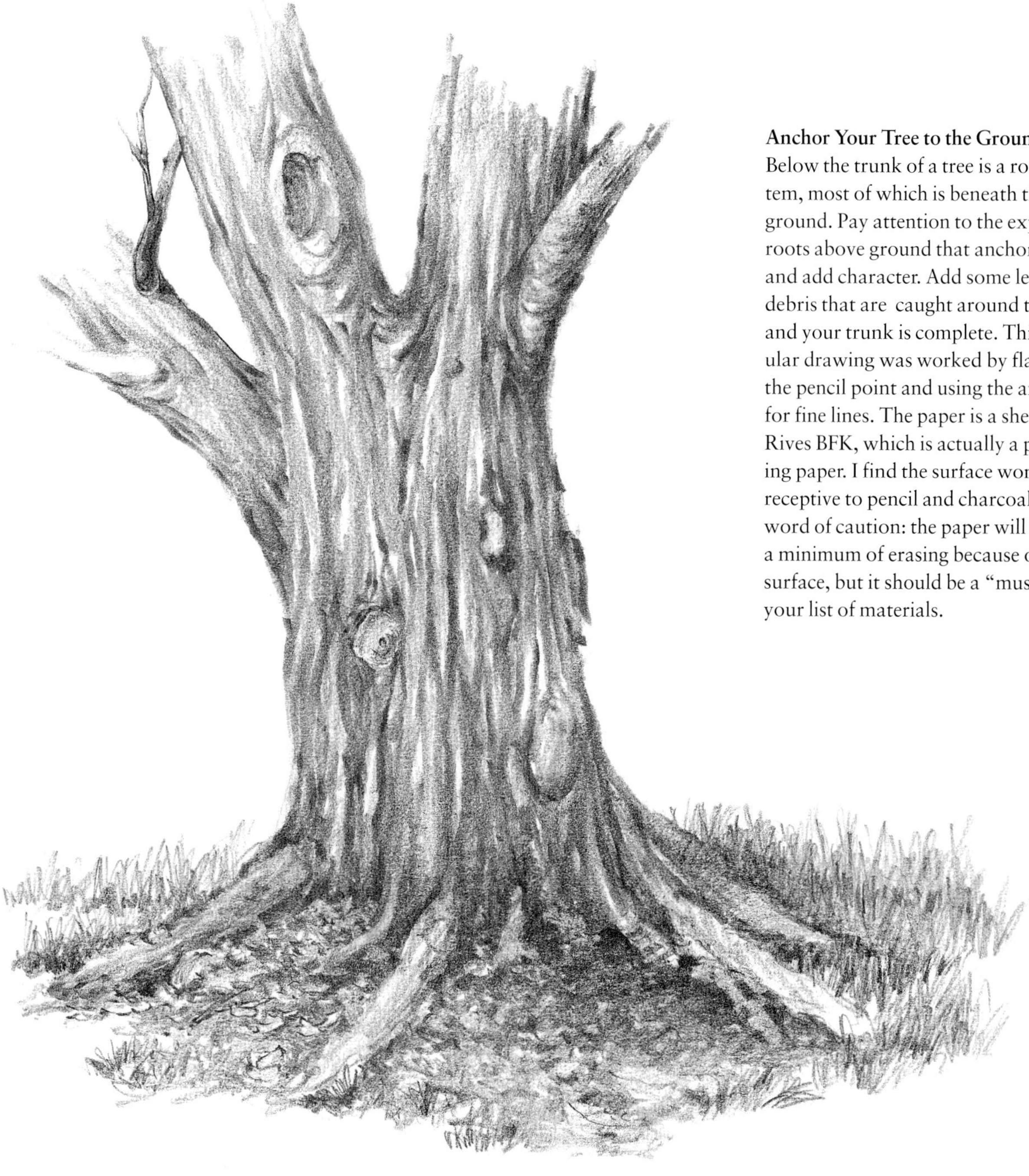

Anchor Your Tree to the Ground
Below the trunk of a tree is a root system, most of which is beneath the ground. Pay attention to the exposed roots above ground that anchor the tree and add character. Add some leaves and debris that are caught around the roots and your trunk is complete. This particular drawing was worked by flattening the pencil point and using the angle side for fine lines. The paper is a sheet of Rives BFK, which is actually a printmaking paper. I find the surface wonderfully receptive to pencil and charcoal. One word of caution: the paper will only take a minimum of erasing because of its soft surface, but it should be a "must try" on your list of materials.

THE SHAPES OF TREES

There is no better time to become acquainted or to familiarize yourself with our woodland friends than in the winter when the shapes of the leafless trees are bared and most obvious to the eye.

Trees With One Main Trunk

All trees are made up of one or two distinct outlines readily identifiable by the growth or shape of the trunk. Some trees have one main trunk with branches growing out of the sides, such as the canoe, or paper, birch (above right) and the Lombardy poplar (below right). Both trees have a main trunk with outward growth appearing in various shapes and contours.

There are many other trees with one trunk, such as the scarlet and pin oaks and the American beech, to name a few. I mention these trees because you probably have noticed them already. Birch trees have peeling bark and black triangles marking previous and present branch growth, while poplars, usually planted on property boundaries or for wind breaks, have one stem and many branches cupped like a hand. All of these characteristics are waiting for you to observe and capture.

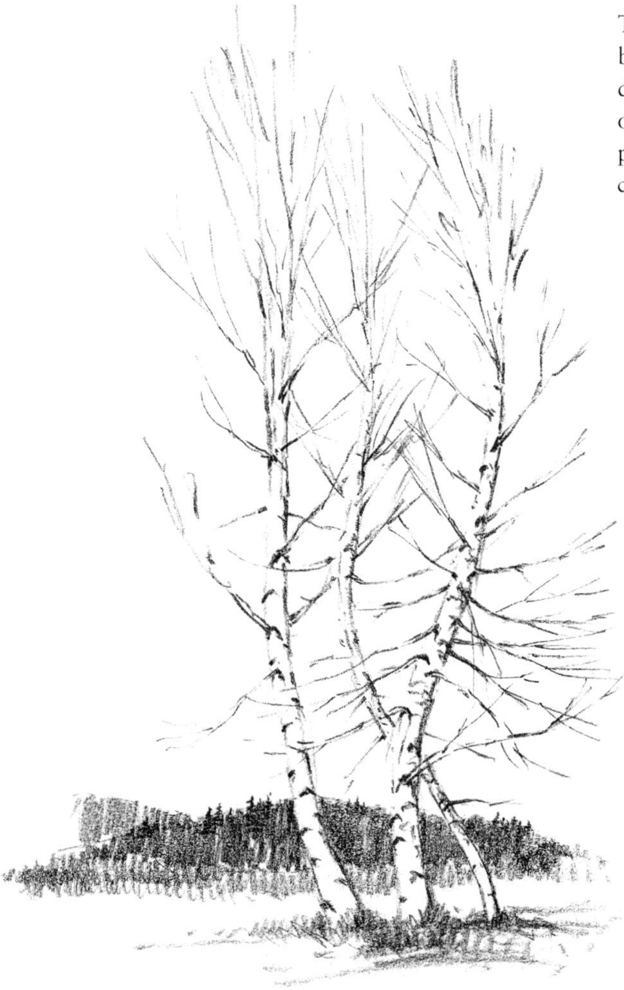

These paper birches were drawn on a piece of Rives BFK paper with a 2B charcoal pencil...

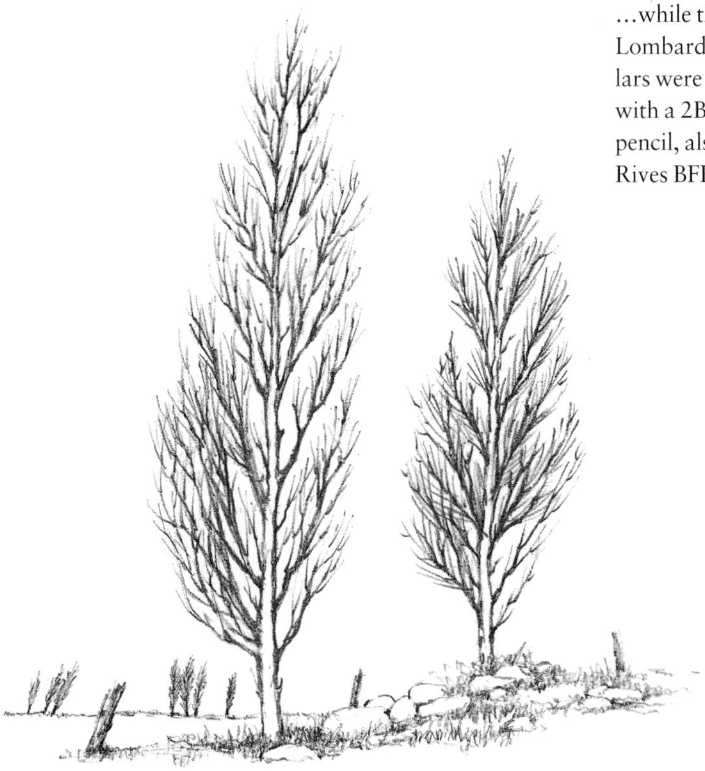

...while these Lombardy poplars were drawn with a 2B graphite pencil, also on Rives BFK paper.

Trees With Multiple Main Trunks

As often as you see trees with single trunks, you will also notice trees with trunks divided into two, forming Vs or Ys. To the above right is a relatively young common locust in the winter. Notice the double trunk with the boughs and branches growing in an angular manner.

In summer the locust has a distinctive leaf pattern. Picture a feather spine with barbs going off on each side. Well, here you have a stem with about five or six leaves growing on each side, plus a very fragrant flower which attracts a variety of insects — good and bad.

As the locust matures, the bark becomes loaded with wonderful patterns. Unfortunately, these patterns, with their crevices, create excellent hiding places for insects, causing the locust to lose many boughs and branches. Although it's rough on the tree, it does result in many shapes of interest for you.

The white pine is another tree that commonly splits into two major trunks (as shown to the right). It is quite a handsome tree, with large boughs and branches that gracefully sweep out horizontally with the ends curving upward. To determine whether your subject is a white pine, check the needles; they should be about 4 ½" to 5" (11cm to 13cm) long with white lines underneath.

The white pine is a magnificent tree to draw, with the bottom branches offering numerous opportunities for design potential. Some branches lose their bark, while others keep a portion, and delicate twig patterns emerge that look like lacework when caught in the right light.

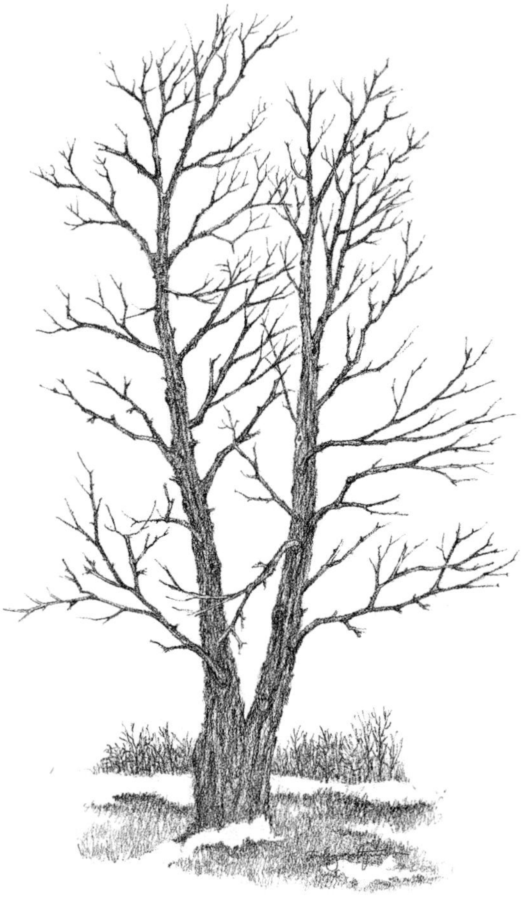

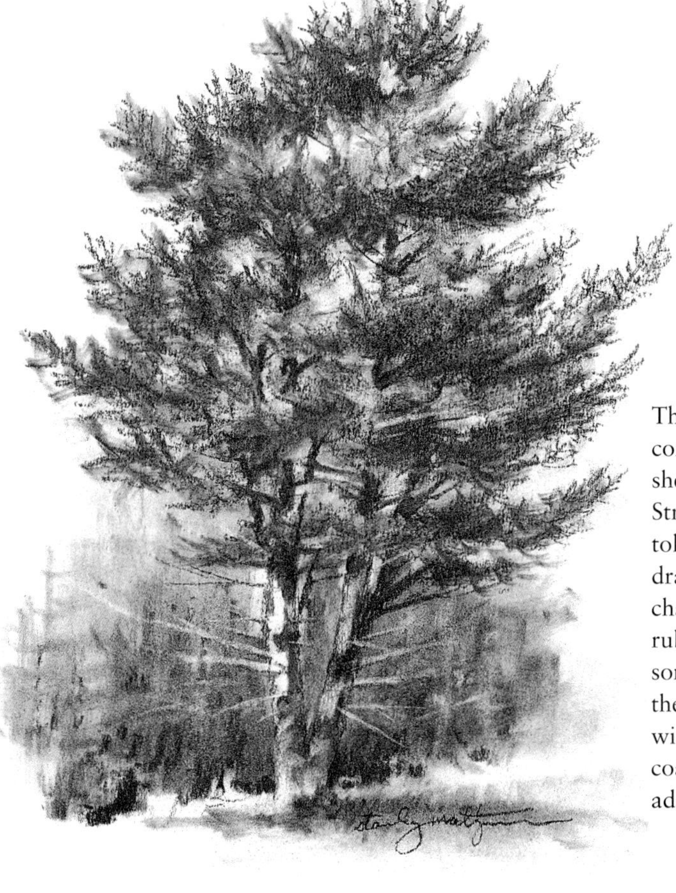

This drawing was completed on a sheet of 3-ply Strathmore Bristol. I first made a drawing with vine charcoal, then rubbed it to add some modeling. I then went over it with a 4B charcoal pencil for added emphasis.

BOUGHS

Boughs are the largest of the main branches. As you observe them, notice how they provide balance to the tree, creating poise and character. Also note the minimal effort put forth to support the other foliage and branches.

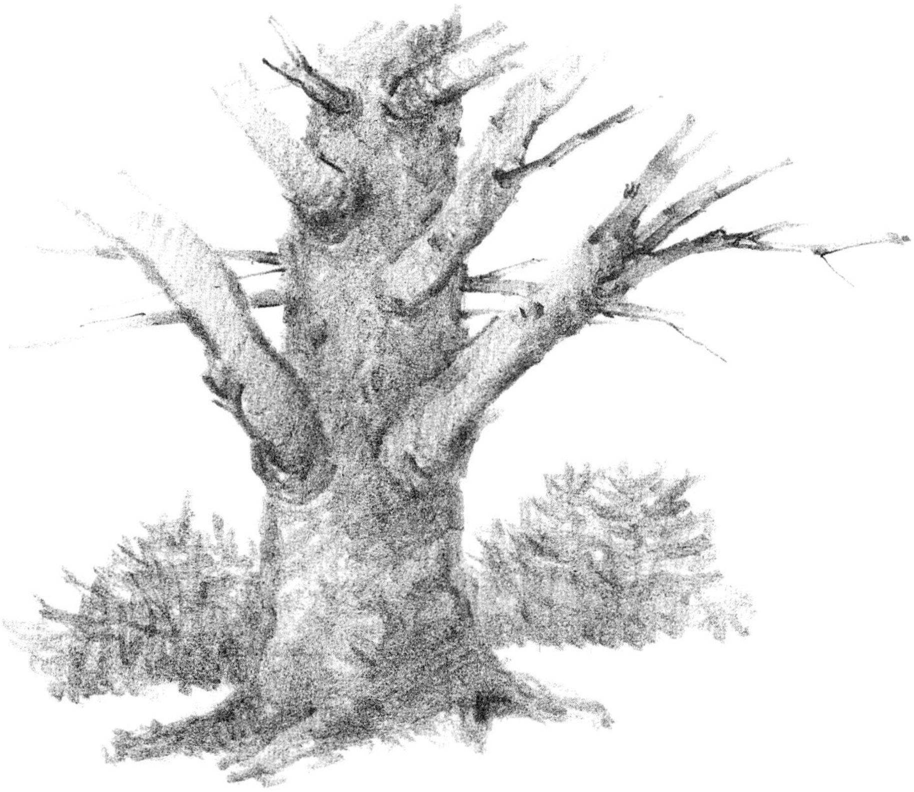

This illustration, created on a sheet of Rives BFK with a 6B graphite pencil, shows a mature tree with boughs fanning out in various directions. Quite often trees will lose boughs through storms, disease, insects and so on. The trees compensate by growing additional branches and foliage to maintain balance. For artists, this creates odd shapes of interest to include in their works.

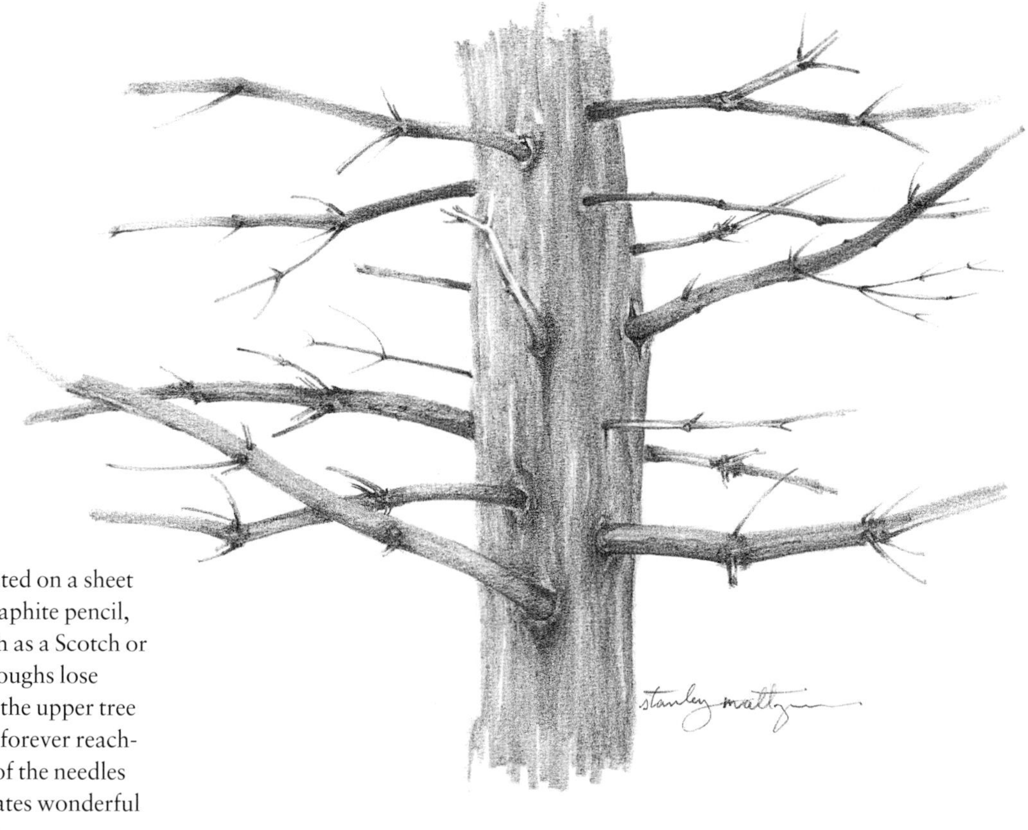

This illustration, also created on a sheet of Rives BFK with a 6B graphite pencil, shows a younger tree, such as a Scotch or white pine. Even spruce boughs lose their lower needles, while the upper tree continues to be green and forever reaching for the light. The loss of the needles on the branches again creates wonderful designs for you to observe.

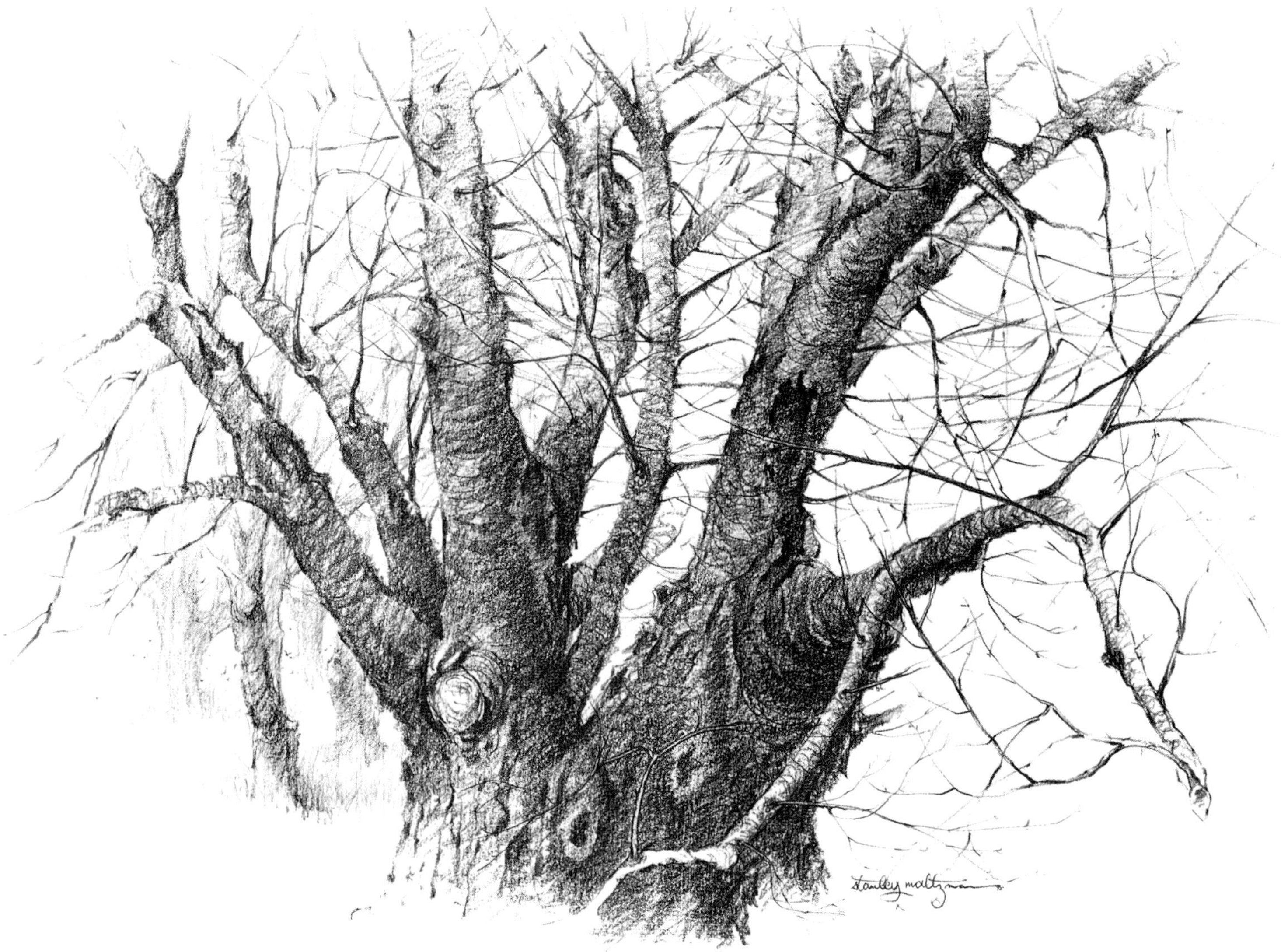

Gladiator II, 22" x 30" (56cm x 76cm), charcoal on handmade Japanese paper. Collection of Jaap and Jettie Penratt.

Here you have a wonderful old character oozing with everything you are interested in: a double trunk with knotholes where boughs once grew, living boughs, branches — some growing and some without bark — and twigs sprouting out all over, but placed so as to create a frame for the main or heavy wood. This tree has something for everyone! Here I drew the main elements of this picture — the trunk and branches — quite accurately, but I freely added and deleted the twigs, placing them to create an interesting design and picture. Always keep in mind that you do not have to make an exact copy. A resemblance inspired by your feelings is what you should reach for.

BRANCHES, TWIGS AND SHOOTS

Branches are a subdivision of the trunk of a tree. Branches add to a tree's characteristics and give you interesting shapes to draw. Your trees do not have to be anatomically accurate; a ballpark representation will suffice to start with. Some branches grow horizontally to the main stem, such as a red pine, a short leaf pine or a red oak (as shown to the right). Notice how the branches grow at an upward angle.

Smaller branches are called twigs, branchlets or shoots. Below is a small branch from a paper birch illustrating this growth. Notice the buds (bumps) along the twigs. These buds will produce flowers, leaves and growth for the tree. Nature prepares for this phenomenon in the fall, and only when the buds are snugged away for next spring's debut do trees shed their leaves. With all of the trees' energy spent on future growth, the trees are now ready for the autumn equinox. This process of shedding and growth creates forms and shapes which you as an artist will be interested in.

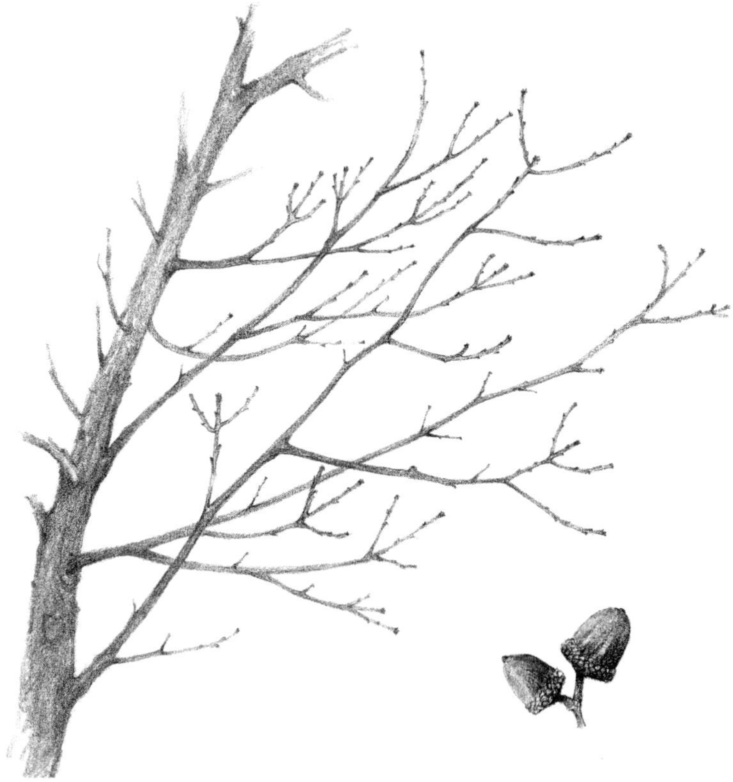

A hint that you are looking at a red oak is the size of the acorn; it is the largest in the oak family and sets in a shallow cup.

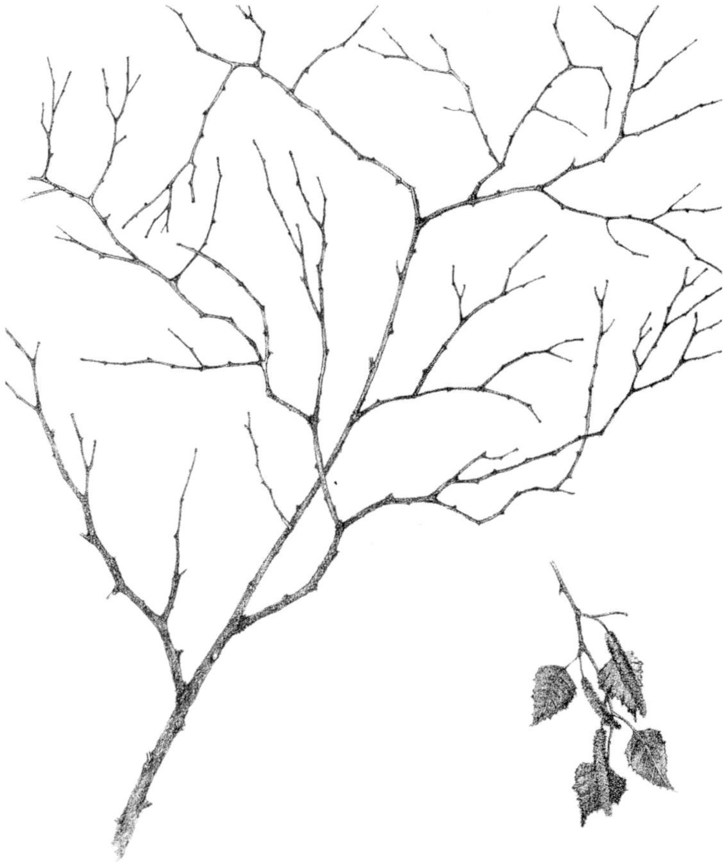

This drawing of a small paper birch branch shows some of the products of buds — leaves and fruit called *catkins*.

HOW FOLIAGE GROWS

Now that we have discussed boughs, branches and twigs, I thought you would like to know how these elements come about: thus, the bud. Diagram A shows a twig with buds. The placement of buds may vary with the different species of trees. From these buds grow young shoots and leaves, adding new growth to the tree and foliage.

Diagram B demonstrates one technique on how to draw foliage. Using an HB charcoal pencil, start with a light scribbling stroke to indicate an overall shape or grouping. Then add a light tone, or leave white paper that will eventually create your highlights.

As shown in diagram C, apply more pressure with your pencil, or use a softer pencil, such as a B or 2B, and begin to add darks to indicate shadows and more shapes to your leaves.

Finally, add more darks, as shown in diagram D, by applying even more pressure, or use a 4B or 6B pencil. Remember that the higher the number, the softer the lead and the darker the value. Then add additional darks to your mass that will give depth and dimension to the foliage. Add a few protruding sticks or twigs to further create the impression of a mass of leaves. Do not overdo the leaves — you only want to suggest them, not indicate every leaf.

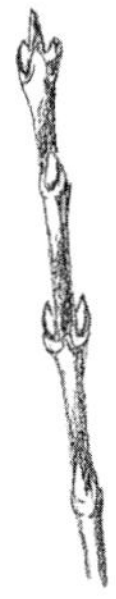

A.

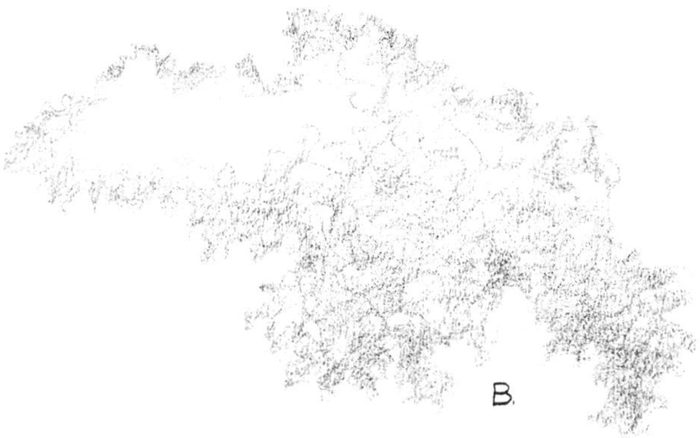

B.

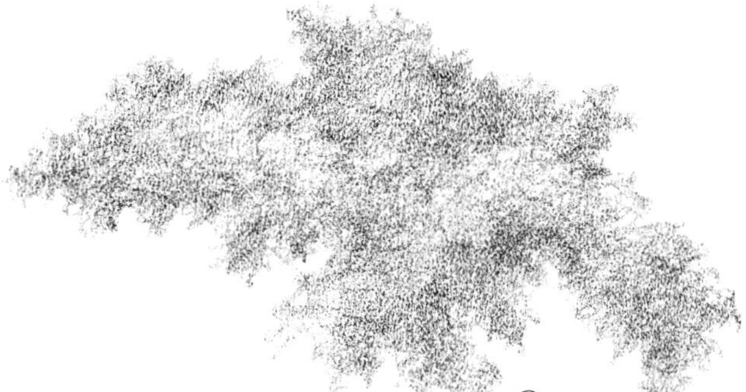

C.

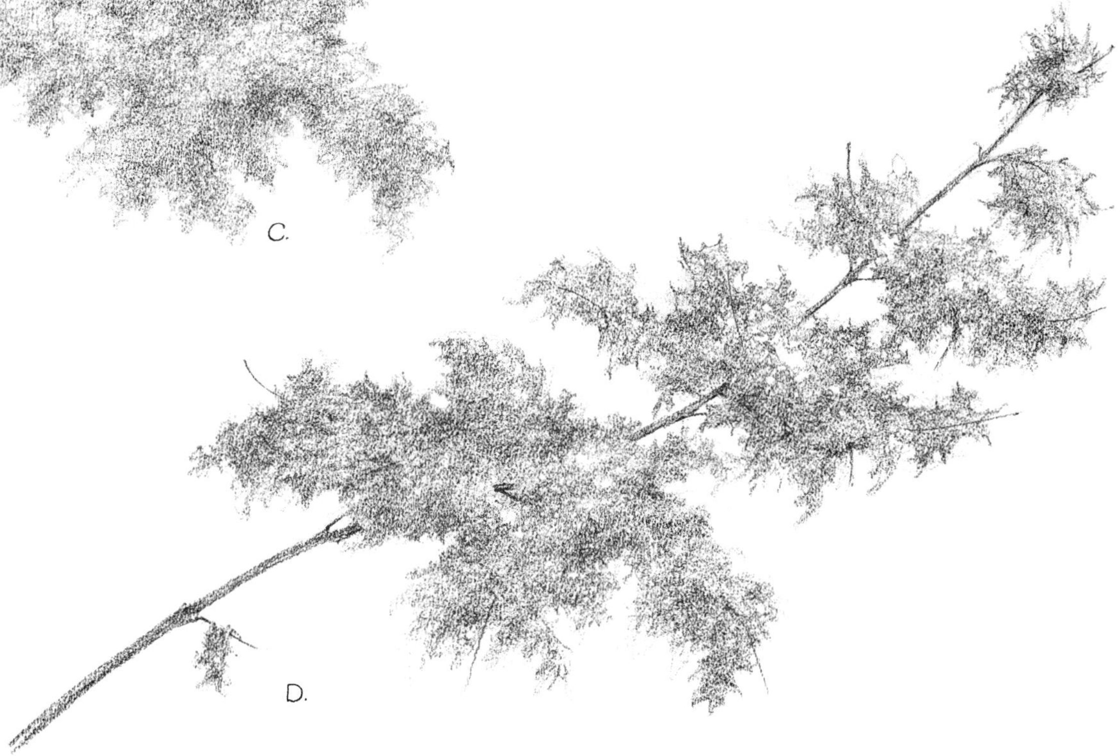

D.

Here is an American larch or tamarack tree. It is of special interest because it is a deciduous conifer. A deciduous tree is a tree that loses its leaves annually, and conifers are members of the pine tree family which do not lose their needles in the fall. The tamarack , however, loses its needles every autumn — most unusual for a conifer. The needles turn a beautiful yellow-orange color before dropping. It is a splendid tree with a delicate and distinctive appearance, reminiscent of patterns of lace.

Diagram B illustrates a portion of a stem (actual size) with small cones about 1" (2.5cm) high, and buds where clusters of needles and cones will grow.

In the winter, the tree is very distinguishable by the clusters of cones and every branch and twig covered with buds waiting for next spring.

As an assignment, find a larch and observe the changes during the seasons. It is a rewarding experience that will have you reaching for your sketch pad.

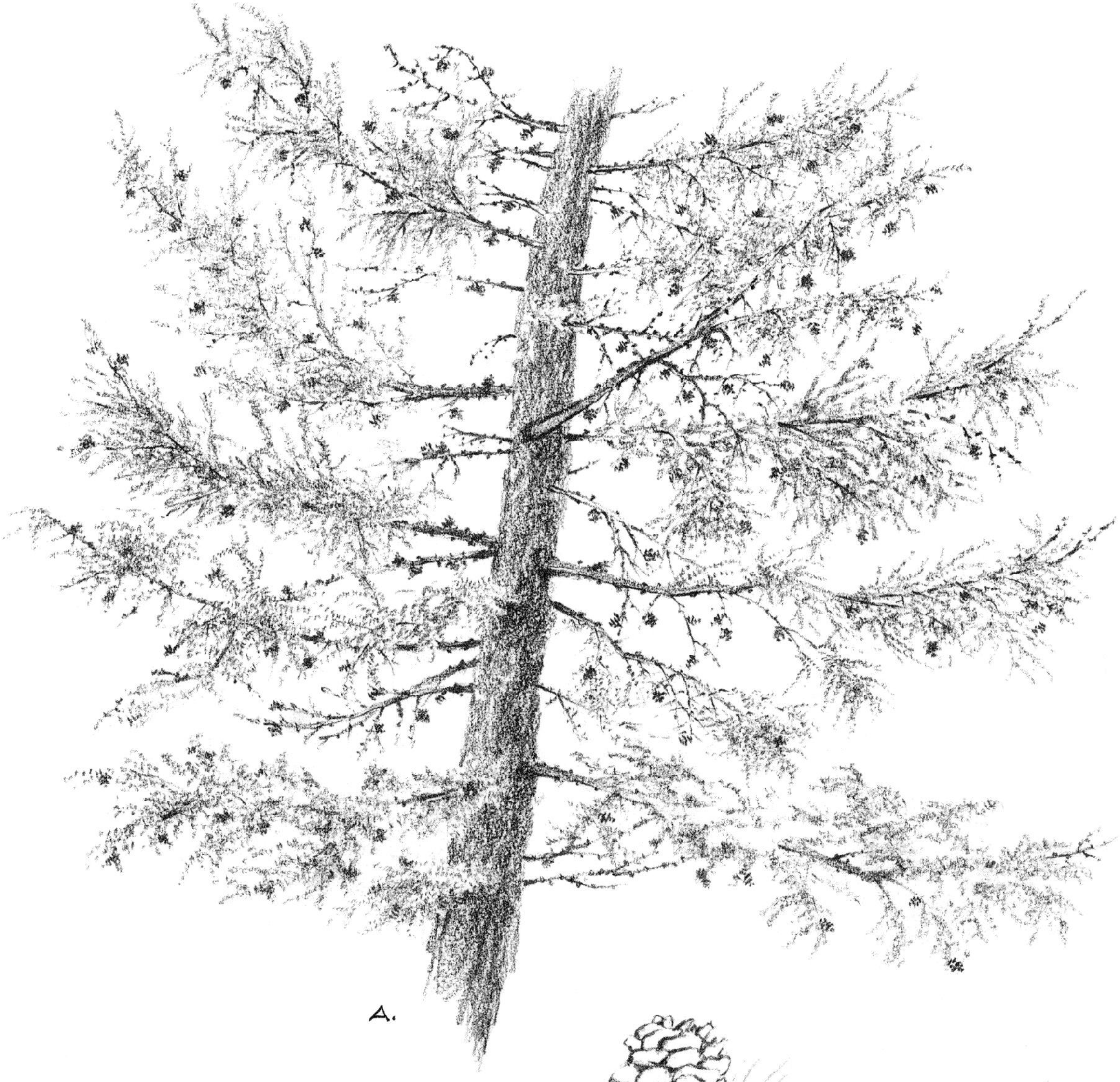

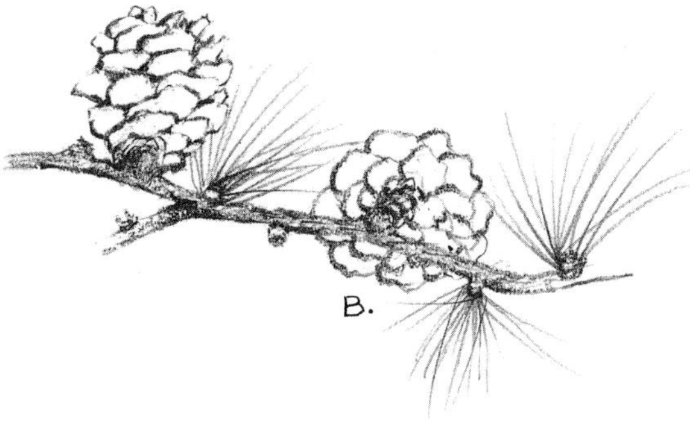

This drawing was made using 4B and HB graphite pencils on Daniel Smith archival printmaking paper.

SAPLINGS

This sketch of a sapling with foliage is not of any specific species, but the thin stem, branches and light leaf treatment can only signify a young tree. I sketched the trunk and branches with a 4B graphite pencil and the foliage with a 4B ½-inch graphite stick. If the graphite stick softens your branch strokes, go back with your pencil to bring out the eradicated or softened lines.

The illustration below shows a wooded area of young saplings. To create this effect, tone the background by lightly shading it with a 2B graphite pencil, then blend it with a stomp to create a soft gray tone that will accept pencil lines over it. Take a 6B pencil and sketch the saplings with thin single lines, keeping your pencil point sharp so as not to get too heavy. Then if you wish, add some white to suggest birches or poplars. Create an indentation with your fingernail or stylus, not cutting the paper's surface. Then when you tone the background, the graphite will miss the indentations you made, thus leaving a white line.

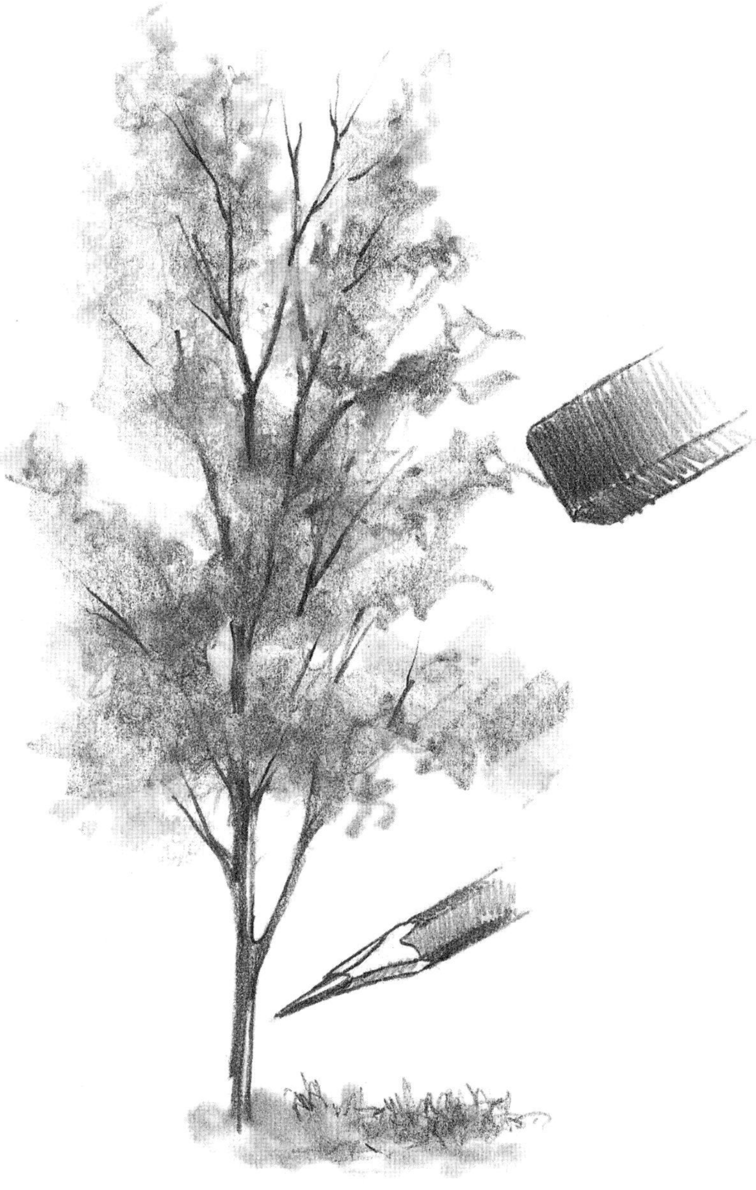

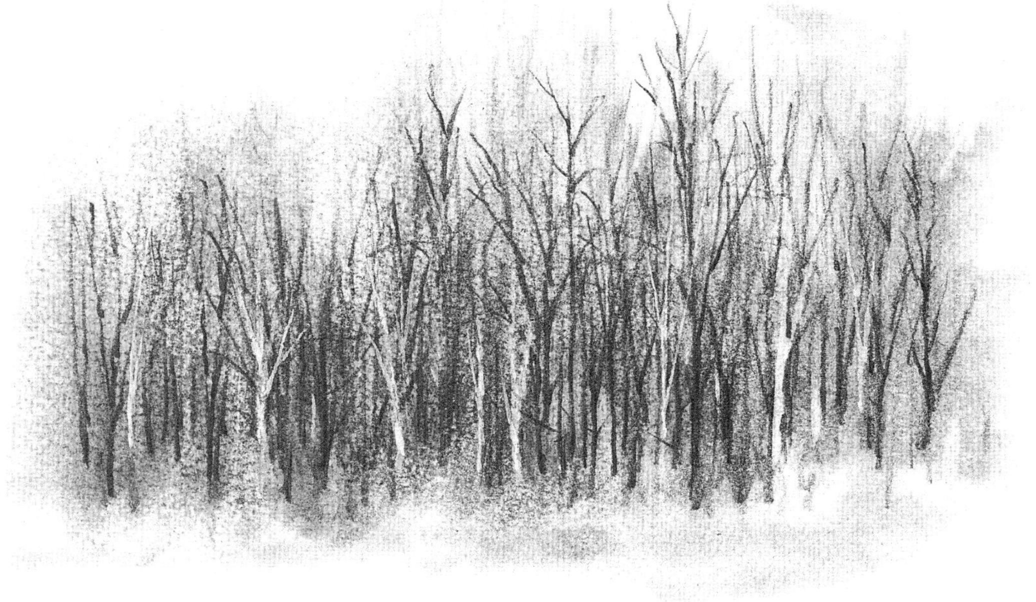

OLD TREES

Old trees can be a wonderful source of inspiration since they come in a wide variety of shapes and sizes. There are very few painters (except maybe for some figurative artists) that have not at some time or other been in awe of a mighty tree, be it an oak, pine, maple or whatever.

Old trees can be awesome, feminine or masculine looking. They can also suggest strength or weakness. In short, they will become what you are inspired to make of them.

This old timer is a maple that caught my attention because of the angle at which it was growing. Upon further investigation, I discovered it was under attack by some borer or other insect and was losing some branches and foliage. My first attempt was a 6" x 9" (15cm x 23cm) pastel, but I felt the tree deserved more, so I changed to charcoal and drew it on a larger scale.

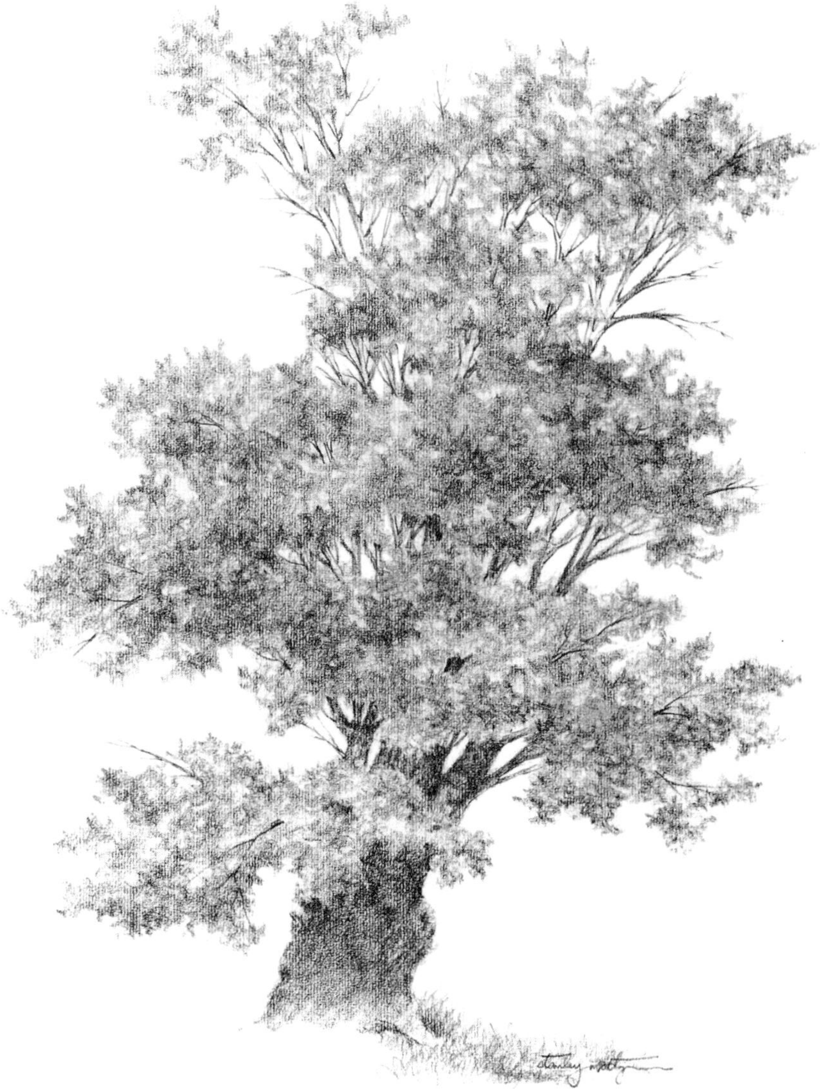

Hunter Mountain Maple, 16" x 20" (41cm x 51cm), charcoal on J. Barcham Green handmade paper.

This drawing was executed on a piece of cream-colored paper called Tovil, a handmade paper by J. Barcham Green of England and watermarked 1986. I started with a piece of vine charcoal, sketching the overall shape and design of the tree, adding the trunk, some branches and shapes for the foliage. Vine charcoal lends itself to easy corrections because it can be easily removed with tissue or your hand. It also makes luscious blacks. The drawing was finished with a 6B charcoal pencil by adding details — more branches and emphasis on some of the foliage. For me, this drawing created a memorable tree portrait. I hope it will help you to start noticing tree shapes.

GUEST PLANTS

In addition to birds and countless insects that attach themselves to trees, you will also find climbing plants. The drawing below (left) is of one such visitor. Woodbine, or Virginia creeper, can be identified by a cluster of five serrated-edged leaves. In the fall these leaves turn a brilliant red — which could possibly be the reason people mistake it for poison ivy. The leaves grow on a vine that attaches itself to the bark, creeping up the length of the tree.

The drawing below (right) is of another climber. This is poison ivy, and as you will be sketching and painting outdoors often, you should familiarize yourself with it.

Note the shape of the leaf — shiny with three lobes to a single leaf. It is also a climber, but you can easily see the difference. Woodbine has a cluster of five leaves, and poison ivy has a cluster of three. If you are in doubt, avoid and go around it.

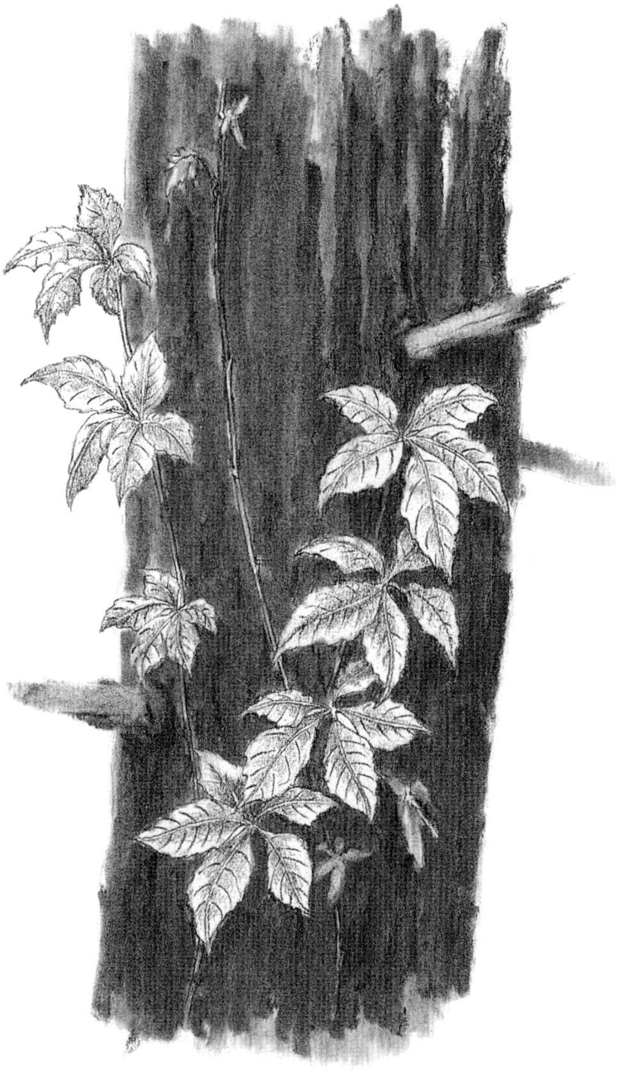

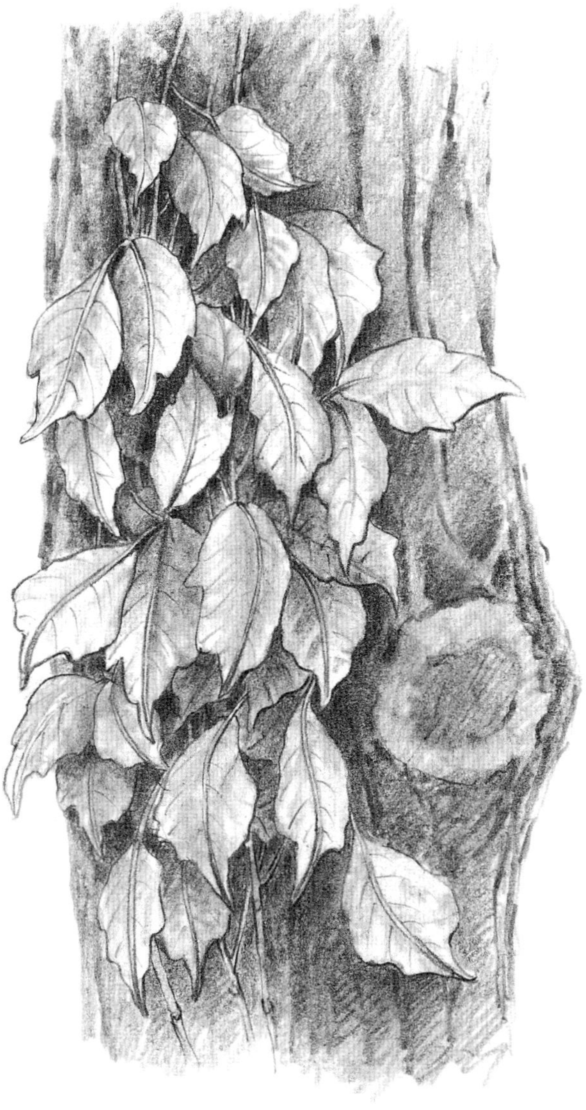

The plant shown here, though not poisonous, is a killer. This is wild grape, which sends vines out in all directions, attaching to and climbing on everything in sight. It literally suffocates a tree through its sheer weight and amount of foliage it places on the host tree. Eventually the excessive weight will cause branches to break, prevent natural growth and cause the tree to die. I have seen vines 3" (8cm) in diameter growing up trees. When beetles attack the grape leaves, they create interesting designs for the artist, but the plant is still a definite menace to trees.

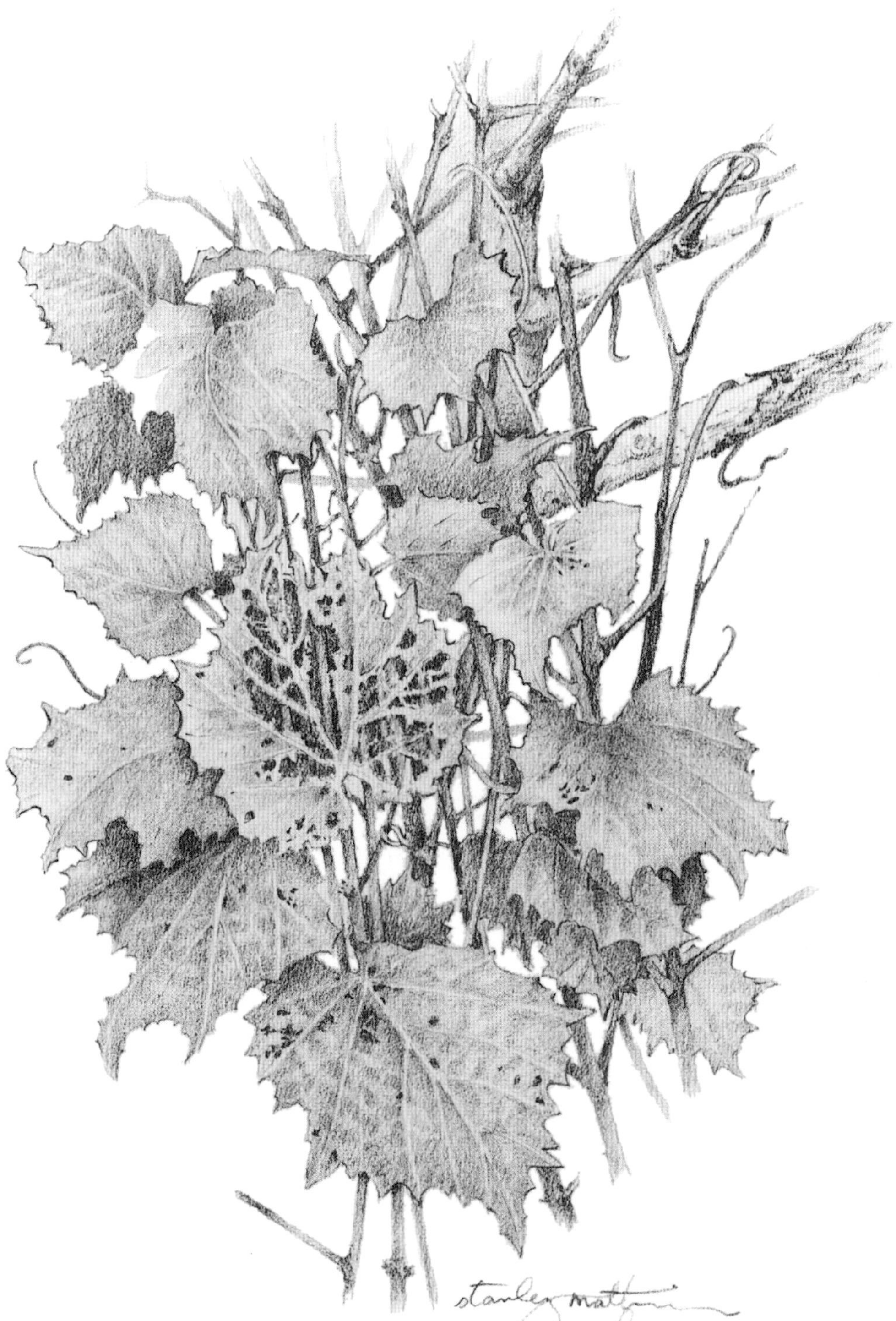

Uninvited Guest, 11" x 15" (28cm x 38cm), graphite on Strathmore Bristol.

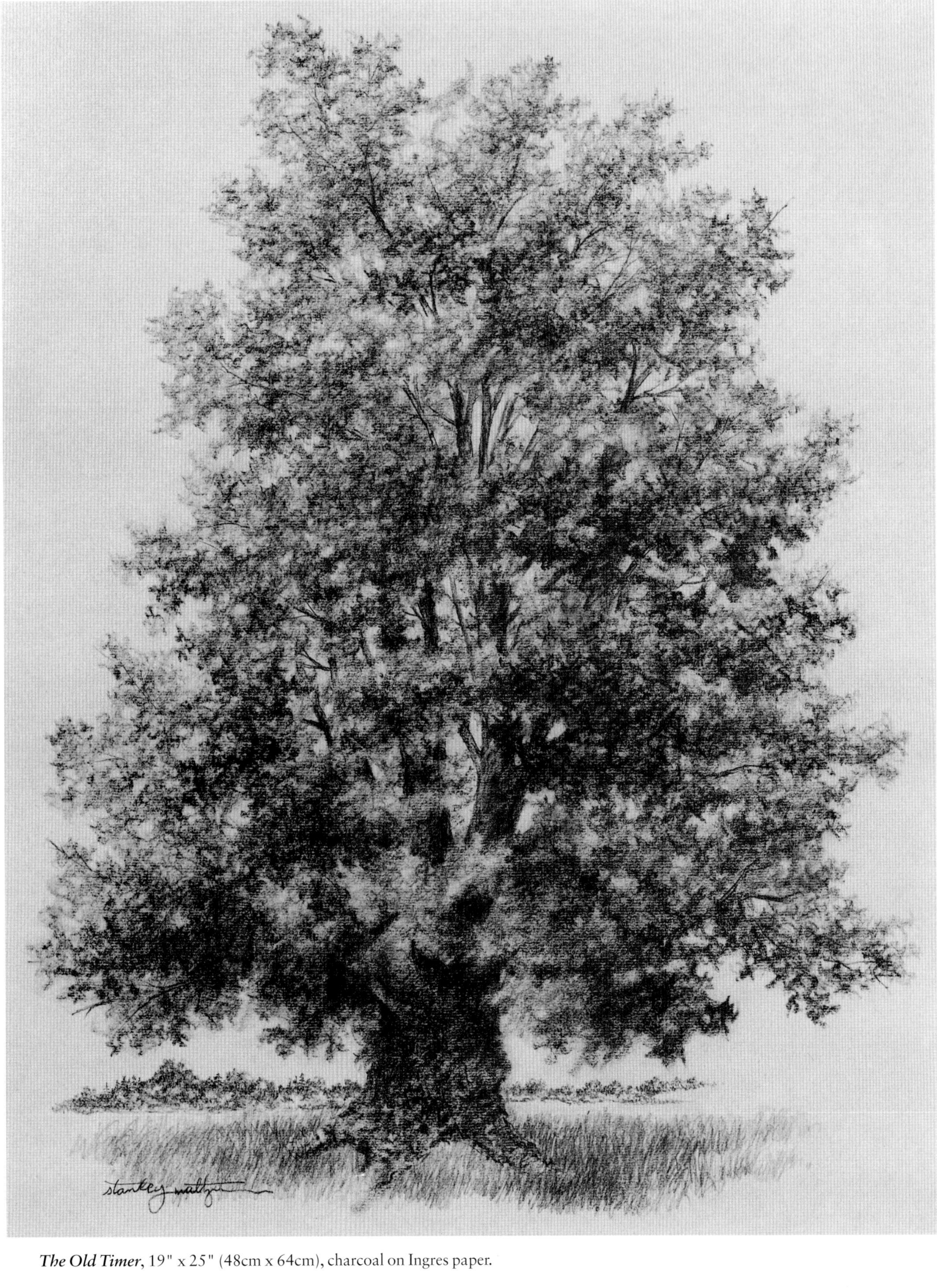

The Old Timer, 19" x 25" (48cm x 64cm), charcoal on Ingres paper.

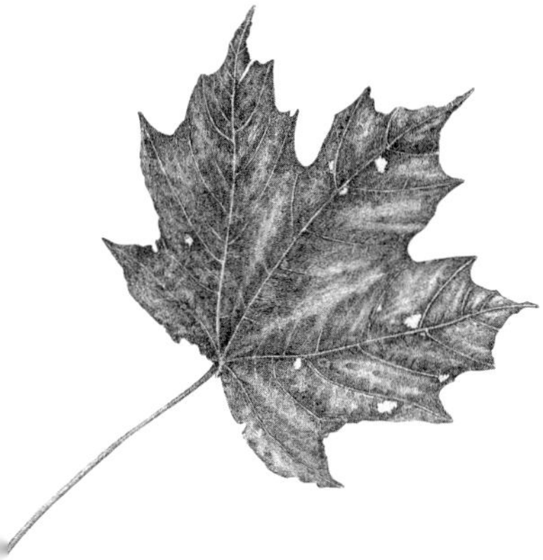

CHAPTER THREE

Drawing Individual Trees

Before you attempt to draw a tree, try familiarizing yourself with the subject at hand by walking around it. Touch it, smell it, and finally sit down and study it some more before you start to work. In short, become a part of the tree you are going to draw. You will be surprised at the contribution the time spent doing these simple acts will have on your work.

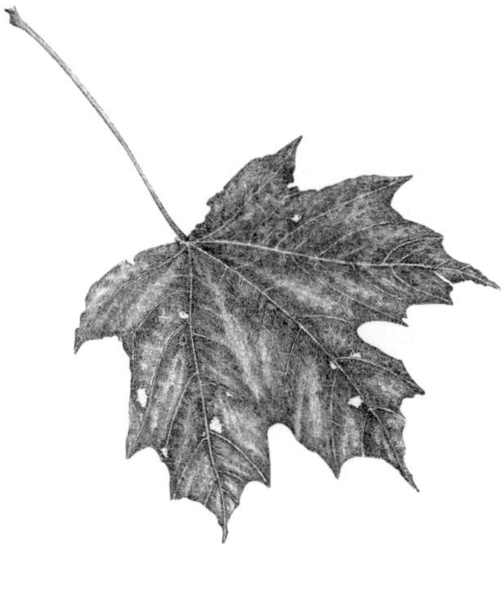

HOW TO DRAW A TREE

When you set out to draw a tree, look for its main structure and forget about adding small branches and twigs. Start by sharpening your pencil to a nice point and sketch an outline like a contour drawing. Remember to keep your lines loose, as shown here with pencil A.

When you have a reasonable facsimile that meets with your approval, use your 2B pencil (whose point you have sanded to an angle for shading) to shape thinner branches with one stroke, using the edge for fine lines as shown with pencil B.

As you shape or as you wear the lead down, it will become wider. Keeping the angle, use that wider lead to shade the wider branches, boughs or trunk as shown with pencil C. When you need finer lines or branches, sharpen the wide lead to the desired width, or keep several pencils sharpened to avoid interrupting your train of thought — one pencil for thin strokes and another for wider ones.

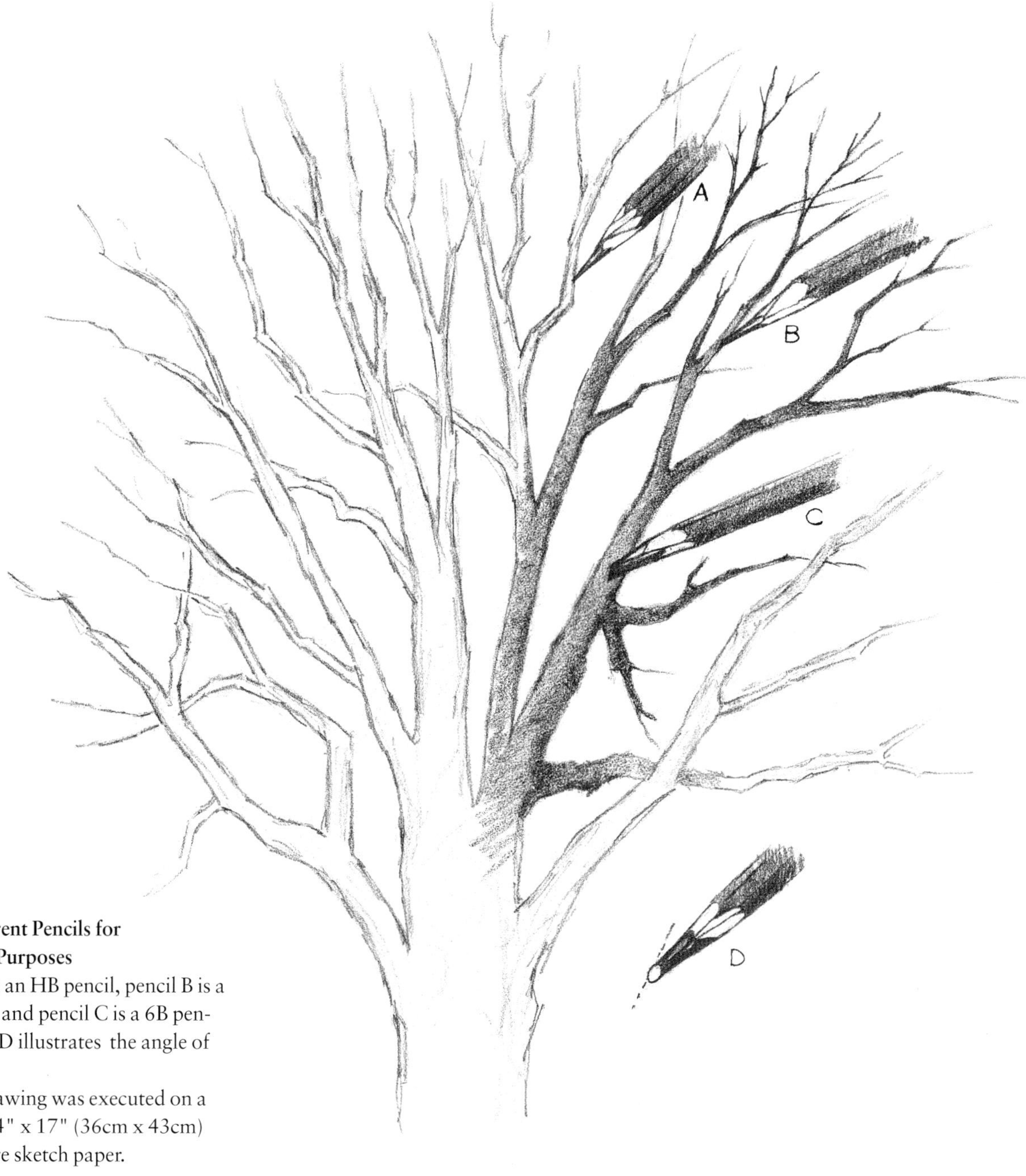

Use Different Pencils for Different Purposes
Pencil A is an HB pencil, pencil B is a 2B pencil, and pencil C is a 6B pencil. Pencil D illustrates the angle of the lead.

This drawing was executed on a piece of 14" x 17" (36cm x 43cm) Strathmore sketch paper.

APPLE TREES

Apple trees provide a wonderment of material for you the artist. In the spring there are buds and then flowers; summer brings foliage and the bearing of fruit; with fall comes the harvest of fruits; and with winter there is the interesting anatomy of the tree. Angular shapes, shoots growing in every direction, old derelicts still alive with amazing hollows in the trunk — in short, there is something for everyone.

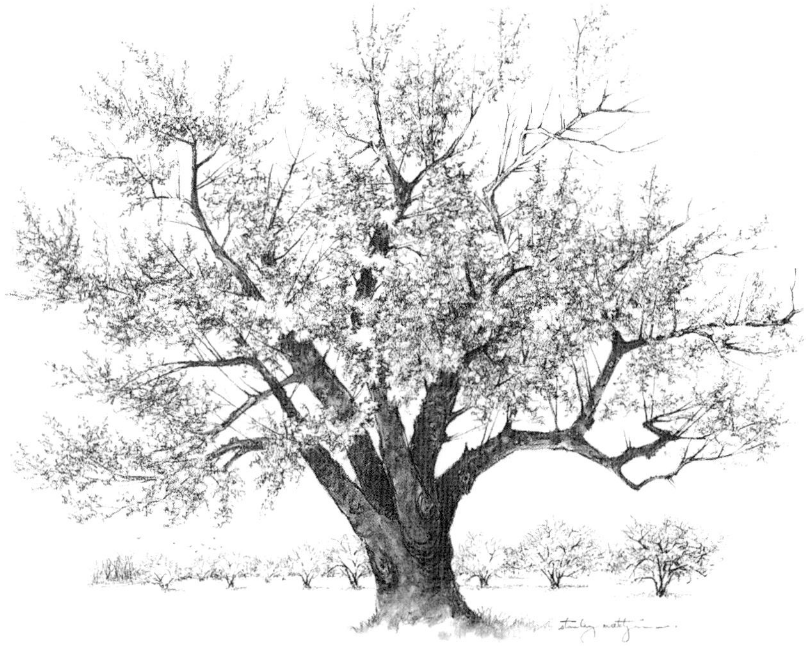

An Apple in Full Bloom
This drawing of an apple tree in full bloom was made on an old sheet of Whatman paper (English) watermarked 1960. To make this drawing, take an HB charcoal pencil and lightly sketch the trunk, branches and foliage. Do not be concerned with extra lines, as they will be covered as your drawing progresses. Remember not to erase much, as erasing causes harm to the surface of your beautiful piece of paper. To strengthen your values, increase pressure with your HB pencil or change to a 2B pencil and continue building shapes. Finish your strongest darks (values) with a 4B charcoal pencil.

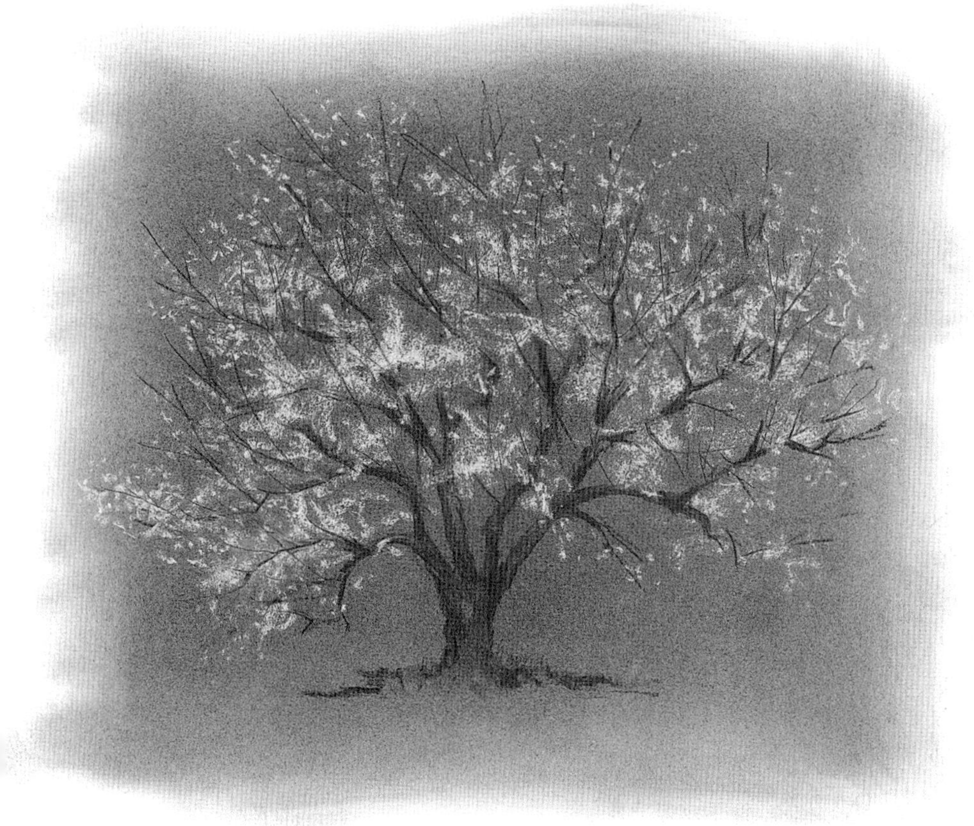

An Apple Tree in the Spring
To create this drawing of a spring apple tree in bloom, take charcoal dust that you can collect as you sharpen your pencils, or purchase some. Dip a small piece of cotton into the charcoal, shake to remove the excess, then, using light pressure in a circular motion, apply to your paper. As the paper becomes covered, increase pressure in a circular motion to get an even tone.

Congratulations, you have just toned a sheet of paper! Instead of charcoal dust, try pastel dust or a stick of soft pastel to achieve a colored background (this is in lieu of colored papers). With a 4B charcoal pencil, draw the branches and trunk. Use a piece of white pastel to suggest flowers. In this case I used a Schmincke soft pastel. Be careful not to overdo the flowers; no detail, just suggest. Let the viewers use their imaginations.

Sketch Lightly

The drawing at right shows a preliminary sketch of another apple tree. With your HB or B charcoal pencil, lightly start your sketch. When I say lightly sketch, I mean caress your paper with your pencil (or whatever you are working with). My beginning sketches here will always appear darker than they should because I want you to be able to see them. If I worked in my usual manner (just caressing the paper with my pencil), you might not see my initial drawing. So remember, just lightly touch the paper.

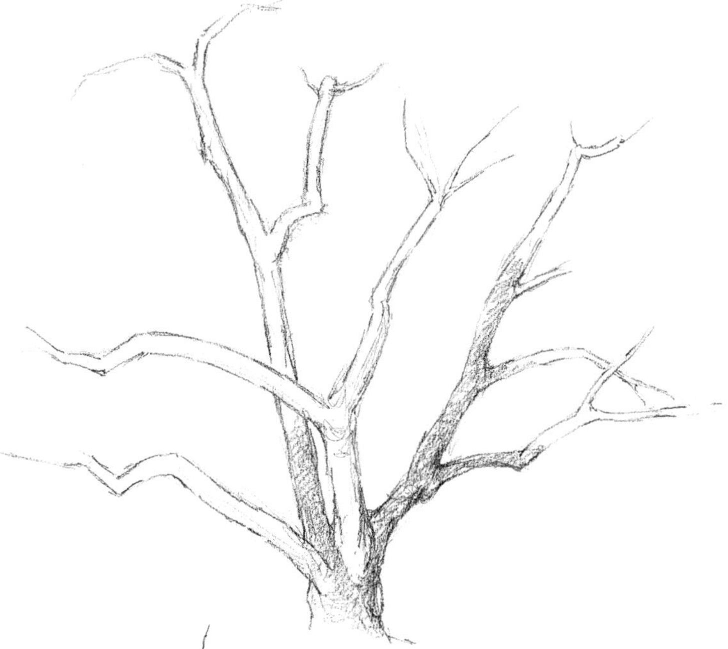

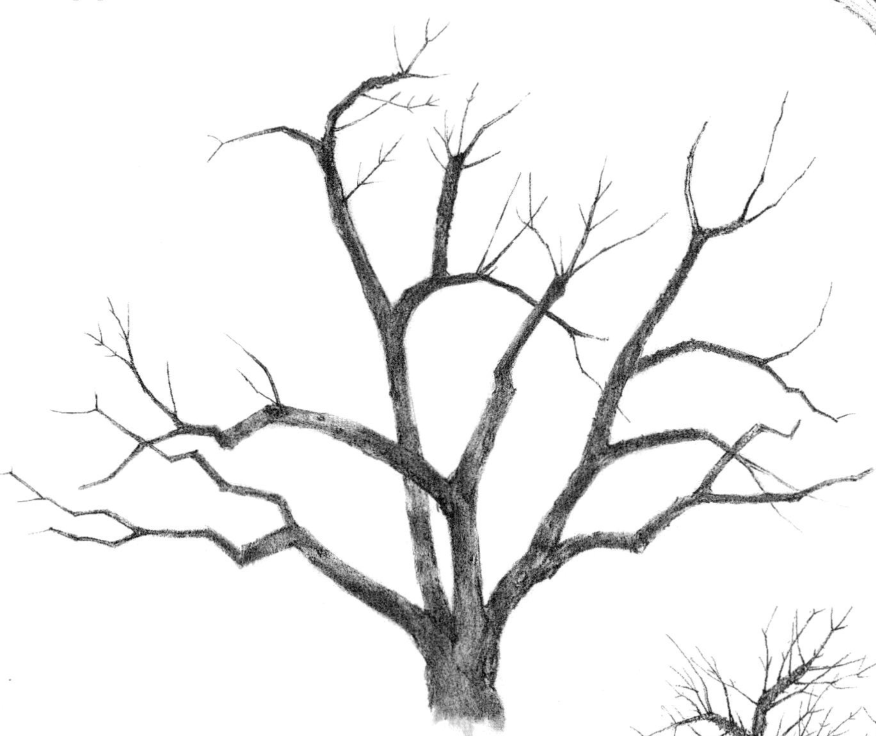

Add Values

The drawing at left illustrates the adding of values using a 2B charcoal pencil, then stomping it to create tone and texture. You can also use a kneaded eraser to create values by pressing it into the charcoal to remove areas that will be highlighted. Wipe the residue you remove onto a clean sheet before applying the eraser to your drawing again or you will end up pushing the residue back into the drawing. Then add some indications of knotholes and tree growth.

Add Details

Here is an apple tree in dire need of pruning, but with an attractive design due to all the overgrowth and overlapping shoots. Use an HB pencil with a sharp point and add twigs and shoots. Start at the top and then skip around, building all over. This method will keep your picture flowing rather than having one part finished and another looking like it does not belong.

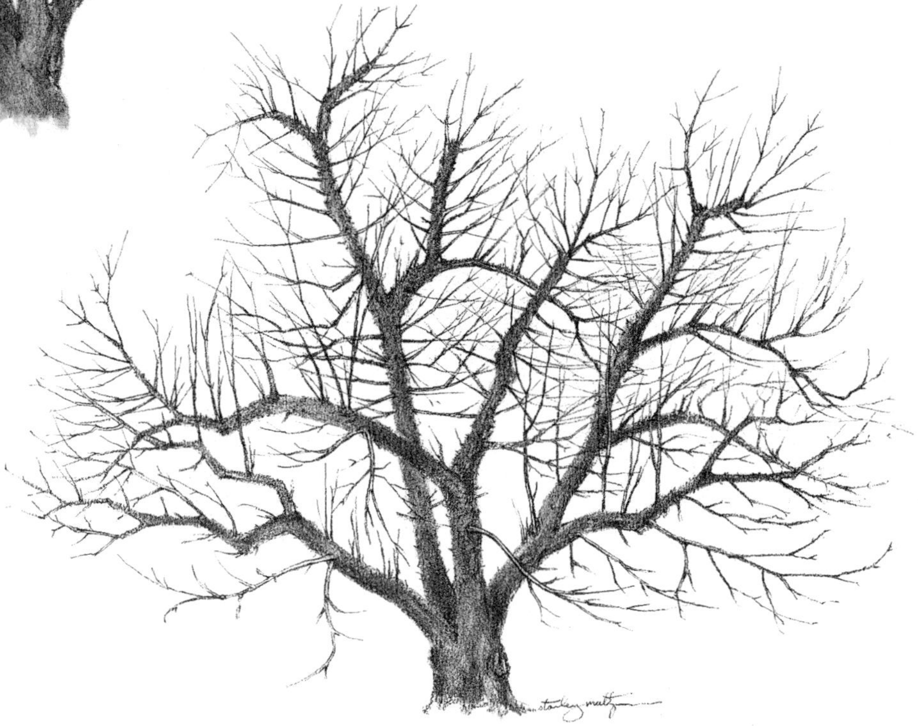

CHERRY TREES

Two of the more common varieties of cherry trees are the black cherry and the sweet cherry. The black cherry tree is distinguishable from the sweet cherry because it has a more tree-like form than that of a large shrub or bush, like the choke cherry. The black cherry's leaves are also thinner and its fruit is sweeter — a delight for birds and humans. Talking with one of the icons of my area, I was informed that the black cherry was also once known as the rum tree because of the liquid delight one could make from the fruit when placed in a crock and left to ferment.

The sweet cherry tree in full bloom is always a memorable sight. Notice that in the drawing below of this beautiful tree, I did not draw a single individual flower or petal. The whole idea is to simulate and suggest without drawing everything, so that your drawing looks like it has it all. In reality, you are leading the viewer to assume that every flower is there, which makes for a very successful picture.

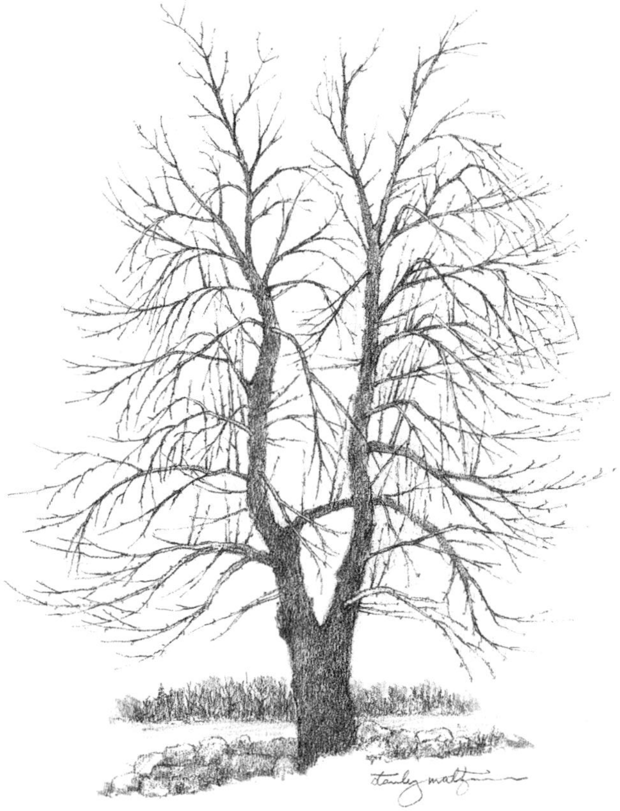

Black Cherry
This is a charcoal drawing of a black cherry tree — growing in the wild woods close to where I live — which I was fortunate enough to find. The drawing was made on a piece of 2-ply Strathmore with a 2B charcoal pencil and a bit of stomping with a felt paper stomp.

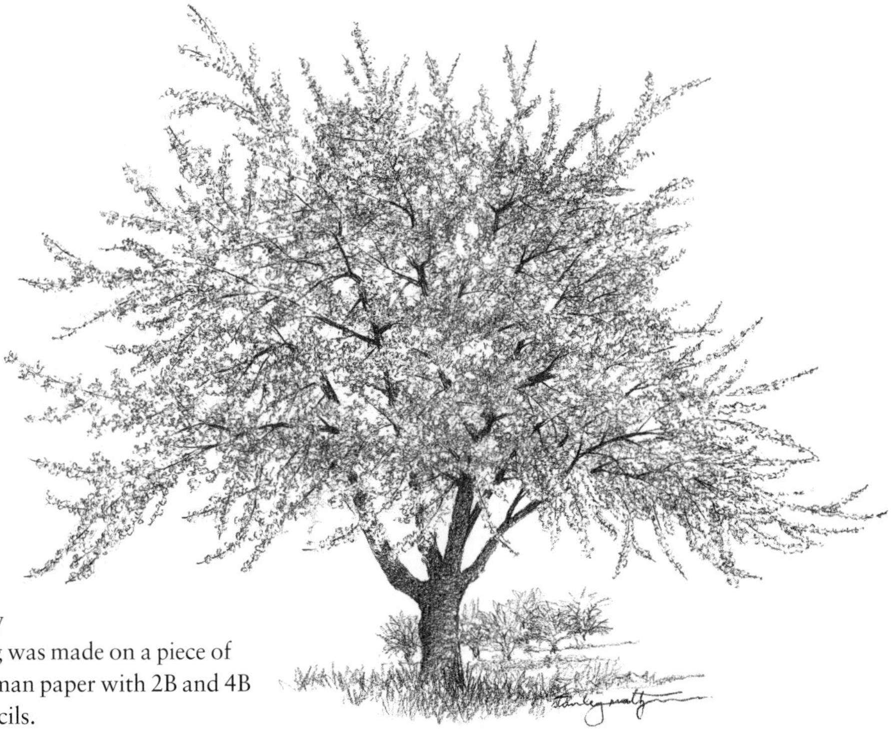

Sweet Cherry
This drawing was made on a piece of 72-lb. Whatman paper with 2B and 4B charcoal pencils.

BLACK WALNUT

The black walnut has a variety of shapely branches and nuts that might be used for a still-life composition. These stately looking ladies can grow to lofty heights and branch outward to create interesting shapes and offer good shade. I planted one near my studio and welcome the shade it offers every summer.

The fruit of the black walnut is a hard, delicious nut encased in a greenish-colored husk. If you take the husk, place it in water and let it soak a while, you will end up with a light tan-colored substance that can be used to tone a background sketch. (Note that this has not been tested to determine if the result is of archival quality.)

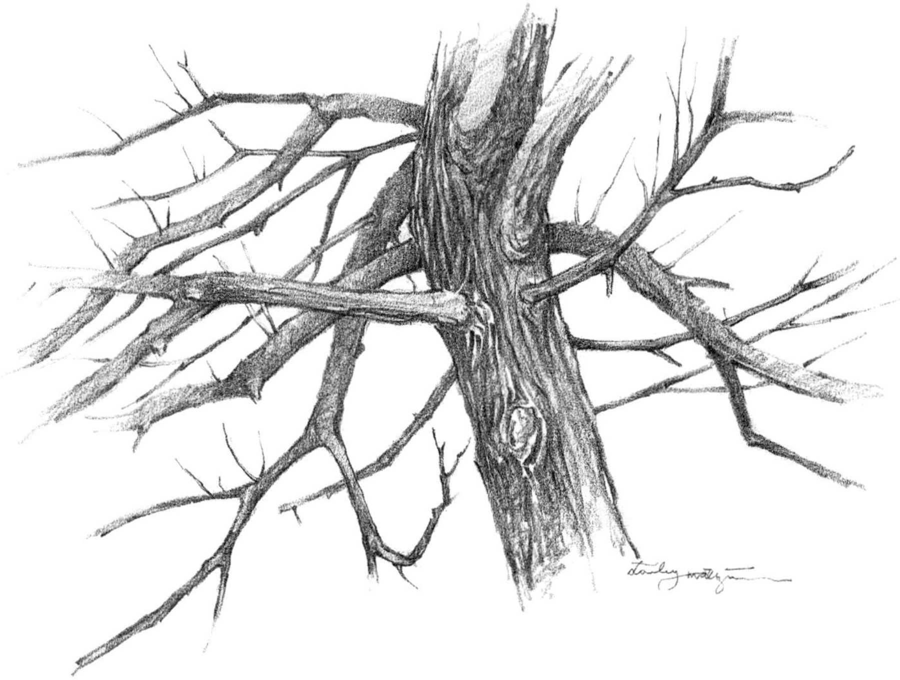

Walnut Trees Provide Interesting Shapes
Here are some of the interesting shapes you can find in a walnut tree. This drawing was created with a 6B graphite pencil on Rives BFK paper using the flat of the lead for shading and turning to the side for fine lines and accents.

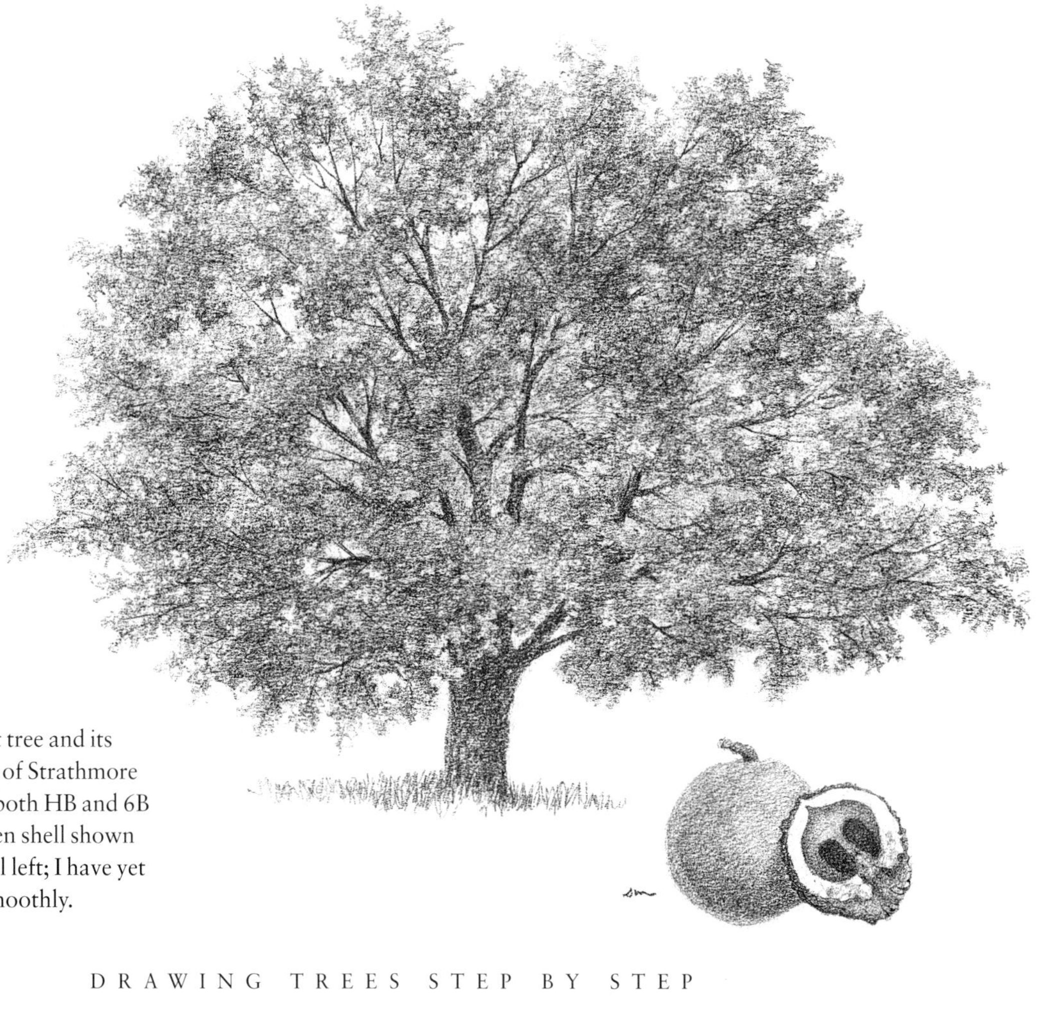

The Black Walnut
This drawing of a walnut tree and its fruit was done on a piece of Strathmore Bristol 2-ply paper with both HB and 6B charcoal pencils. The open shell shown here is what a red squirrel left; I have yet to break one open this smoothly.

OAK TREES

One of the many beauties of the oak family is that they add wonderful color to our winter woods by retaining their leaves. Through most of the winter months, you can see browns and reds — a bonus for you the artist.

Pin Oaks

The pin oak is readily recognizable by the downward angle of the bottom branches and the straight trunks of younger trees. It also has many intermingling twigs, more so than other oaks like the swamp white oak, whose leaves are also quite different.

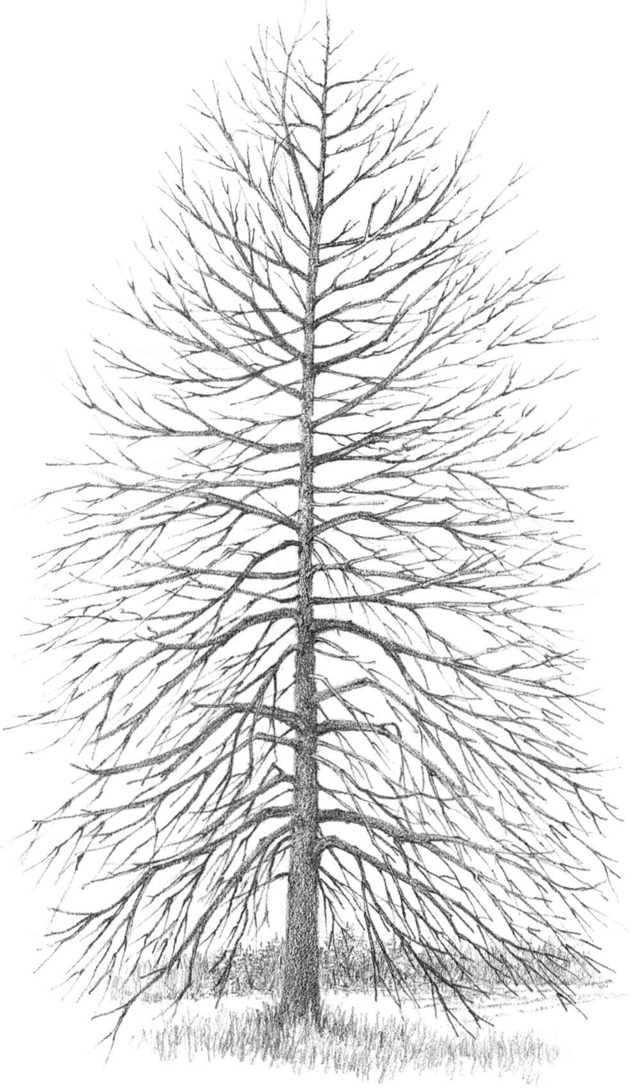

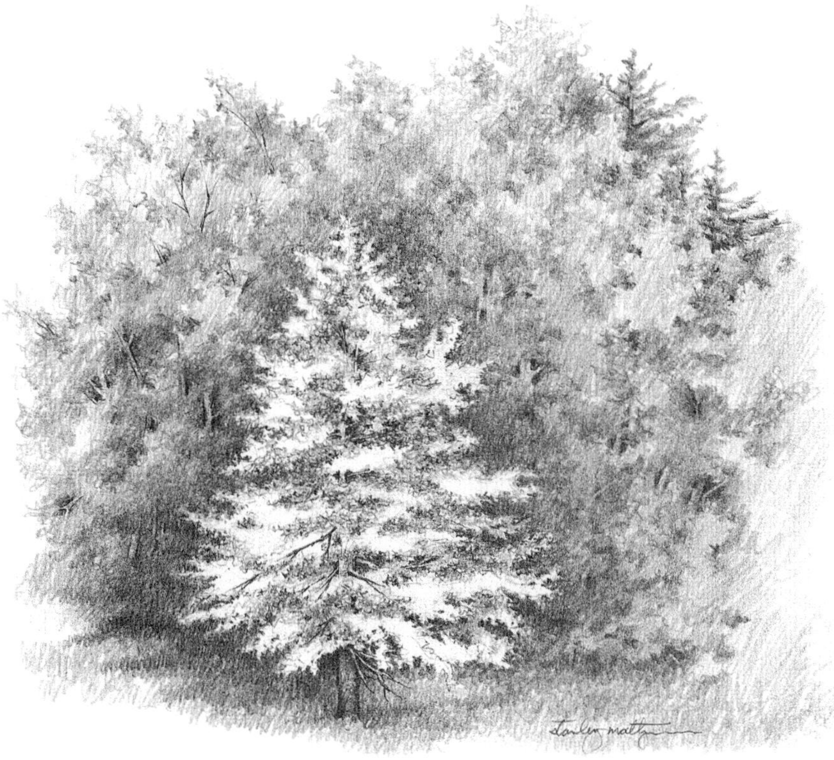

Use Negative Space to Bring a Tree Forward
To make the pin oak shown in this drawing come forward, make the most of negative spaces. Leave most of the tree silhouetted without much shading against a darker background, creating a positive color (the white of the tree) against the negative (various grays and darks) background. Do this in a subtle manner and the subject (in this case, our tree) will blend into the overall picture nicely, like it belongs, and not resemble a cutout pasted in your picture.

White Oak

If ever there was a tree that could be thought of as majestic, it is the white oak. It grows to great heights with massive boughs, and the trunk easily measures four feet or more in diameter. This strength that it portrays makes it a favorite among writers and artists.

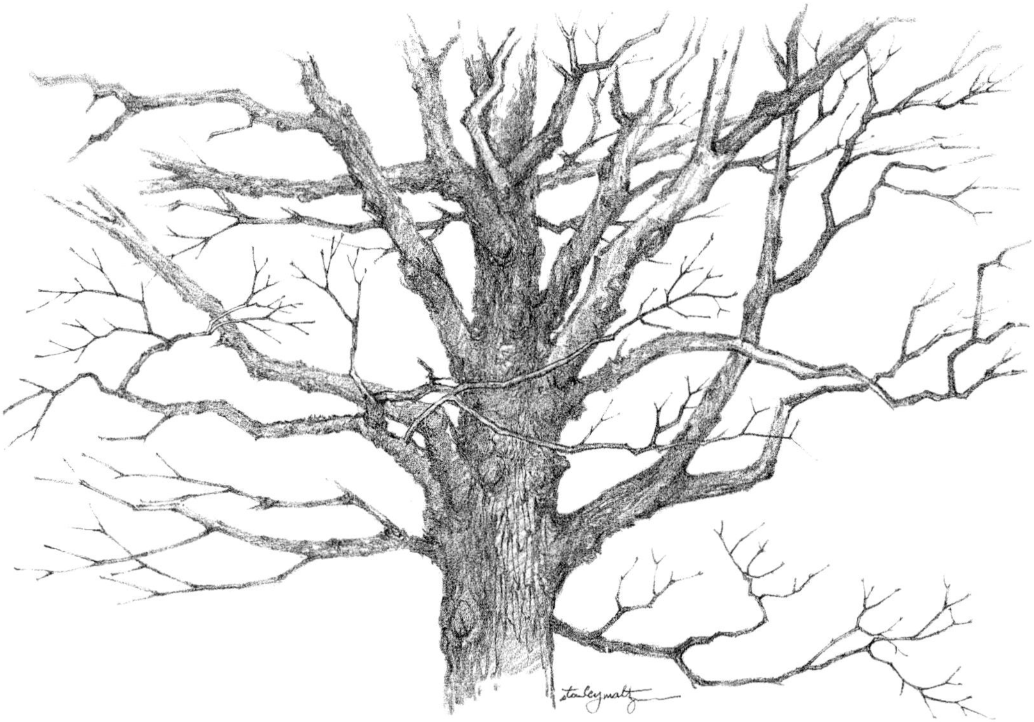

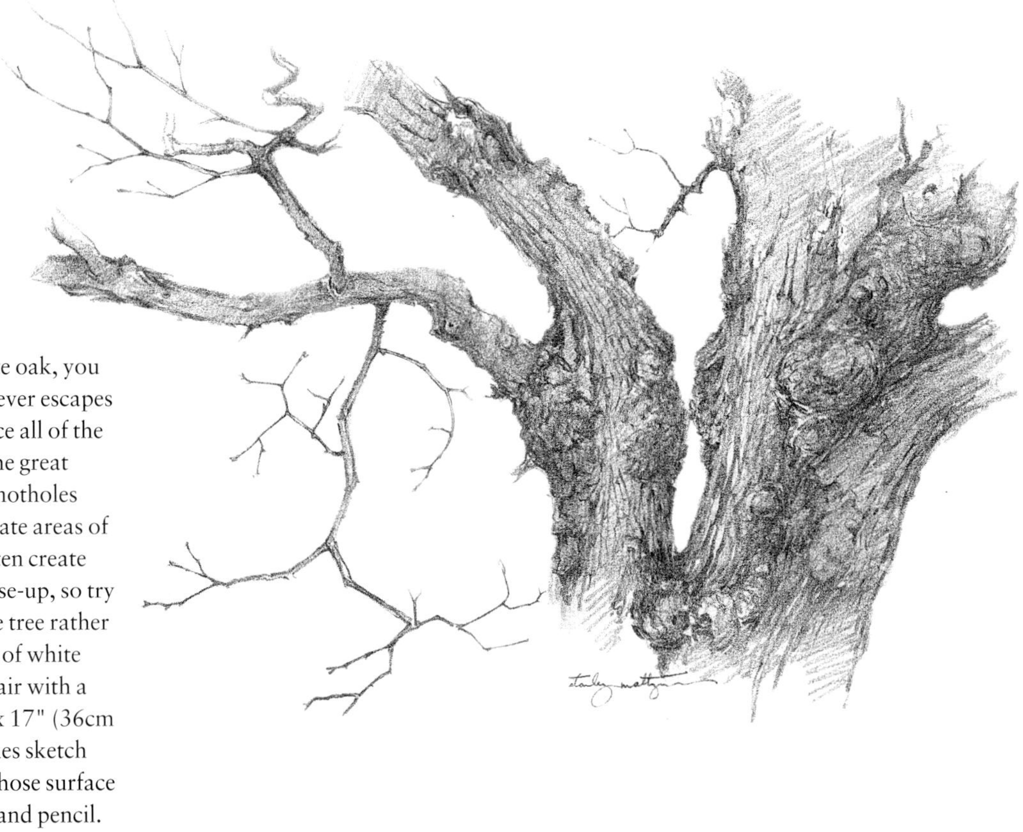

The White Oak in Detail

In these two studies of a white oak, you can easily see how this tree never escapes the interest of an artist. Notice all of the possibilities it has to offer. The great branches, the growths, the knotholes and the many textures all create areas of interest. Your subject will often create even more interest with a close-up, so try to sketch just a portion of the tree rather thanall of it. These drawings of white oaks were executed en plein air with a 6B graphite pencil on a 14" x 17" (36cm x 43cm) Strathmore 400 Series sketch pad, an inexpensive paper whose surface complements both charcoal and pencil.

Red Oak

The red oak is a beautiful tree that will grow quite tall and have a good spread of dark foliage. The leaves turn deep orange and red in the fall, making it an interesting tree to include in your landscapes. An important observation for you to keep in mind when drawing large oaks are the sky holes. These are the spaces between your clusters of leaves that let the atmosphere show through, especially on the uppermost twigs. Sky holes will add more depth to your pictures.

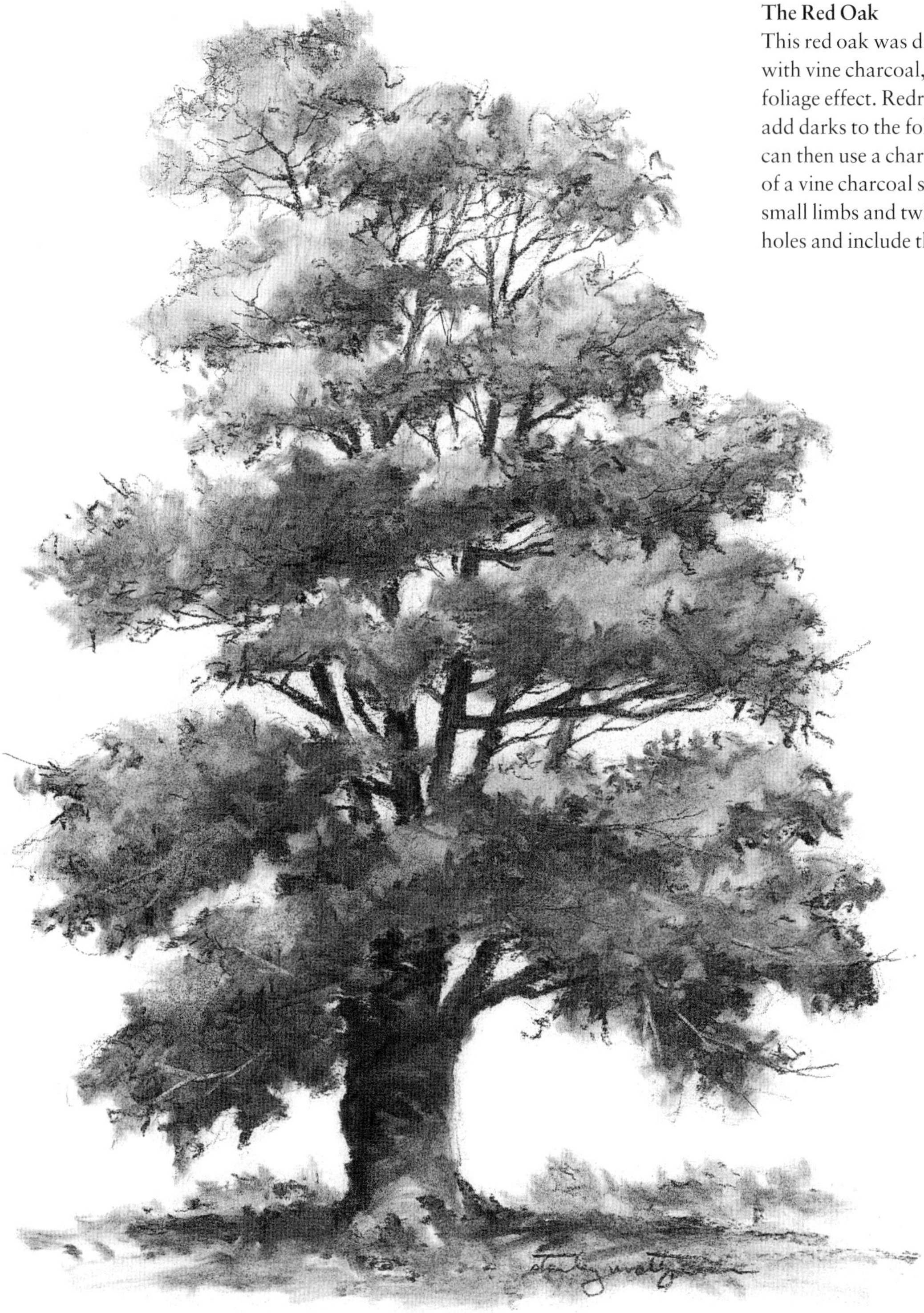

The Red Oak

This red oak was drawn on 2-ply Bristol with vine charcoal, then stomped for a foliage effect. Redraw with charcoal to add darks to the foliage and wood. You can then use a charcoal pencil or the side of a vine charcoal stick to finish off the small limbs and twigs. Note the sky holes and include them to add depth.

WHITE WILLOW

The willow is very conspicuous because of its yellow blooms that add great color to the landscape, especially against the darker greens of other trees, like conifers. Often found with more than one trunk, white willows can grow quite tall and, unlike the weeping willow, its twigs do not hang down to sway in the wind quite as much. Nevertheless, it remains quite an attractive tree.

Usually found near some source of water, be it a stream, pond or lake, white willows root rather easily, and wherever you find one, you're bound to find more. Broken twigs are often caught at the water's edge, then root. The white willow also propagates readily from cuttings.

The White Willow
This drawing of a white willow was created on a piece of 2-ply Strathmore Bristol by first working with vine charcoal on the trunk, then stomping, and finally by returning with a 2B charcoal pencil for finer details, like the branches.

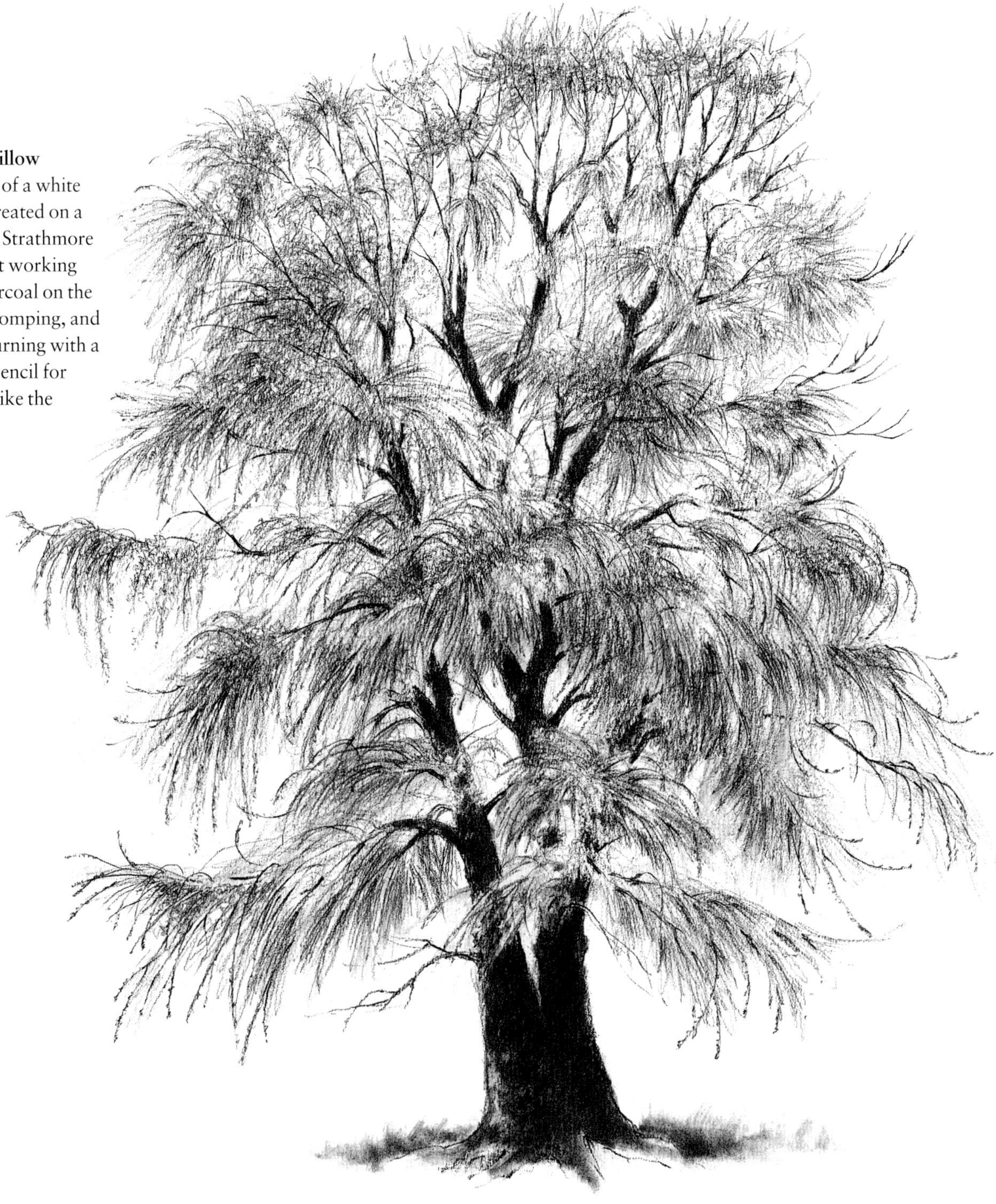

MAPLE TREES

Though there are many varieties of maples, only the sugar maple has a broad leaf with rounded shapes, as compared to the angular leaves of other maples.

To draw a maple like the one shown here, use a piece of vine charcoal to lightly sketch the outline of your tree, as shown in A. Include the overall shape, indications of leaf patterns and, again lightly, the wood (trunk, limbs and branches). Note the angle of the charcoal.

Next, turn the charcoal to the flat part as shown in B, and fill in your shapes or patterns of leaves that you created. Don't fill the entire area; let some white paper show through.

Using your stomp, push the vine charcoal around, as shown in C, to add character to your leaf shapes. Vine charcoal lends itself to being modeled and pushed around. Leave some black charcoal and white paper — you can always cover it if you don't like what you did.

Finally, return to the stomped area with your charcoal to add darks as shown in D. This will give your tree dimension, showing that it is a round, not flat, object. At this point you can alternate your darks with your stomp until you have the look or effect you desire; also add any additional limbs or branches. Squeeze your kneaded eraser to make whatever size branches you would like, and remove some charcoal to create light branches. Variation creates interest.

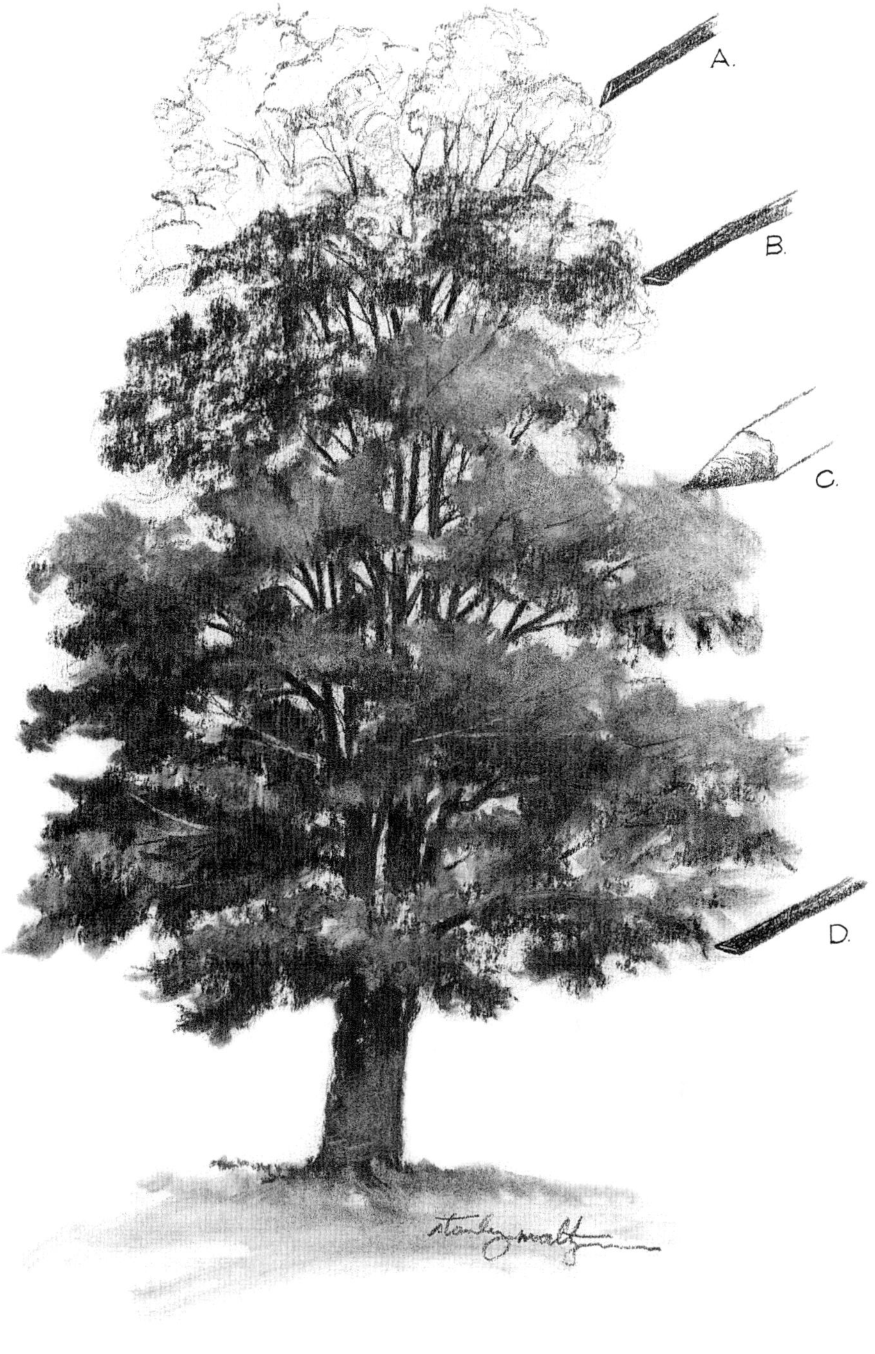

For this drawing, I used 2-ply Bristol because of its hard surface. It will allow many changes to the shapes and additional applications of charcoal, if needed.

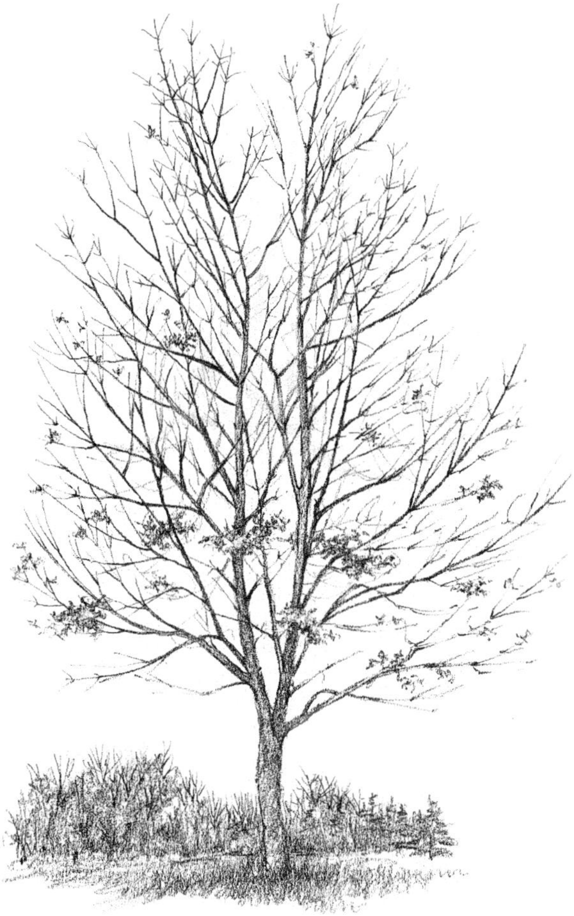

A Young Maple
This drawing is of a young maple with a few clumps of leaves left over from its autumn display. Because this is a young tree, you should remember to keep the wood thin — no heavy trunks, and limbs that grow upward rather than outward.

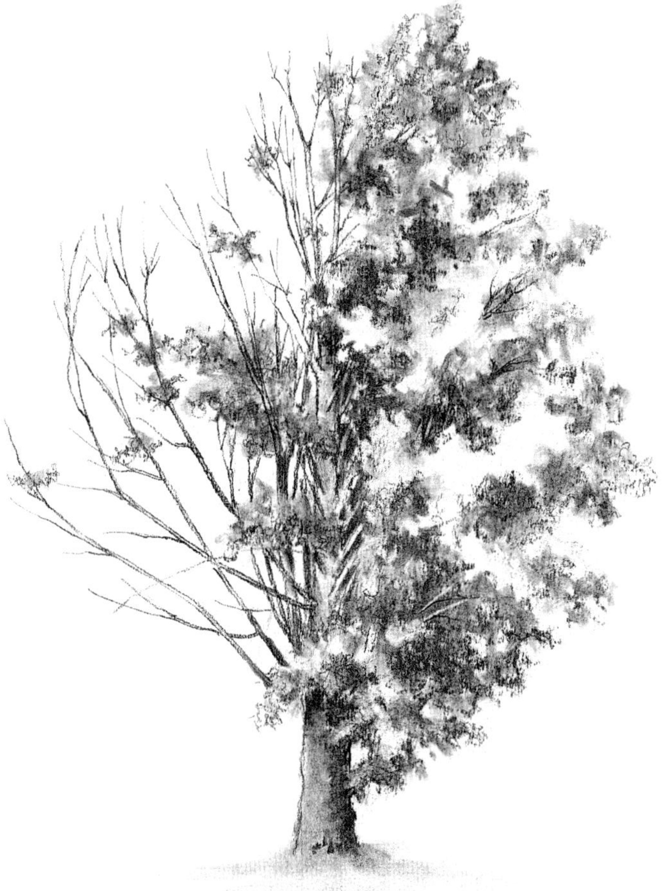

The Maple's Anatomy
I was fortunate to find this maple with half of its foliage missing. It offered a unique opportunity to see the basic upward formation of the limbs and foliage.

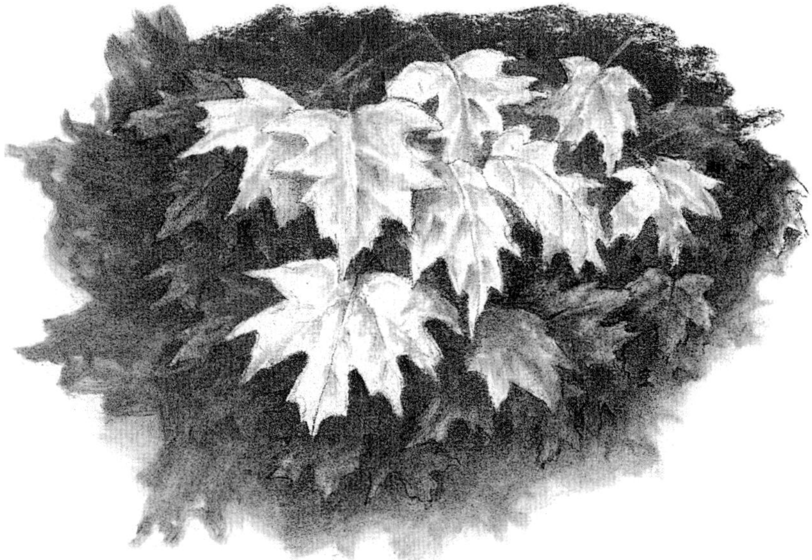

Maple Leaves
This group of sugar maple leaves is a perfect example of how you can move in on a subject and create a picture. I applied vine charcoal to silhouette the white leaves and then pushed it around with a stomp. Then using both a stomp and charcoal, I took away and added in where necessary to create additional leaf shapes. Lastly, I used a kneaded eraser to add stems and to highlight certain areas for additional detail.

NORWAY SPRUCE

When you include a pine or groups of pines in your picture, be sure to familiarize yourself with shapes. Ask yourself, "Do the limbs face up or down, and is the foliage dense or are there many windows exposing the skeleton of the tree?" These are a few important characteristics that you should be looking for. They will help you to place the proper tree in your picture, making it readily identifiable.

The dense conical shape of the Norway spruce makes it desirable for use during the yuletide season. Its twigs are more yellow than the other members of the spruce family, with flatter needles.

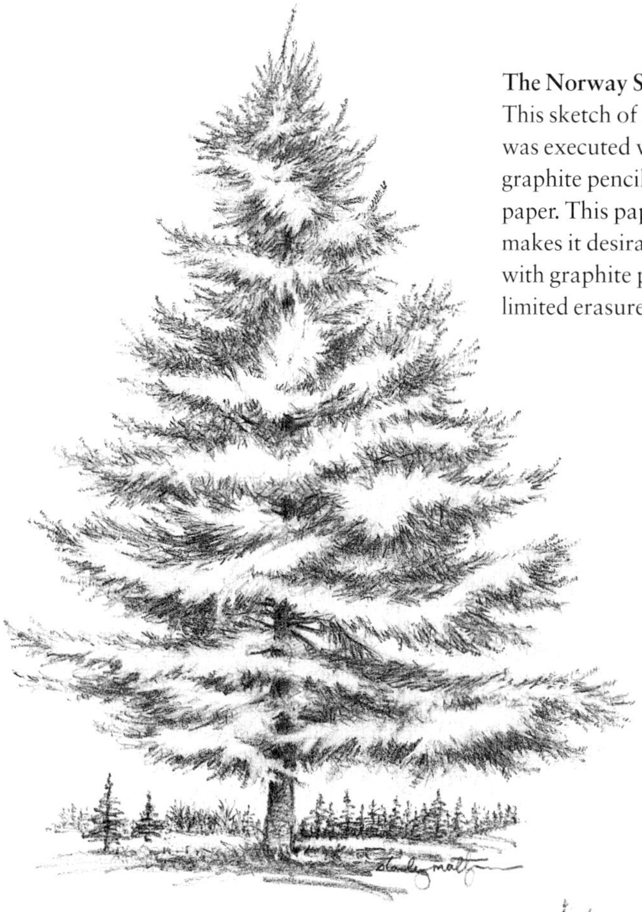

The Norway Spruce
This sketch of a Norway spruce was executed with HB and 4B graphite pencils on Rives BFK paper. This paper's soft surface makes it desirable for drawing with graphite pencils, but requires limited erasures.

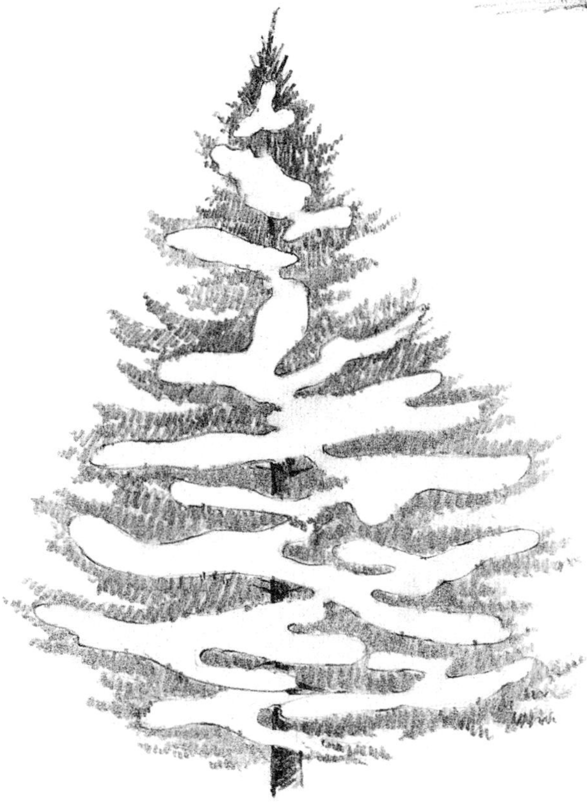

Look for Patterns of Light and Dark
This study shows the patterns of lights and darks on a tree. Every tree, whether it be coniferous or deciduous, will have a pattern of foliage formation. If you remember to look for these light and dark formations, you will find it to be a tremendous aid in selecting the right shapes for your trees.

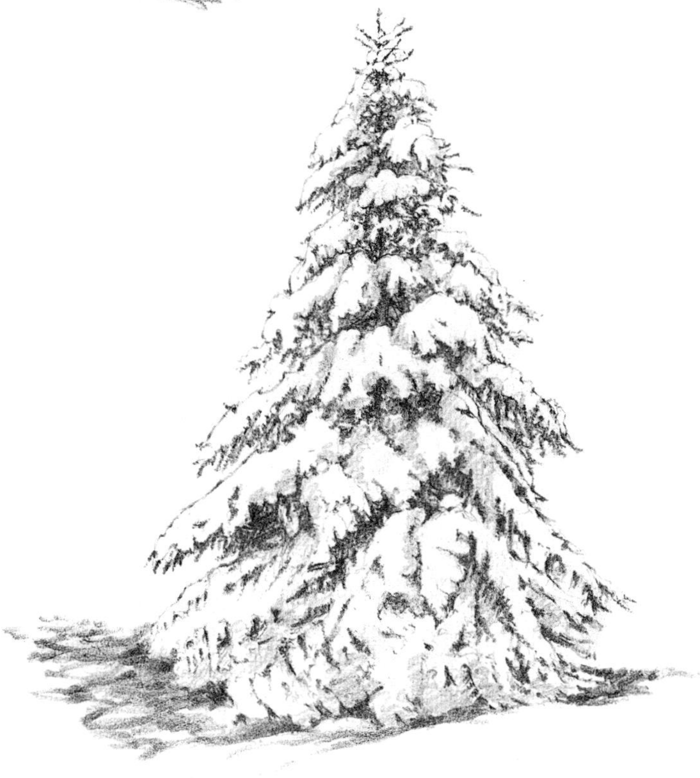

Putting Patterns of Light and Dark to Use
This drawing shows a tree after a snowstorm. Notice the difference between this sketch and the previous one of the pine. To create the appearance of snow, use soft lines with rounded edges. Create the impression of mounds rather than angular lines as used to portray the sharpness of pine needles.

WHITE PINE

The white pine is a tree of beauty that can be spotted from great distances. It has long graceful boughs curving outward and upward, giving the tree a very distinctive appearance, with lots of windows for great design potential. White pines grow quite large, and if you look at the underside of the needles, you will find a distinct white line.

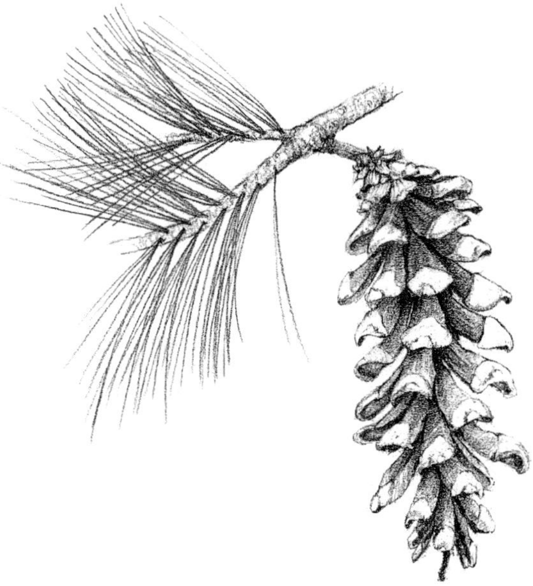

White Pine Needles
This illustration shows a small section of the white pine. The needles grow in groups of 5, each about 3" to 5 ½" (8cm to 14cm) long, with a long thin cone that can reach 8" (20cm). To preserve the fine needle detail in this type of drawing, select a hard surface paper, such as 2-ply Strathmore Bristol, and use an H graphite pencil. The cone, however, is drawn with H and 2B pencils.

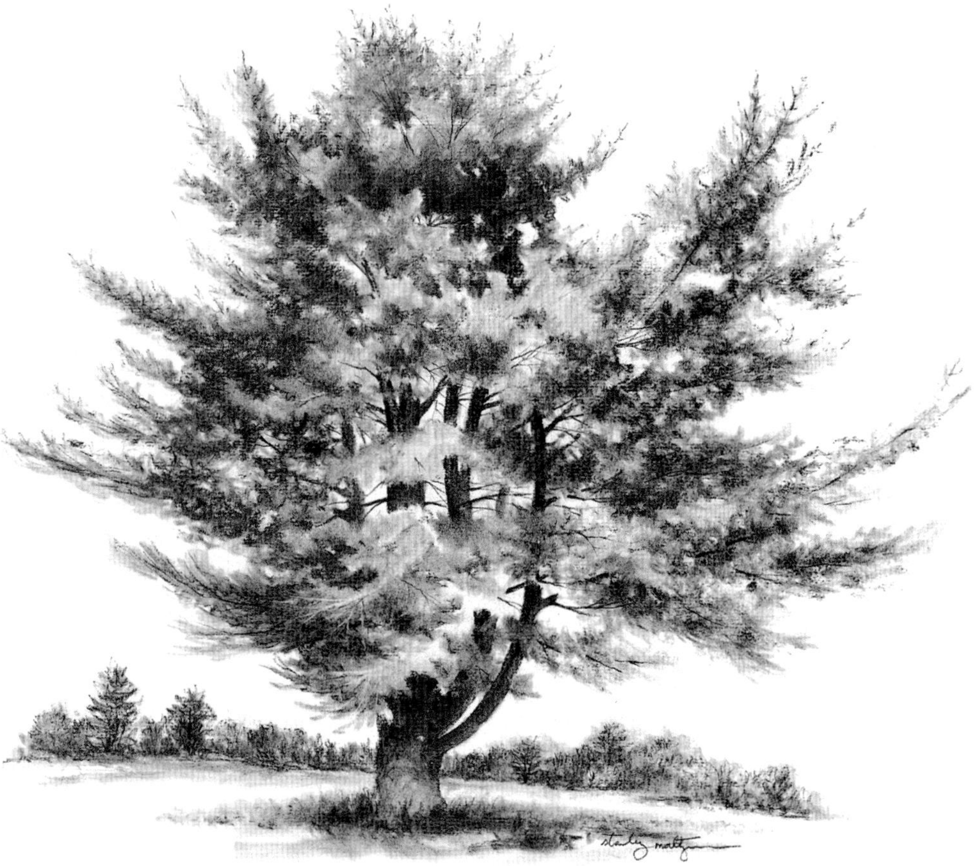

The White Pine
This white pine was drawn on a handmade sheet of Tovil paper by J. Barcham Green of England. The paper, called *laid paper*, was chosen because of its lined texture, which is caused by the screen used when producing the individual sheets of paper. When the paper dries, it keeps the lines of the screen and is excellent for grabbing soft vine charcoal. For this drawing, I pushed the charcoal around with my fingers and a stomp. Remember, when you shape with one side, you are also creating an angle on the other for working thin lines.

BIRCHES

If ever there was a tree that could remind one of a lady of the woods, I think the delicate birch would earn that distinction.

There are many varieties of birch, such as the white birch, paper birch and canoe birch. A distinct telltale of the paper birch is the thin strips that constantly seem to be peeling from the bark. Imagine the interesting picture a birch could create silhouetted against a dark woodland background.

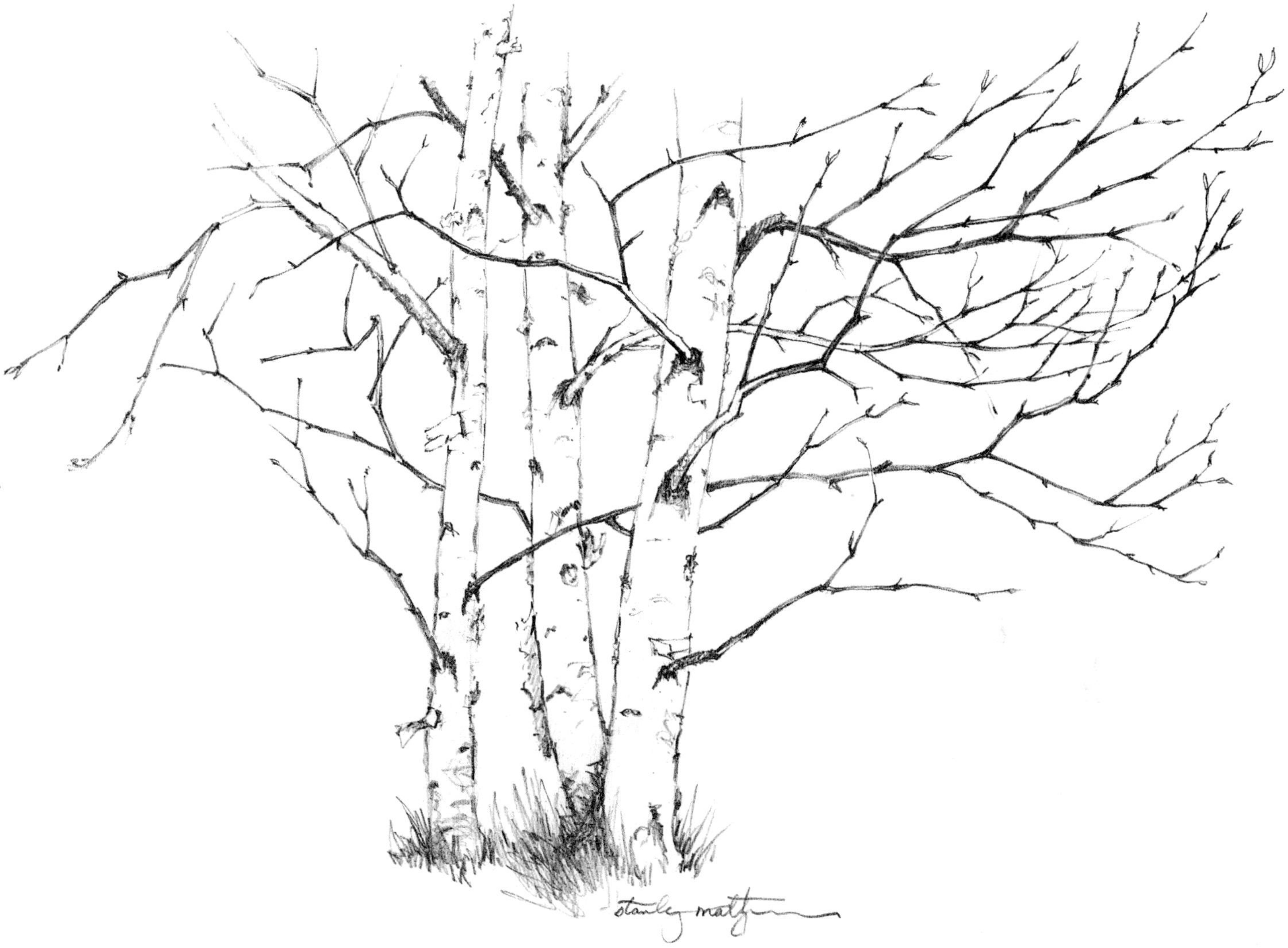

The Birch
This drawing of a birch was executed with a 2B graphite pencil on a sheet of Rives BFK paper. Note the thick/thin contour lines of the main trunks and the fineness of the lines that indicate the ends of the branches. This delicacy of line helps give the birch the feeling you should strive for.

ASPEN

Though similar to the birch, aspens are distinguishable in several ways. One is by the color of the bark, which is a beautiful pale green against the white of the birch. The leaves are also more fanlike, and it is interesting to see the way they seem to spin in the slightest of breezes. Don't confuse the aspen, however, with the poplar, which has a gray bark and vertical marks that resemble wrinkles.

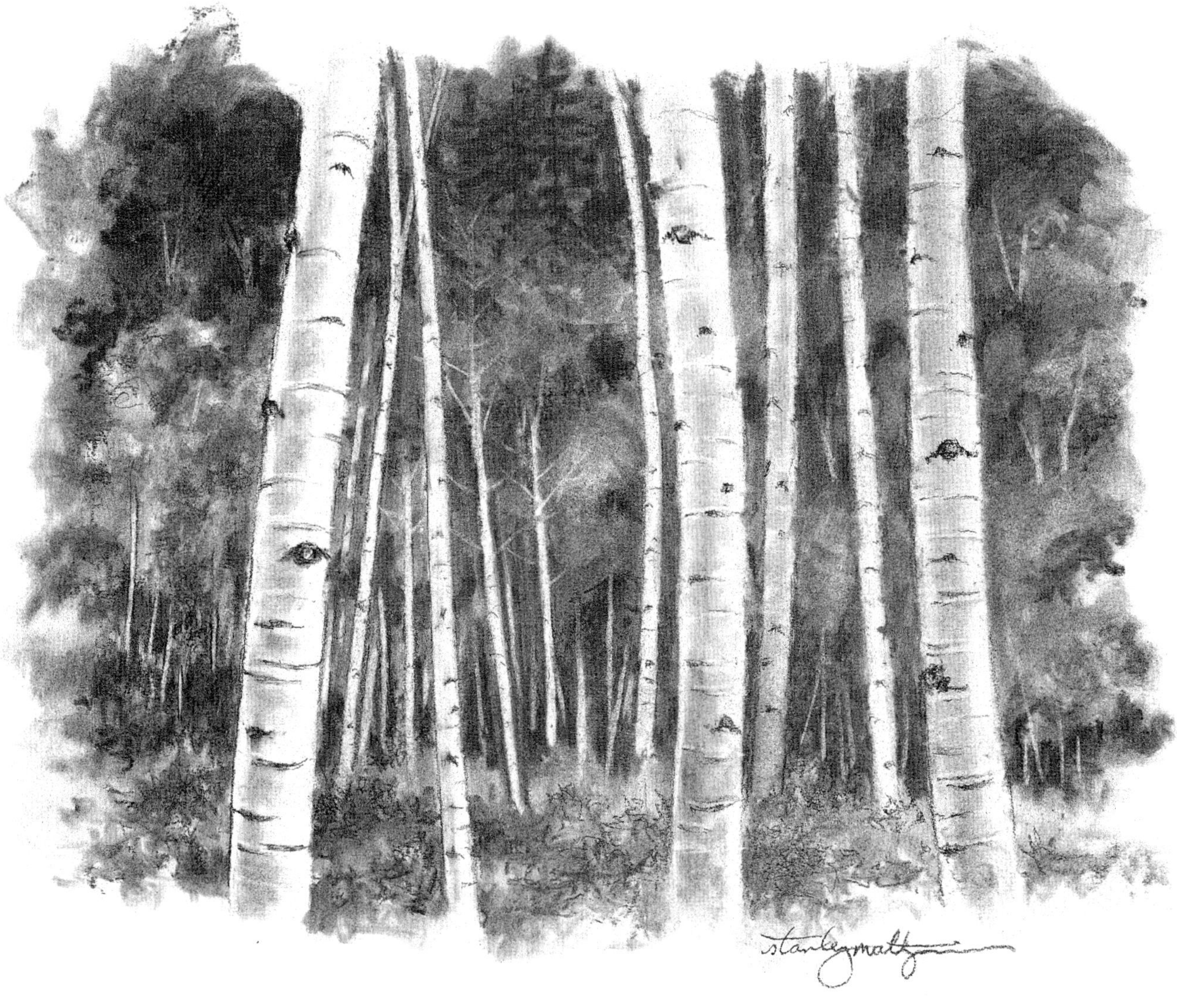

The Aspen
This drawing of an aspen in a wooded area was done on 2-ply Strathmore Bristol, again chosen because of the surface durability and being able to take more punishment than soft papers. I used a piece of medium vine charcoal, being careful to leave the white paper for the larger trees. After shaping the background forest by applying both medium and soft charcoal and by stomping to create tree shapes, I took away and added more charcoal until I was satisfied with the shapes. Then I squeezed my kneaded eraser into various thicknesses and removed even more charcoal, thus creating the thin background trees.

SYCAMORE

The sycamore, or buttonwood tree, as it is also known, is a very special and unique tree for artists to work with. Its beautiful white wood looks as if it had been bleached. Running up the boughs and branches are blotches of brown bark attached in a most interesting and unusual array of shapes. These varying shades of brown make a subject with countless possibilities for you to draw or paint.

Another outstanding characteristic of the sycamore is the angular way in which the branches and twigs grow. Take a little extra time to study this tree to get a feel for the unusual placement of these growths so that you do not overwork the oddity of the formations. In short, simplify.

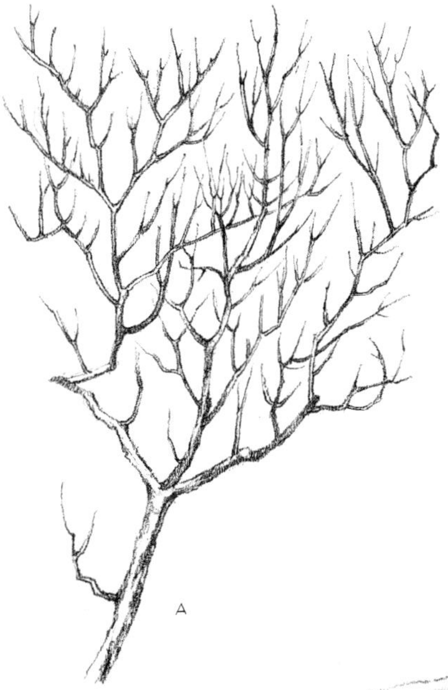

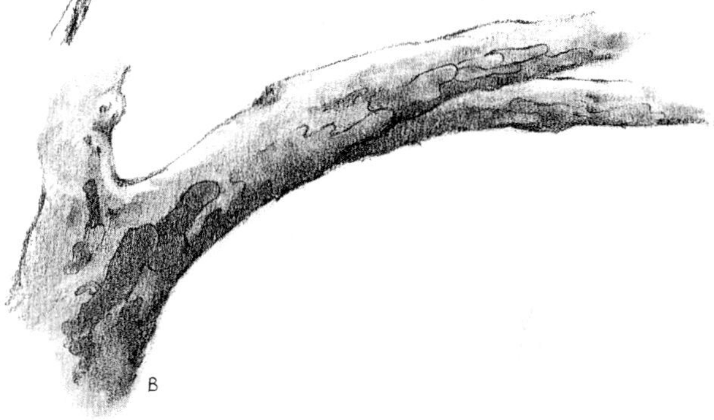

Sycamore Details
Drawing A above shows the two outstanding features of the sycamore: the angular shapes of the branches and the growth of the twigs. When you step back and look at the tree, notice the brushlike appearance of the upward growth, especially when the sun is hitting the crown of the tree. Drawing B shows the boughs with the odd-shaped brown blotches. Remember to keep it simple. Do not overwork the beautiful design of the bark.

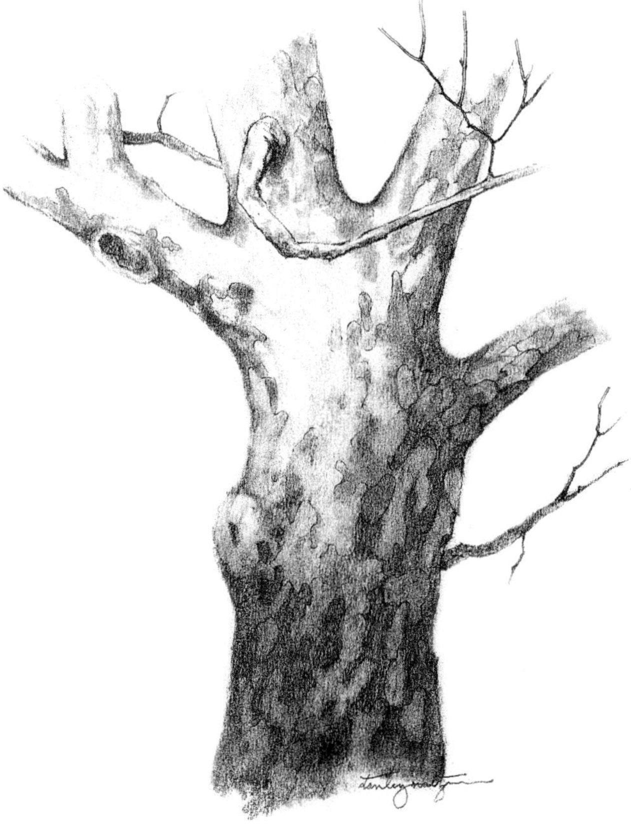

The Sycamore
This drawing (left) was started in the usual manner — an HB graphite pencil and a light sketch of the subject and bark shapes. I used a sheet of Strathmore 2-ply Bristol, knowing that I would be adding and deleting a great deal of graphite; thus a hard surface was more desirable. With a 6B pencil I applied tone, and with my stomp I distributed the dark and light values. I added more dark where needed, and used my kneaded eraser to lighten other shapes.

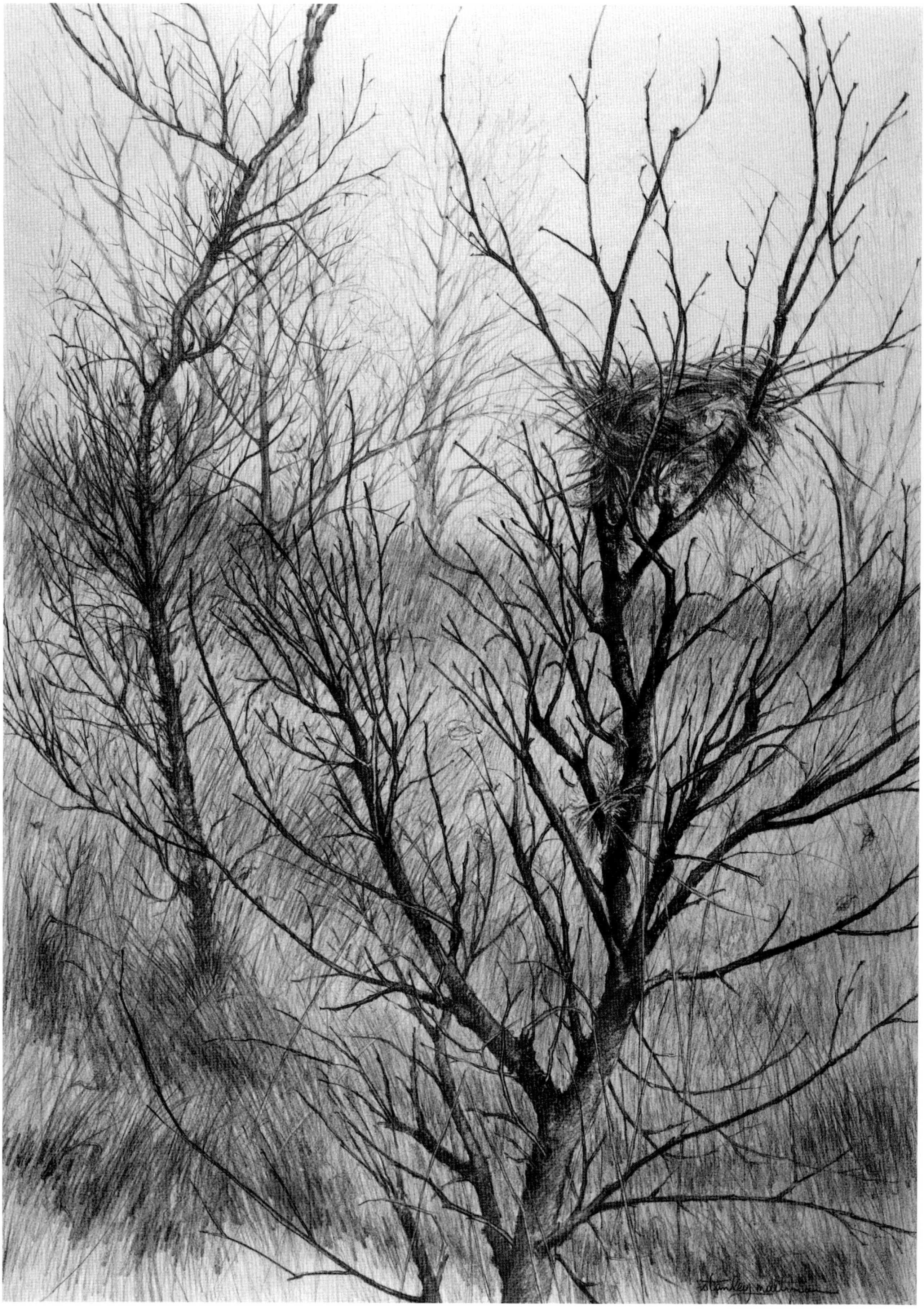

Gone South, 22" x 31" (56cm x 79cm), charcoal on handmade Japanese paper. Collection of Arlene and Joel Savitsky.

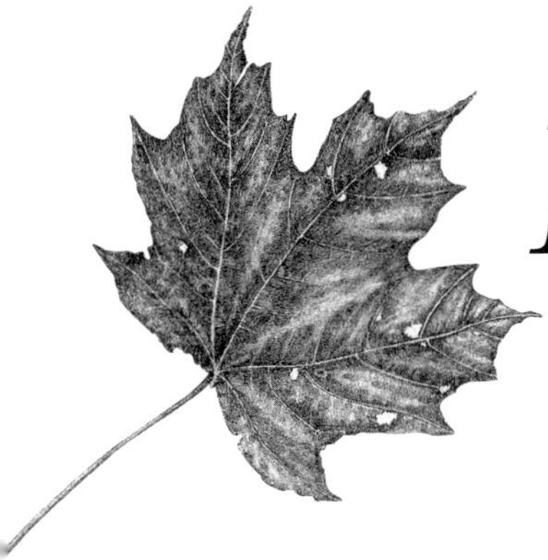

CHAPTER FOUR

Drawing Forests & Tree Groups

When you look at a forest or group of trees, you see big and small, wide and thin, and coniferous and deciduous trees. Drawing these trees in a mass is not as difficult as it may sound. Out of this mass you create a design, a pattern of lights and darks. Look for the shapes of various trees silhouetted against one another. Be liberal with your sketches, and try to capture a reasonable representation rather than an exact copy.

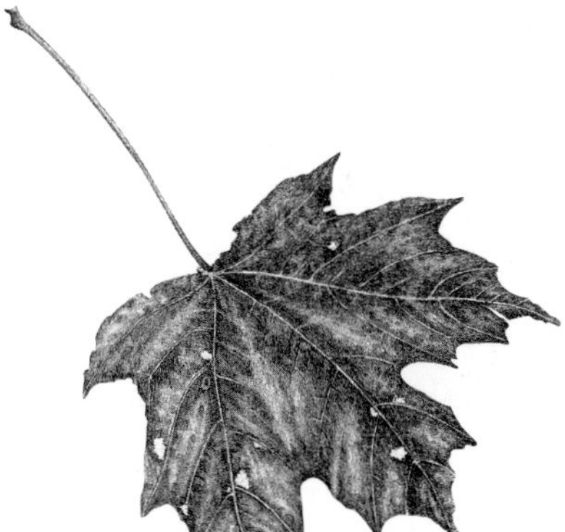

DRAWING TREE GROUPS

In the four simple steps shown below, see how easy it is to get from rough idea to finished drawing.

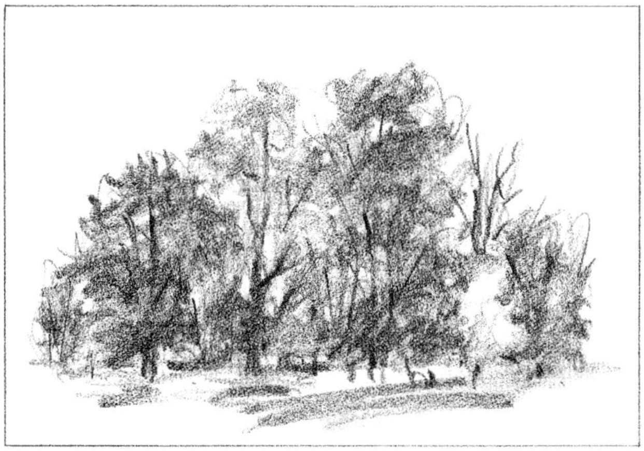

1. Sketch Your Ideas
This is a good example of a rough thinking sketch for a simple group study of various trees. As I've mentioned previously, you should always do a study or a series of small sketches of your different ideas to see what works best. They do not have to be articulate, but should be a sort of blueprint for your drawing.

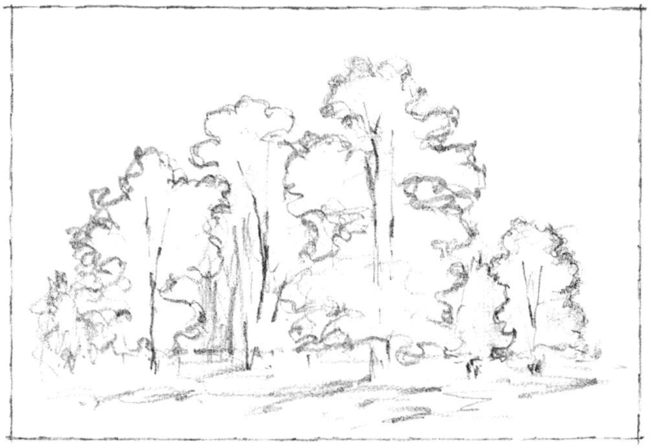

2. Use Your Best Idea
Once you have decided which idea or composition is best, lightly sketch it out on good paper.

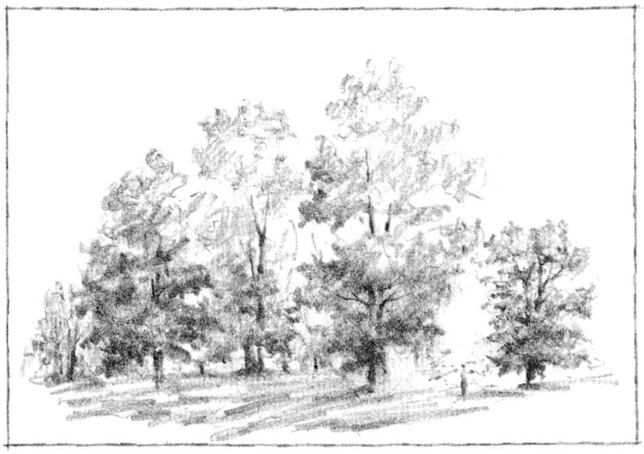

3. Build Your Values
Build up your drawing by adding shading and various values.

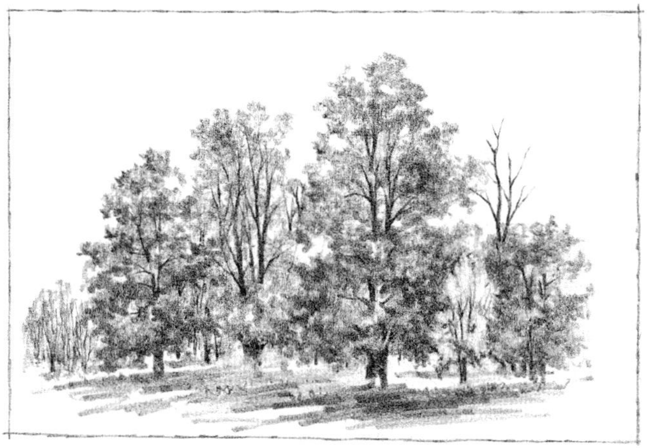

4. Add Details
By adding details and a few additional trees to create depth, you will complete the drawing nicely. This example was drawn with only a 6B graphite pencil. By varying pencil pressure, you can create various tones from just one pencil. The paper I used is a sheet of Japanese paper called Hosho. Though primarily used for printmaking, it has an extremely soft surface that readily accepts charcoal and graphite, but will not tolerate much erasing. In spite of this drawback, you should try it sometime.

DRAWING DISTANT WOODS

Having found an area of woods that appeals to you, the next step is to narrow the scope of the view so that it does not become overpowering. A viewfinder, which can be nothing more than holding your left and right hands together to form a frame, will help you select the area you wish to portray in your drawing.

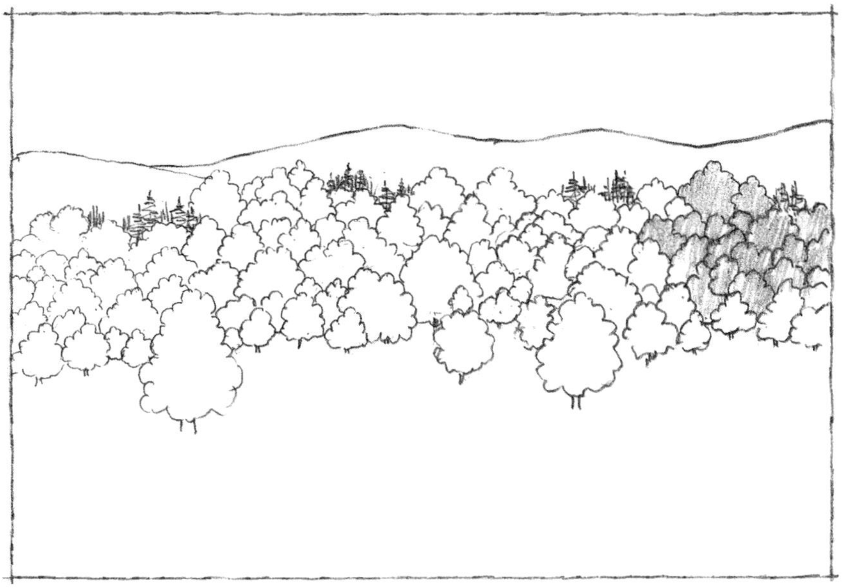

1. The Initial Sketch
Make a light sketch that will serve as a guide for your drawing. Once sketched, add an overall light value as is shown on the right side of this drawing.

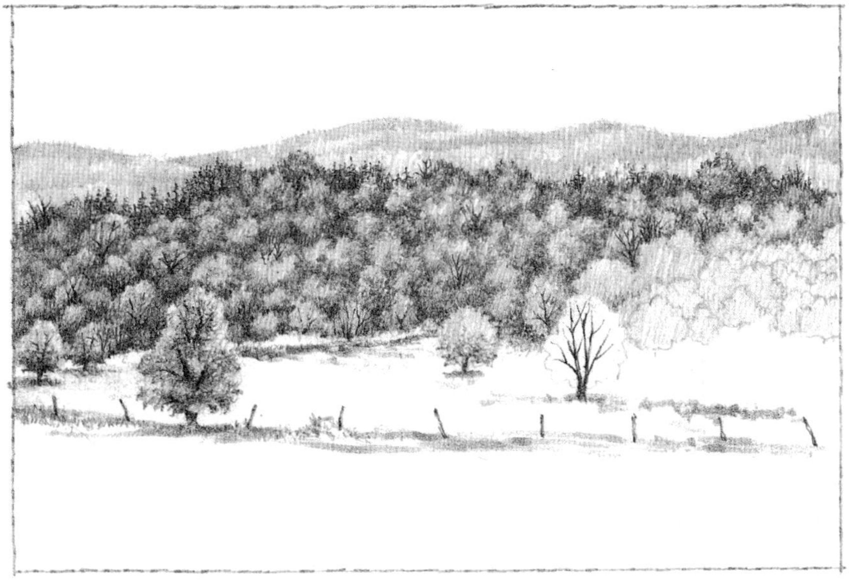

2. Add Tones and Details
Here the drawing is progressing through the addition of tone around the tree shapes. The right corner shows the remaining overall value laid down before giving the tree shapes more character. Give thought to this procedure, and make certain you do not have too many repetitive shapes close to each other. Add some pine trees and include some skeleton shapes to further the feeling of woodlands. By placing trees in the foreground you will create the feeling of space, while the mountain and fence posts add to the overall scenery. This particular piece was made with a 4B graphite pencil on Japanese Hosho paper.

DRAWING BACKLIT WOODS

One of the first things that will add more impact to your composition when moving in close to a wooded area is backlighting. Interesting effects can be achieved through its use. Pay close attention to allowing light to come through when you draw backlighting. Draw some foliage in front of your trees, and add some branches that will lean forward in the front of the picture. This will break up the monotony of a straight line. Also remember to leave a little light flickering through onto the ground. These little details will make your picture stand out from the usual.

1. Allow Light to Come Through
This drawing shows the primary shapes of the trees with their foliage. Leave sufficient space from the base of the tree line to the bottom of the foliage to allow for the appearance of light coming from behind the tree. The lower right corner of the drawing shows the beginning indications of foliage and ground cover. Add in some trunks and saplings; be sure that you vary the thickness of the tree trunks.

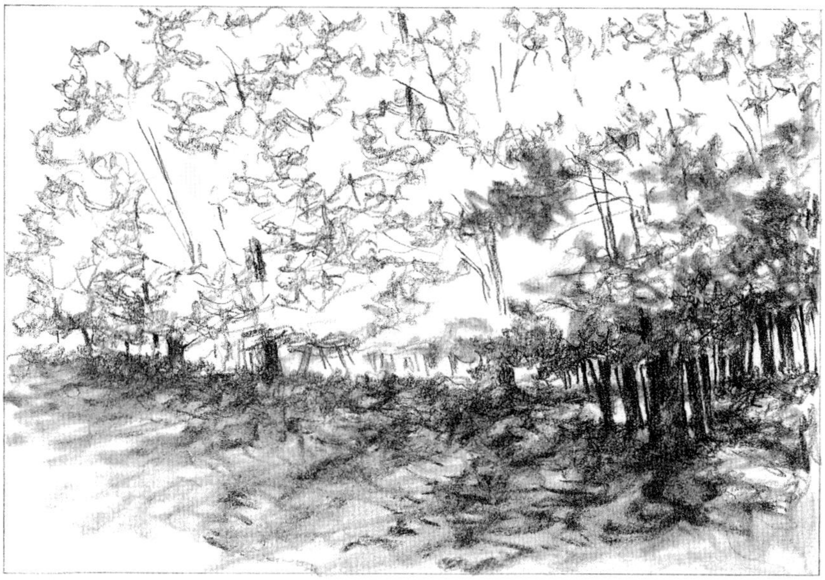

2. Add Details and Highlights
To achieve the backlit effect shown here, lay in your sketch with vine charcoal and spread it about with your stomp or finger. Then work over your initial drawing with 2B and 6B charcoal pencils, and add details to the foliage, trunks and branches. Finally, use your kneaded eraser to pick out highlights and some lights on the ground to give the appearance of sunlight flickering through. This particular drawing was executed on a paper called Hammermill Text, a remnant from my commercial art days. It has a little tooth that takes charcoal and pencil very nicely.

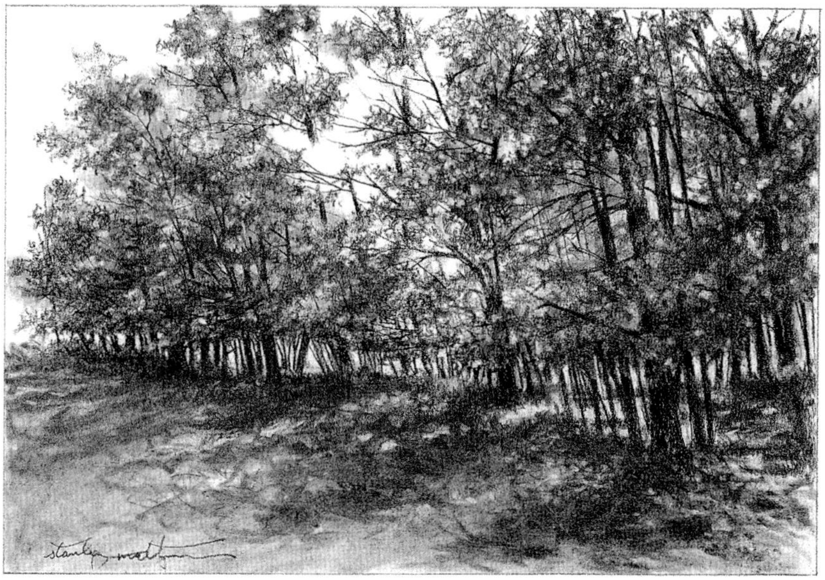

DRAWING WOODLANDS WITH REFLECTIONS

1. Lay in Basic Forms and Shapes
With a piece of vine charcoal lightly lay in the lights and darks of your composition. Use a dry (not moist) finger or stomp to push the charcoal around and form shapes and values approximating the picture you have in mind, but with no details at this time. Then model a little more with your vine charcoal.

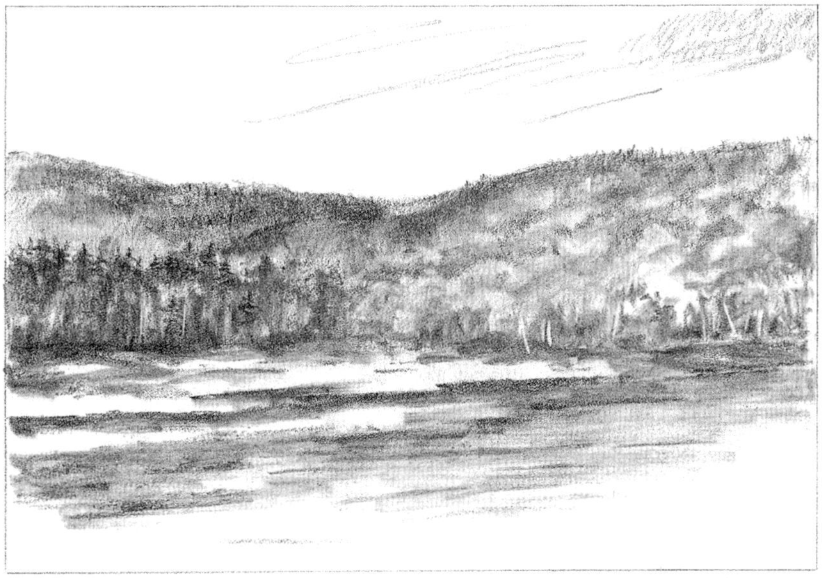

CHOOSE YOUR PAPER CAREFULLY

If you know that you'll be using water with your drawing, choose a paper that will not buckle from the water. For example, 2-ply Strathmore Bristol will take light washes of water quite nicely without buckling.

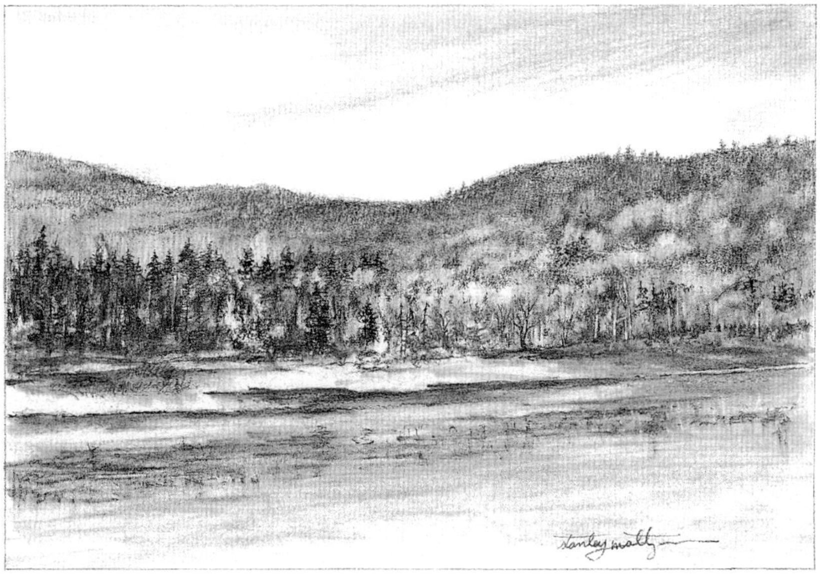

2. Create Reflections and Add Details
Using a soft brush and clean water, create shapes by pushing the charcoal around. For light areas, wash your brush frequently with clean water; dark areas need less cleaning. Once dry, you'll have a nice combination of light and dark silvery grays.

Then with vine charcoal and a 2B charcoal pencil, work over your underpainting to bring out more details. For water reflections, use the side of a flat brush that you dipped in water and then wiped so as to not be saturated, and brush horizontally, left to right, creating lights and darks. Clean the brush frequently. Where the shoreline is light, make a thin dark line, and where it is dark, leave a hairline of white; this shows the separation of land and water. Add some tree shapes in the water with a charcoal pencil. Then flatten your kneaded eraser and, using horizontal strokes, break the shapes you just made to create light ripples on the water's surface.

DRAWING WINTER WOODS

To create scenes that depict winter woodlands, use a piece of charcoal to loosely sketch a horizontal shape with varied tones, leaving spaces that can be interpreted as distant trees. With your finger or a stomp and with some vertical strokes, blend and simulate more tree shapes — some light, some dark and some crooked. Introduce your charcoal pencil over this, and in varied tones suggest more trees in a linear fashion. Randomly add a limb or two branching out from the linear trees you just created, and slowly build your forest. Do not make a straight line at the base of your trees. Rather, to suggest that the trees belong, let the trunks run into the snow; some will be round, some will be at angles.

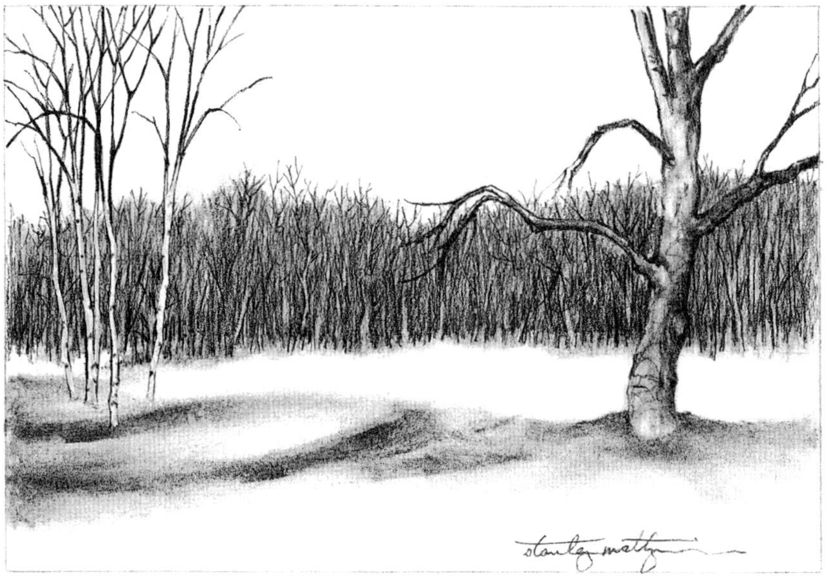

A Winter Scene in Charcoal
Notice how the birches and large tree in the foreground help to add depth. This particular piece was done on Rives BFK paper.

Use Washes for a Wintry Effect

The aquarelle pencil is a graphite pencil that, when brushed over with water, will create washes of various values determined by the intensity of the initial marks you made. By keeping the lines of your sketch light, you'll end up with a light wash that you can still make revisions to, if necessary. Let your first wash dry, then add more details and, if you wish, darker washes.

Once all the washes are dry, add the finishing details. You don't need to use an aquarelle pencil for the details, any degree of graphite pencil will work.

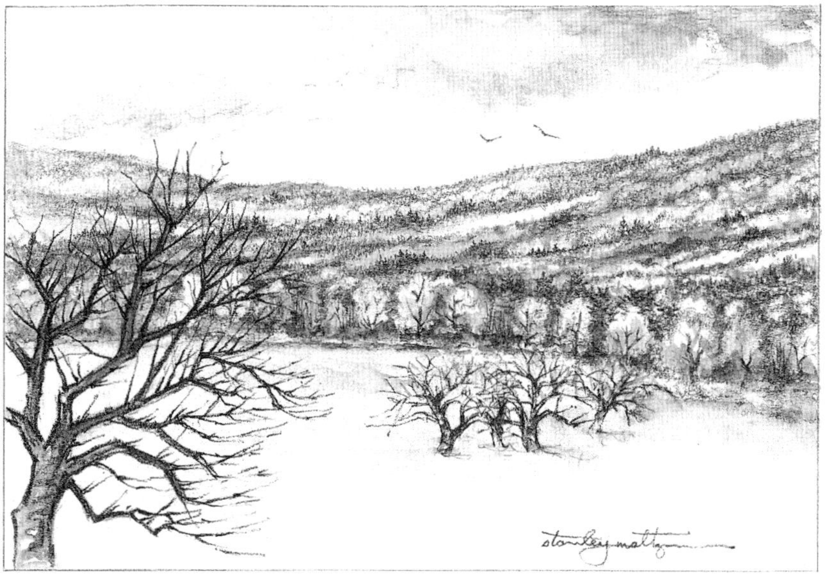

A Winter Scene in Aquarelle Pencil
When you want to go outdoors and travel light to do some quick sketches or studies, aquarelle pencils will do the job very nicely, as shown by this wintry scene. But besides illustrating the wonderful washes you can achieve with these versatile pencils, this picture also depicts aerial perspective, where you look down at the tops of trees and up into the mountain.

STEPPING INTO THE FOREST

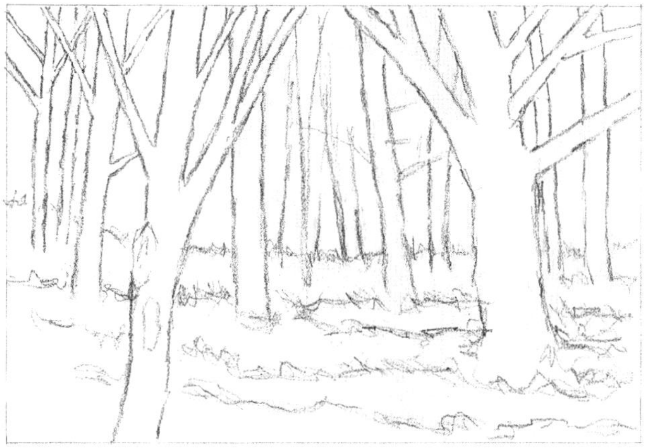

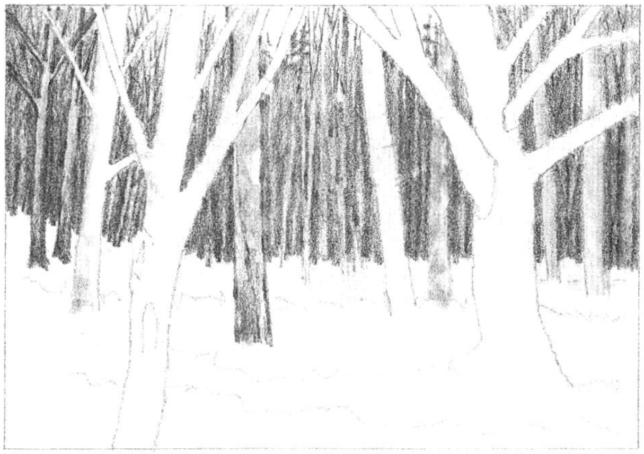

1. Preliminary Outline
This preliminary outline sketch is of a wooded area leading into a forest. Perspective is used here as an obvious ploy in directing the viewer into the woods. By making the tree on the left run off the paper at the base and top, you create an impression of closeness. The large tree on the right brings you in a few more steps by showing the base of the tree but not the top. This particular example was done with 2B and 6B woodless graphite pencils on a vellum-surfaced paper.

2. Create Depth
Continue to create the feeling of stepping into the woods by adding more randomly spaced trees, reducing their width or size as they recede into the denser woods. To achieve the appearance of denser woods, put down a light tone and then a darker value over it to indicate density. Silhouette the larger trees and leave some sky showing to also create the feeling of depth.

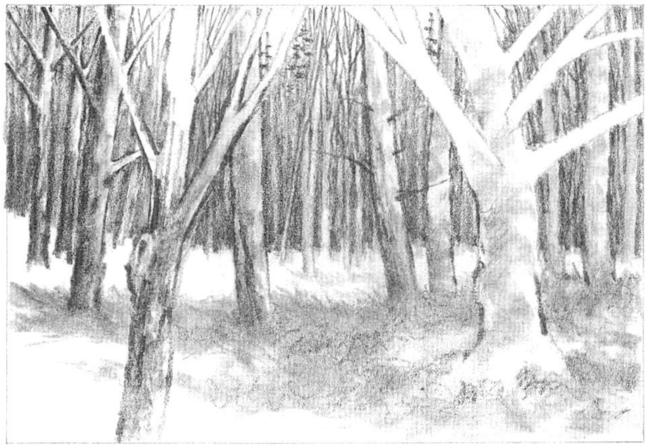

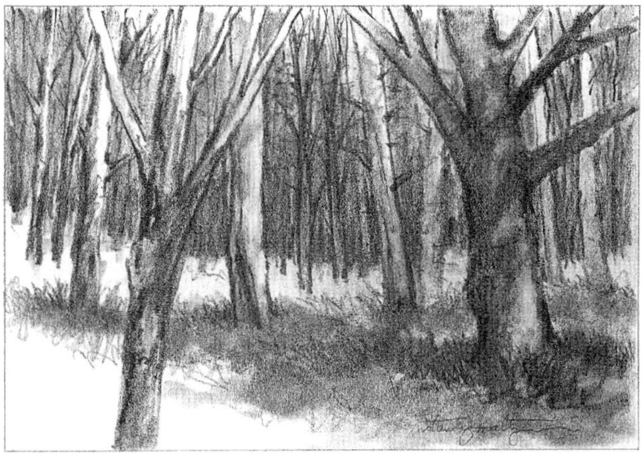

3. Add Tones
Start emphasizing particular trees by adding tone. Use a stomp or, if you like, your finger, as long as it isn't sweaty; a moist finger rubbed on your paper can create a resist which will not allow you to get the best results from your pencil. Start lightly, then add your darks to hold your shapes and shadows. Darken the base of the wooded area some more if you feel it warrants it. With whatever residue is left on your stomp, add some ground debris. If your darks need some help, use your 6B pencil gently — do not lean on it! Use just enough pressure to add some tone to the ground.

4. Finish and Refine
Here's the finished interpretation of stepping into the forest. The richest darks were saved for the two foremost trees. To lead you back into the woods, there needs to be a focal point. Notice the arbor created with the limbs of the two foremost trees which direct you to two more trees, and further back to a couple more. Each tree recedes and becomes smaller as you go back, leading your eyes into the woodland. The foreground is held down by the impression of grass and debris made by stomping the graphite and sort of scumbling (an oil painting term for loosely smearing color over previous color using a brush) with your lead on top of that surface. This gives a nice rich look.

DRAWING HEAVY WOODS

To create an interesting image of a heavily wooded area, you must consider several important elements. Your center of interest: even though it is just a wooded area, your drawing needs a focal point, a pleasant flow and a spirit that makes your eye wander about yet always brings you back to your center of interest. Perspective: make sure you have a clear foreground, middle ground and background. These are just some of the important aspects that you should consider as you make your preliminary studies.

1. Preliminary Outline
Draw a rough sketch to seve as a guide for the placement of trees and foliage that will be in your drawing. Do not include too much detail in your preliminary sketch; it is only a guide to roughly place the elements in position. This particular drawing is on a sheet of 2-ply Strathmore Bristol.

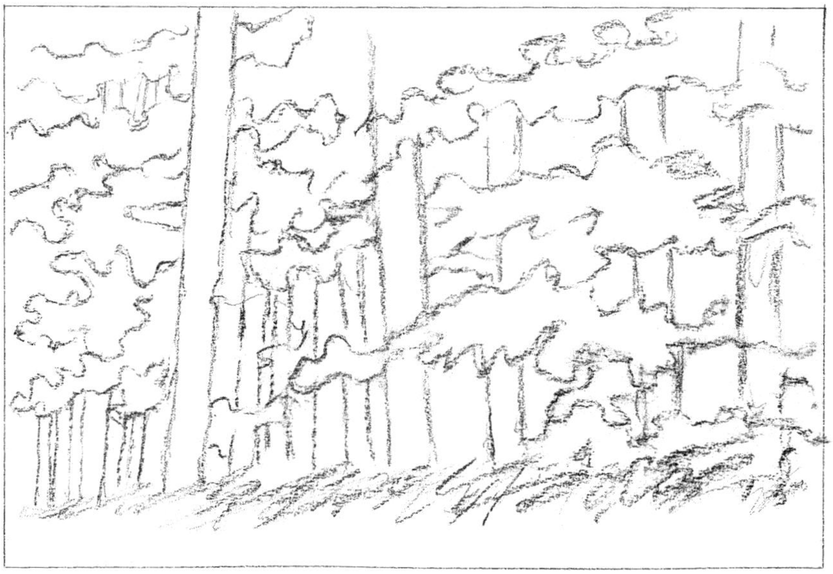

2. Add Values
Place the various values in their respective areas. In this case I used a piece of vine charcoal. The right side of the sketch shows how to loosely and roughly place the charcoal, while the remainder of the picture shows how to initially disburse the charcoal with a finger, tissue or stomp. Notice how the details are still kept to a minimum.

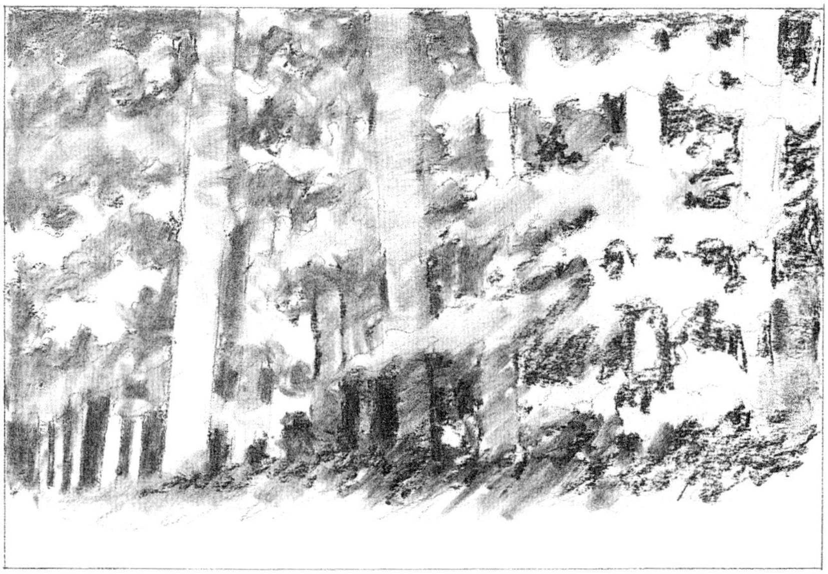

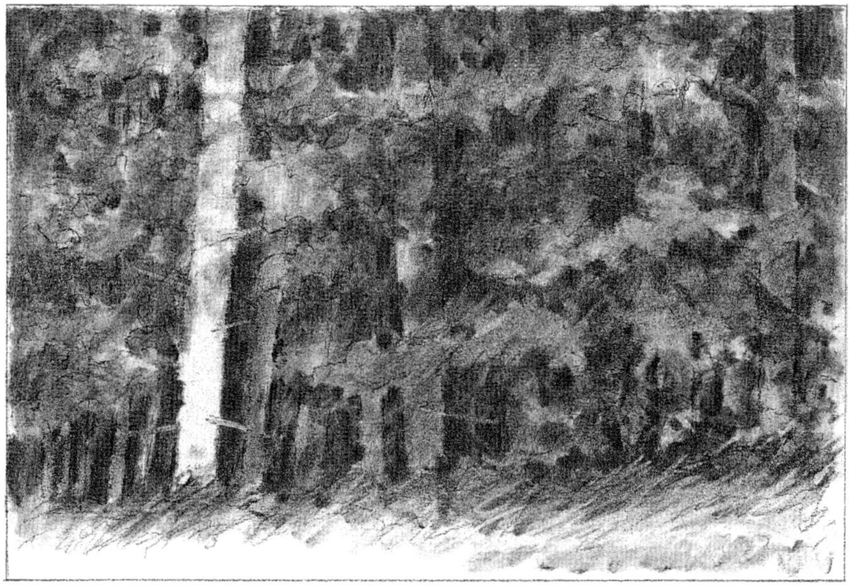

3. Create Forms
Add and eliminate charcoal as necessary to create the various images. Make your trees more prominent, and distinguish the pine shapes by bringing them into focus. Use your kneaded eraser to lighten areas that may have been covered with too much charcoal. Remember that every time you lift out charcoal, however, you must be sure to wipe the eraser on a piece of scrap paper so that you do not push the debris you just removed back into the picture.

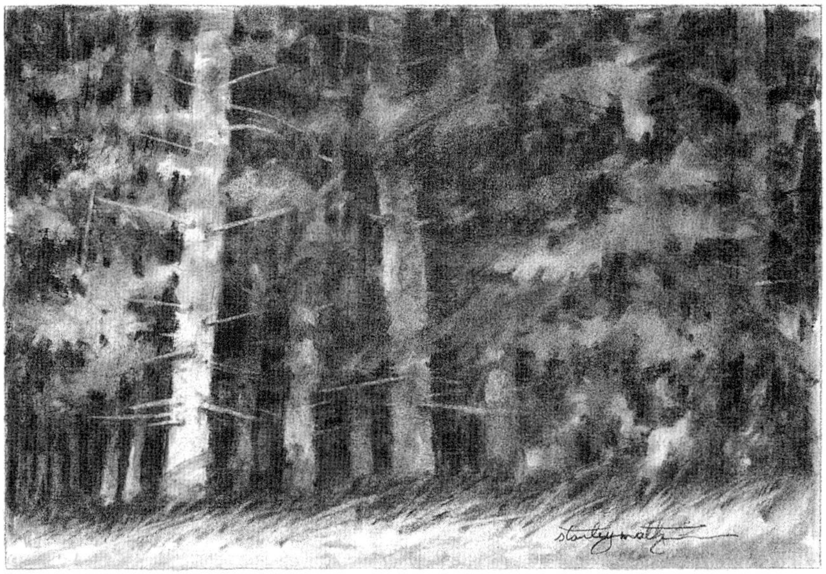

4. Finish and Refine
Notice how the one prominent tree on the left, then the light areas and finally the pines on the right move your eyes across the drawing. The dark base adds depth, the lack of sky holes creates the impression of a heavily wooded area, and the sparkle of light here and there gives the woods interest. Create those sparkles by removing charcoal with your kneaded eraser. You can also use the eraser to create additional elements, such as the pine branches. (You can cut out a paper stencil to work within so you don't disturb any other part of your drawing.) Usually one stroke of your eraser will do the job. Remember to put dark against light and light against dark.

DRAWING FOREST CLEARINGS

1. Preliminary Outline
Sketch out your initial outline to serve as a guide. Here I used vine charcoal and 2B and 6B charcoal pencils on 2-ply Strathmore Bristol. As you work, don't be afraid to make changes to your original idea, as necessary. Always keep an open mind. If you see or feel that a revision will enhance your picture, then by all means do it rather than let something that is not quite right remain as it is simply because you spent quite a bit of time developing it.

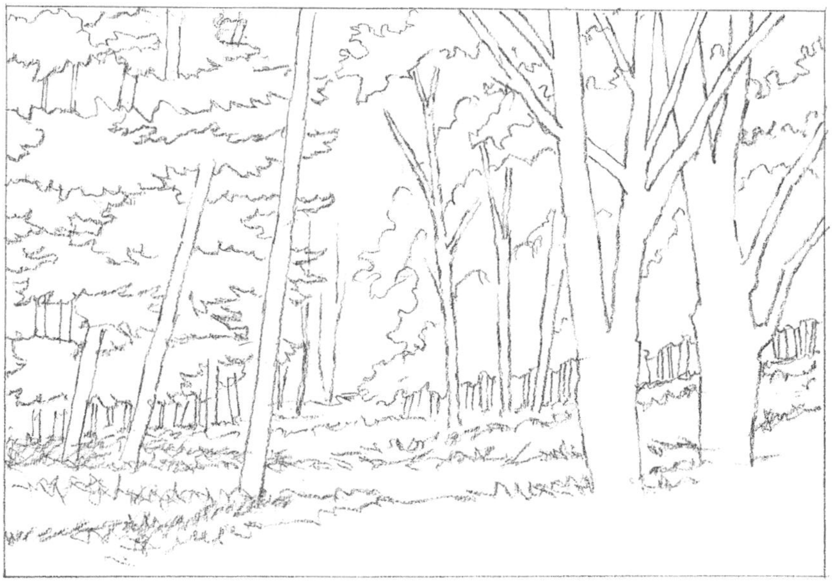

2. Add Values
Lay in the values for the larger areas. Use vine charcoal that has been pushed around with a stomp to create a nice flat tone. Notice that the mass of trees on the right is one value, while the trees on the left are another — a combination of lights and darks. In both areas, use no detail. Create an image that simply suggests your vision.

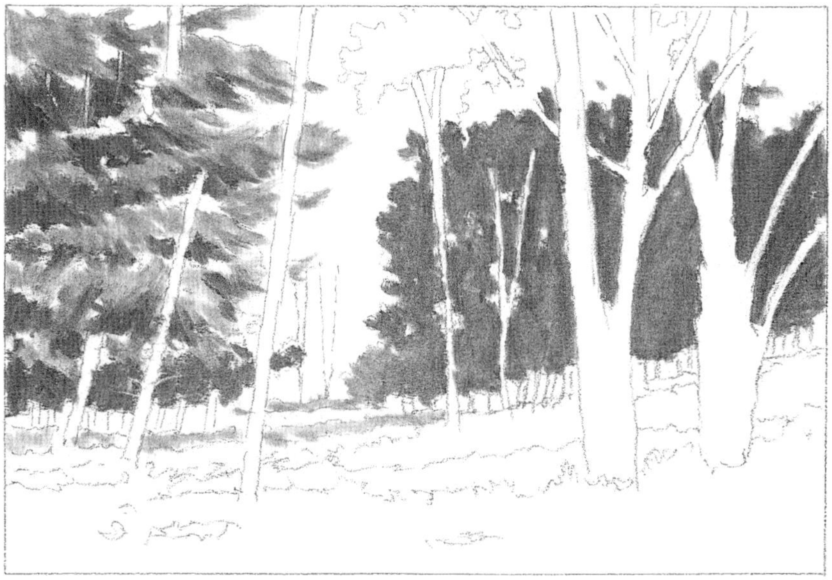

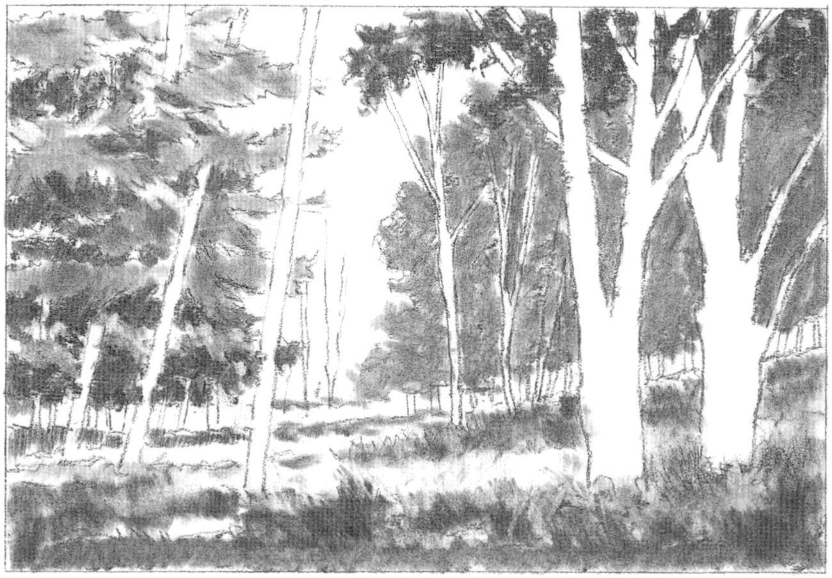

3. Create Depth

Add more values by making the top of the foreground trees on the right darker than the previous value. To begin to give some depth to your picture, add the immediate foreground and a little more definition to the pines on the left. Notice the channel of light that is created by the positioning of your values.

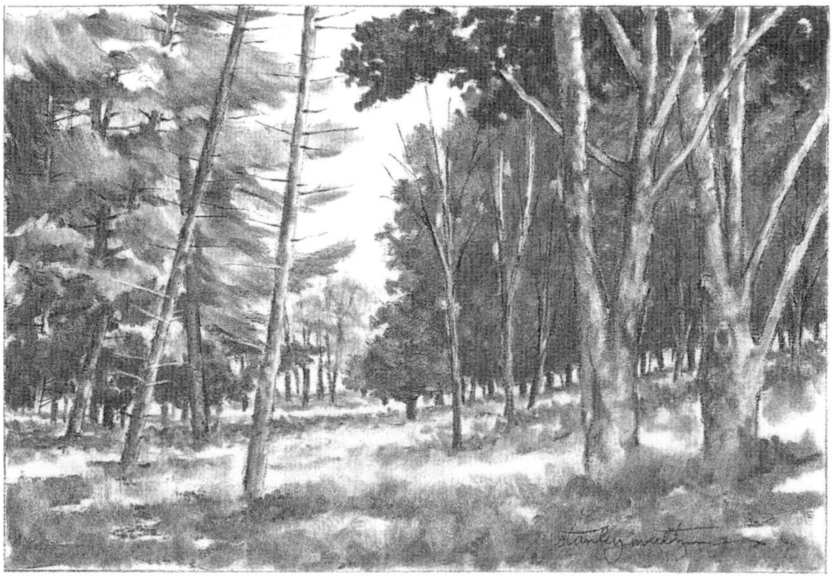

4. Finish and Refine

Add more definition to the pine trunks on the left. If necessary, add and change other tree trunks so that the viewer's eyes are directed to the clearing outside of the woods. Sketch the two large trees on the right with vine charcoal, model them with a stomp for texture, and add some definition with a 4B charcoal pencil.

Notice the ground pattern. A letter Z or a flattened S shape was created with the lights and darks that leads you out of the forest to whatever lies beyond. Every part of the composition is directed to leading you toward the light ahead, yet you can include interesting diversions to make your eyes come back to look at the overall scene.

I think this is a fairly successful drawing. It looks like it has a great deal going on, yet as you study it, it is not that complicated. The trick is to say more with less. Count the different values here: black, white, dark gray, medium gray and light gray. You do not need a lot of different values to make a drawing; five or six will do nicely.

TIP

If you suspect that you will be subjecting your paper to a lot of punishment because of planned erasing, lifting, stomping or pushing around, make sure you choose a paper with a hard surface that can withstand the work and yet still yield the results you are after.

COMING OUT OF THE WOODS

1. Preliminary Outline

Draw a rough sketch of the placement of the elements in your picture. Of course you first made some rough sketches before coming to the composition, didn't you? Take note of how loosely the foliage is sketched to the right. For this example, try using vine charcoal and 2B and 4B charcoal pencils on a vellum-surfaced sheet of paper.

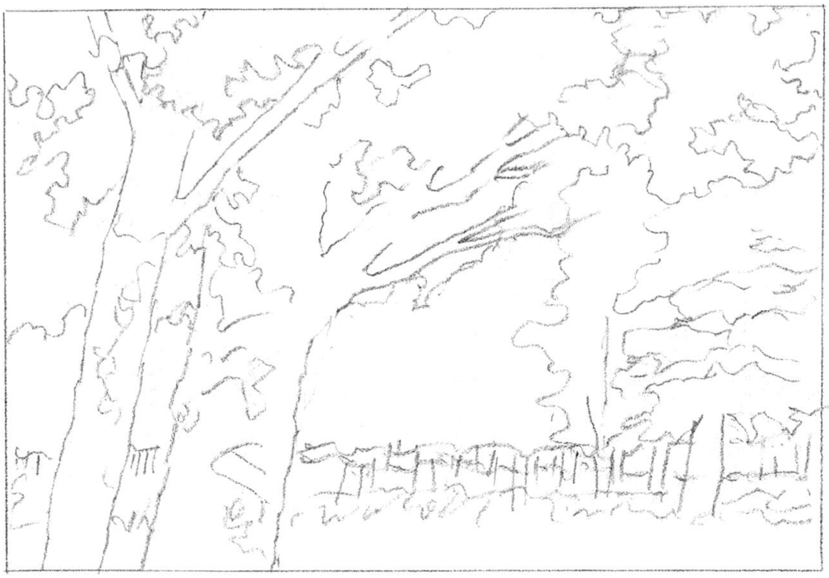

2. Place Initial Values

Lay down vine charcoal for the background trees and move it around with a swab, tissue, stomp or finger. Make the trees a little lighter on top and darker at the base. Trees on the right are a little lighter, with no details as of yet. This way, if you want to move or change an element, it will be an easy task.

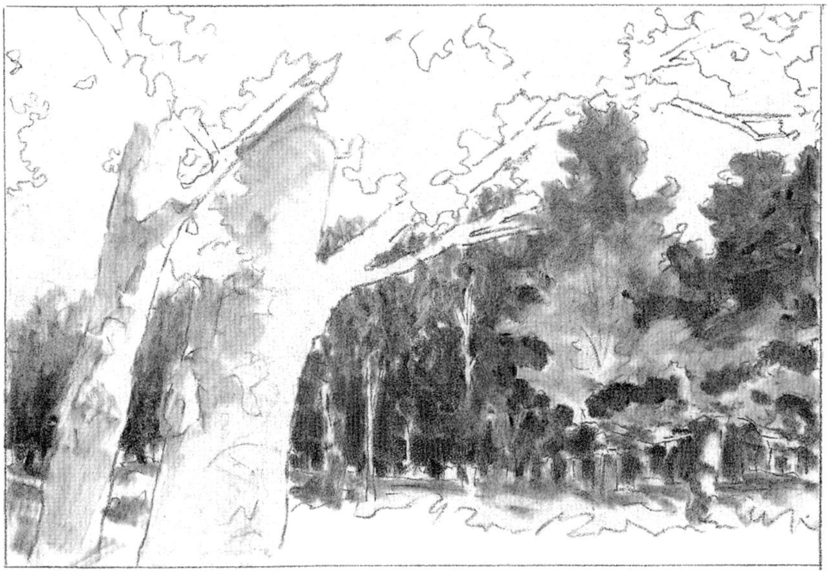

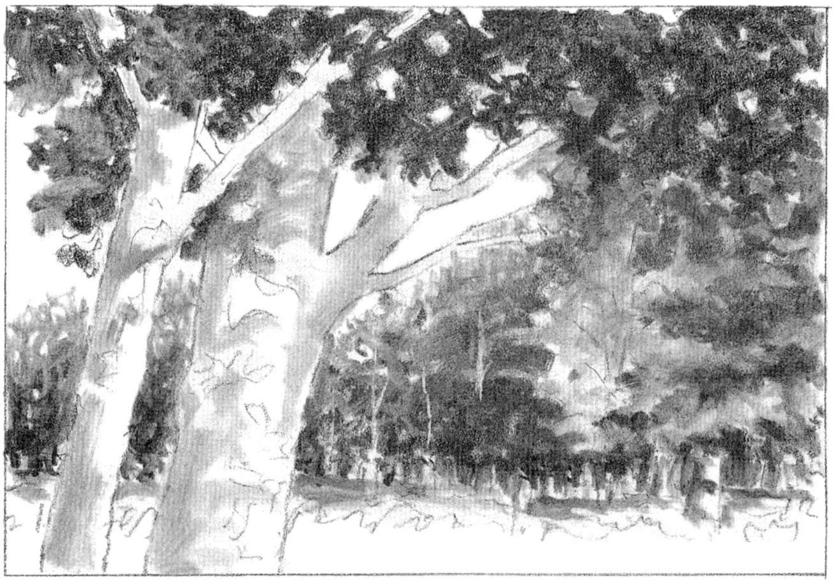

3. Define Your Shapes
Begin to show some definition by adding some darks to the foreground, middle ground and background. Add some more darks to the first mass of trees, and, with a kneaded eraser, sharpen the white tree indications so the trees stand out. With some of the residue left on your stomp, add some tone to the foreground trees.

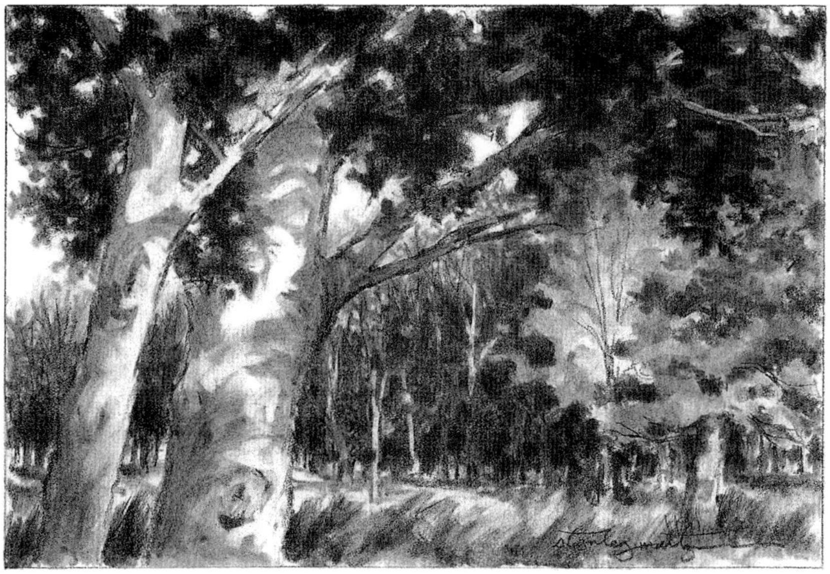

4. Finish and Refine
Add the finishing touches to your forest. Darken the base and add some darks next to the young maple on the right, which immediately pushes it out in front. With a charcoal pencil, lightly add some branches and the trunks of background trees. Add some rich darks to the two foreground trees; they should be darkest because they are closest. Again, with what is left on your stomp, tone the foremost trees some more. If you need more color, add some charcoal and repeat until you are satisfied.

Notice how the light leads your eyes to the left, out of the heavily wooded area. To create the foreground grass, put down some charcoal, then shape it with your finger or a stomp. If you compare the initial sketch with the finished drawing, you can see why it is to your advantage not to put much detail in the preliminary sketch.

DRAWING TREES IN FIELDS

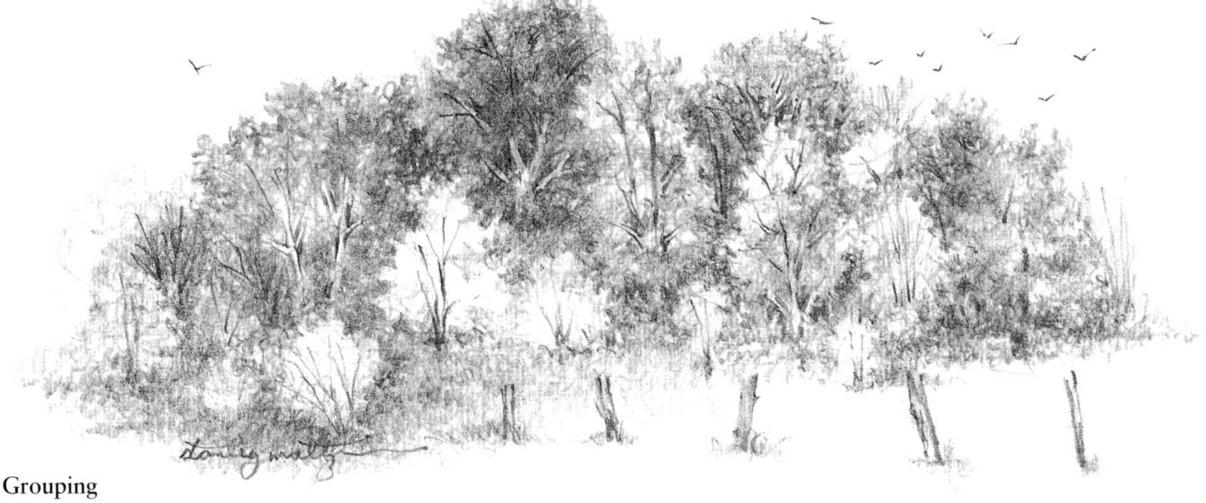

A Farmland Grouping
Here is a familiar sight — a group of trees in a field. A group like this is generally found on farm land, where it takes the place of markers, and is used as a retreat for animals to keep out of the day's heat. This picture was executed on a piece of Rives BFK with a 2B graphite pencil.

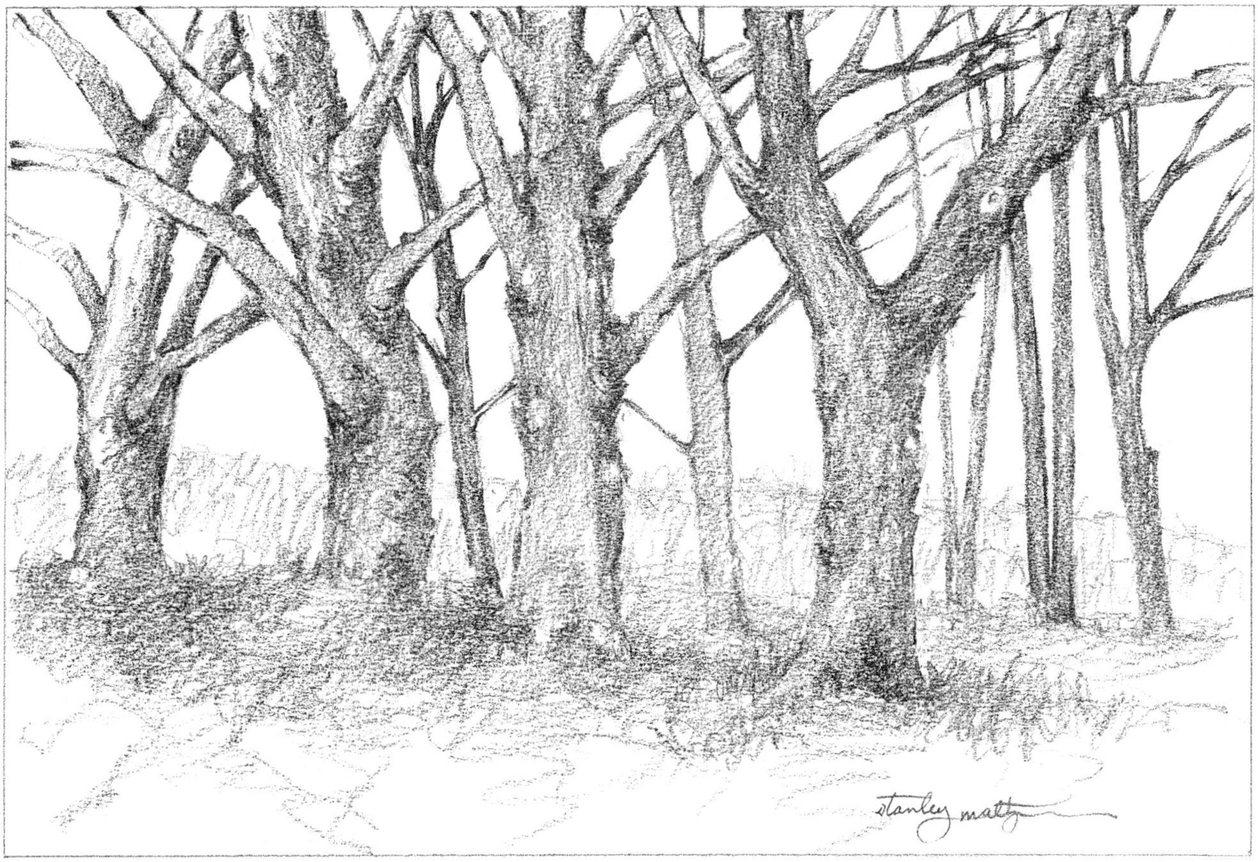

Trees Up Close
This close-up of a group of trees in winter provides a good opportunity to study the anatomy of a tree without foliage. This drawing was done with an aquarelle pencil on 2-ply Strathmore Bristol. To achieve tones like those you see here, vary the pressure of your pencil as you work. And though the aquarelle pencil can be readily used with water, I want you to see that it can also be used nicely by itself.

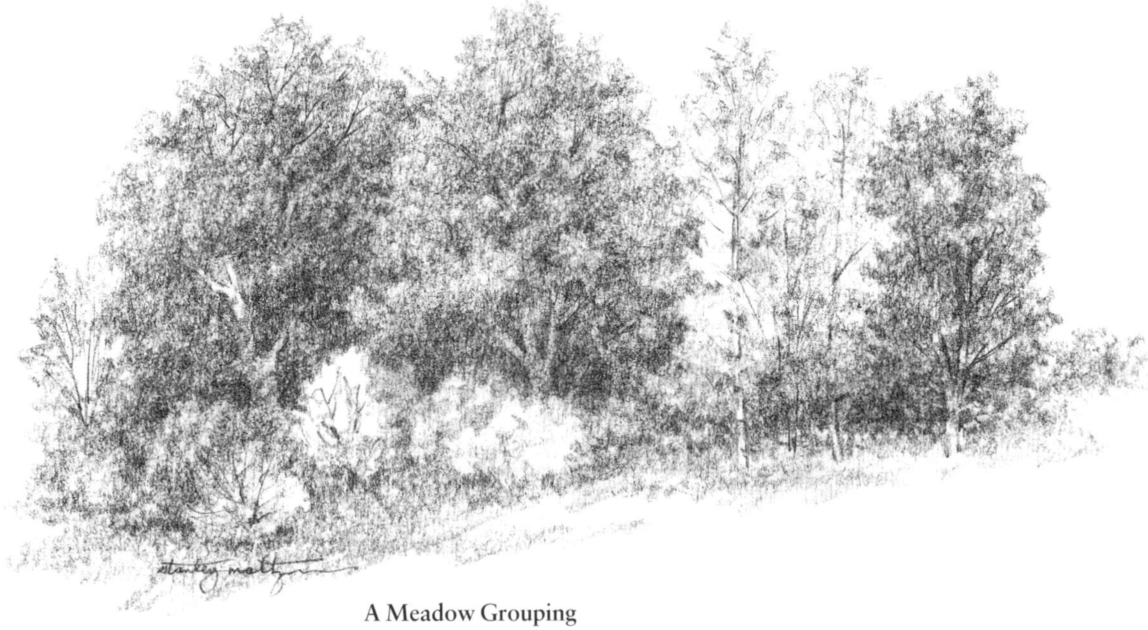

A Meadow Grouping
Here is another group of meadow trees, some maples, birch and ash. This was drawn on a sheet of Japanese paper called Kochi. Though primarily used in printmaking, Kochi paper has a beautiful texture. Notice the sparkle that it lends to the charcoal work, creating the feeling of sunlight on leaves. And although Kochi paper is soft and will not tolerate erasing, it is a must for you to try.

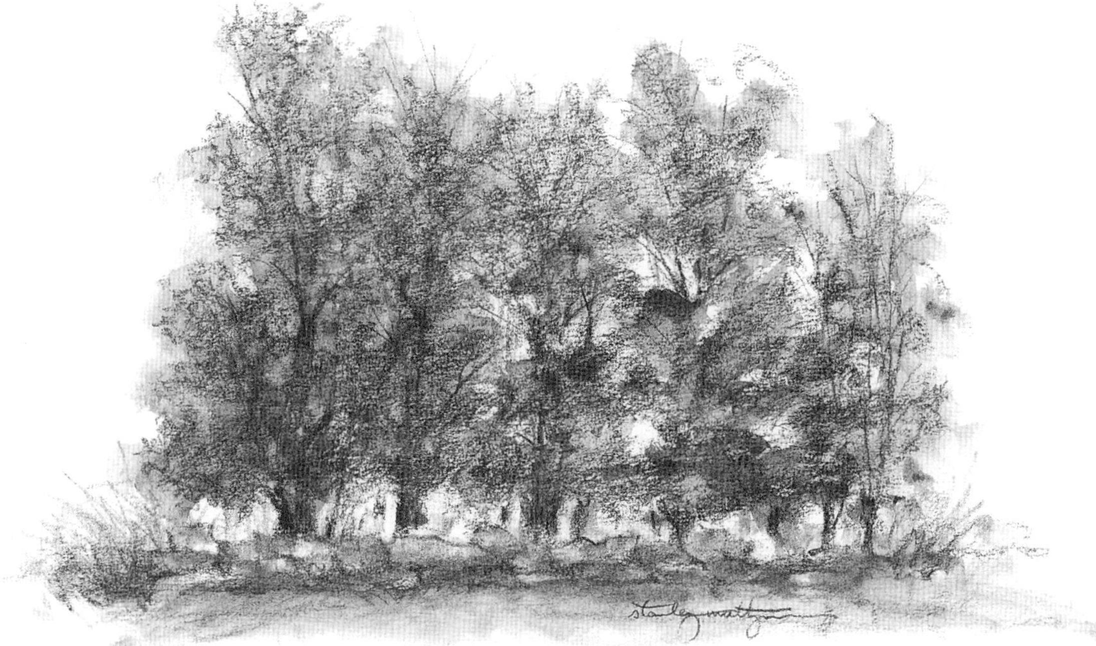

A Charcoal Study
This sketch of a group of maples by a stone wall was created on a piece of inexpensive drawing paper with a soft piece of charcoal. After making my sketch, I took a soft brush, dipped it in water and wiped it gently on a rag, then I pushed the charcoal around into shapes. Remember, where it is very dark and you do not want to spread it, you must wash your brush. (You should wash your brush frequently anyway.) When the washes were dry, I was left with some very pleasant grays. I then used a 4B charcoal pencil to work over and add definition to the subject.

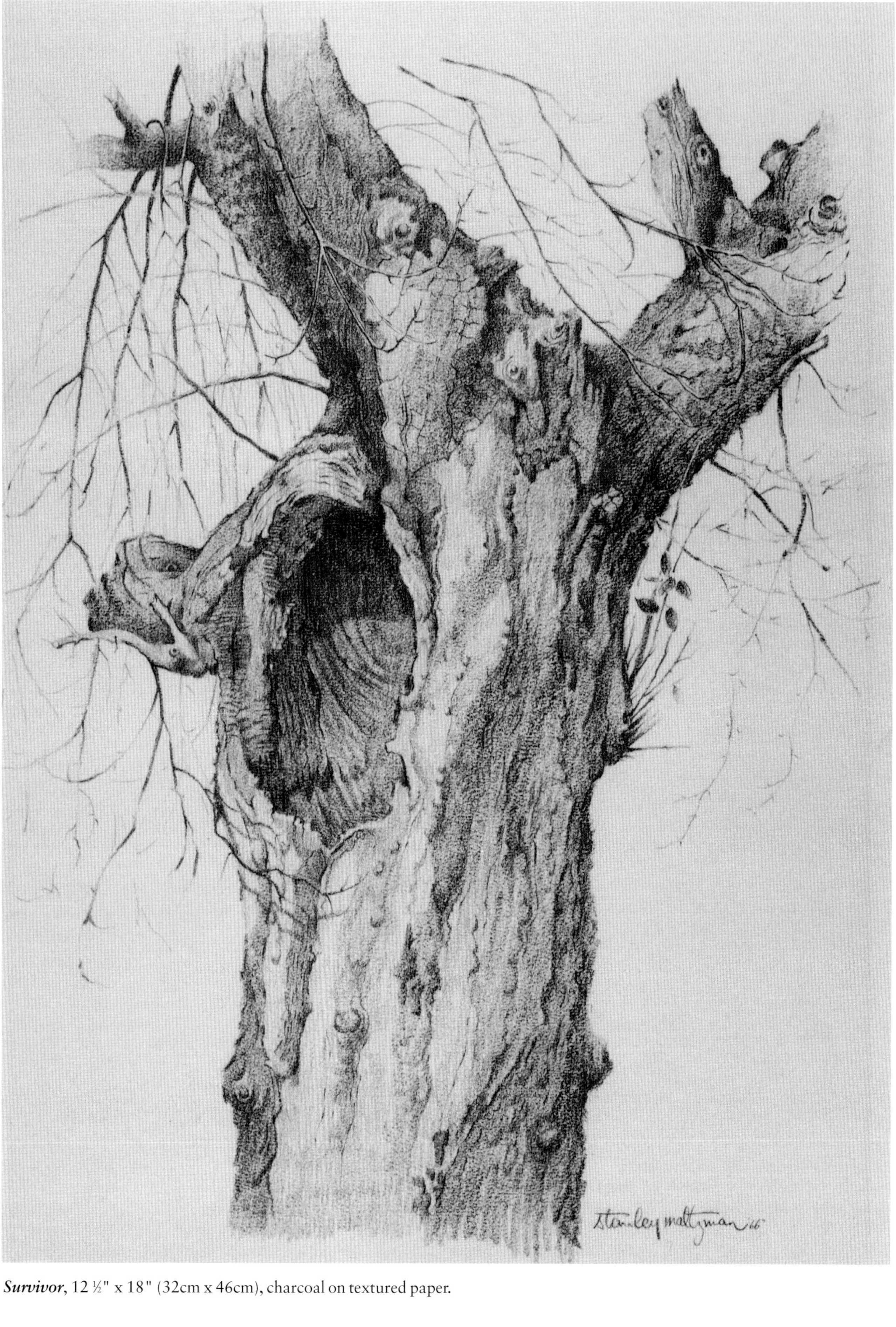

Survivor, 12 ½" x 18" (32cm x 46cm), charcoal on textured paper.

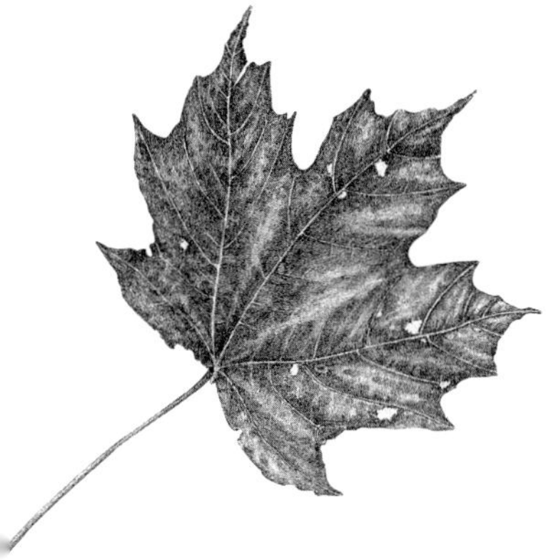

CHAPTER FIVE

Observing Nature's Details

As you become more aware of all the objects of interest surrounding you, your work will reflect a turn toward being more original. Throughout this chapter are many pieces of nature acquired on painting trips or while walking with my canine friend, Buffy, in the woods. They are all over the place, yours for the asking.

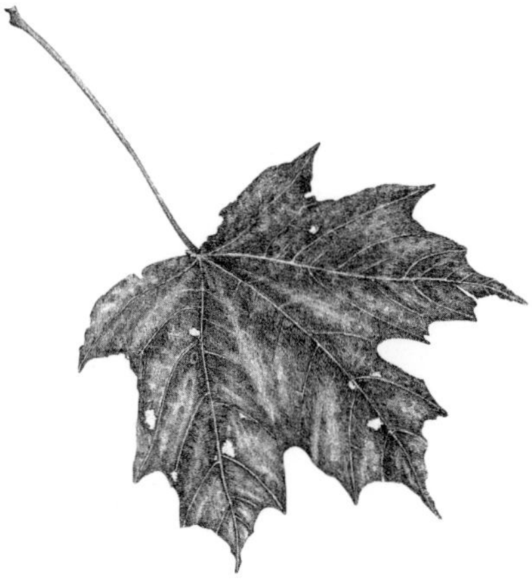

BE AWARE OF THE WORLD AROUND YOU

I have all kinds of nature pieces in my studio. Some I will use, some I will not, but I collect them because there is something about them that gives me a sense of enjoyment. This is all part of learning to see. Look around you!

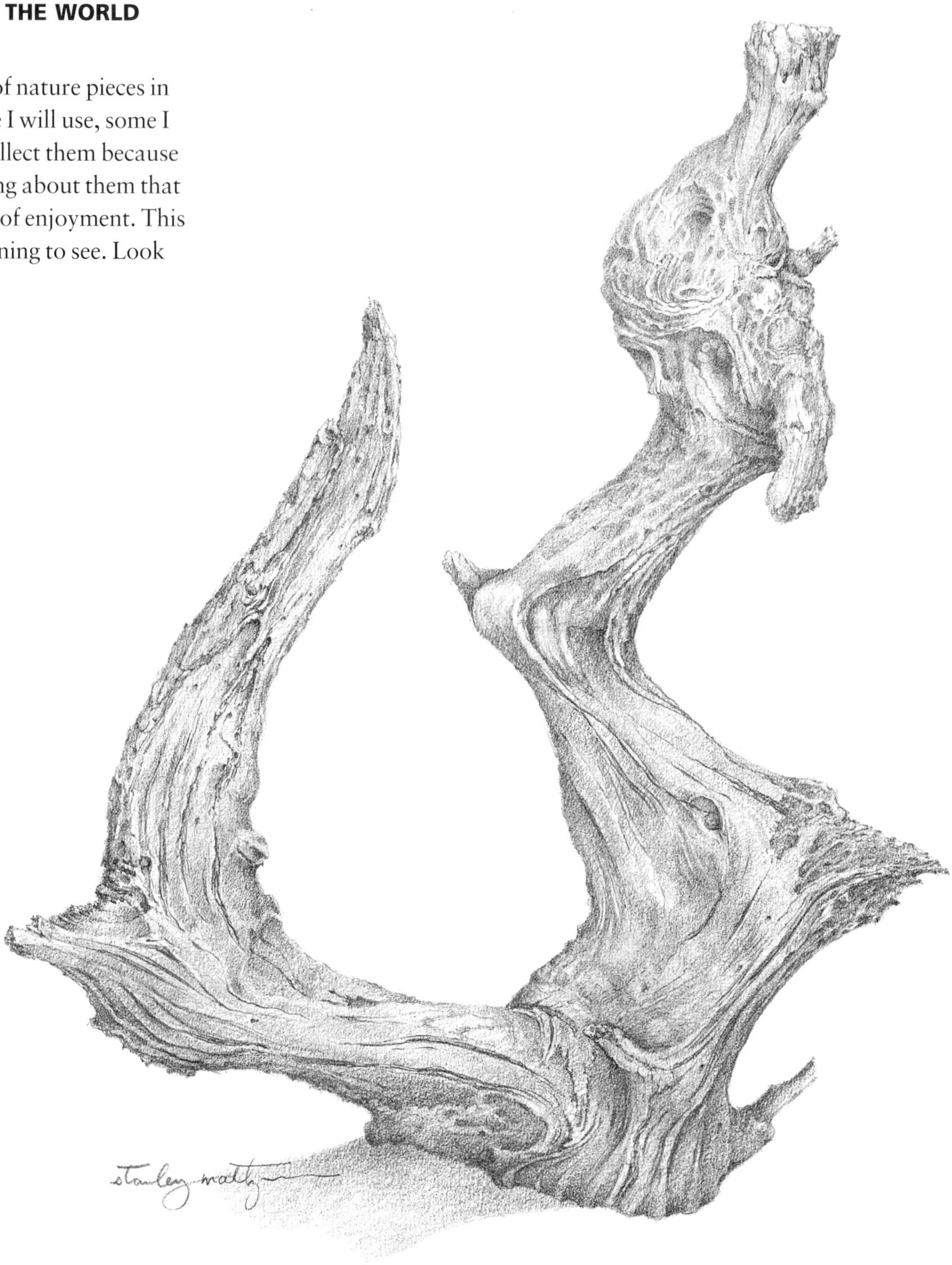

You Just Never Know...
This drawing is of a piece of tree root I found lying on the ground. The root is no more than about 8" (20cm) square, but to me it had a sense of beauty and design that made me pick it up. I think it has been lying in my studio for years, but I knew one day I would draw it, and I am happy to be able to finally share it with you. This piece was done using HB and 4B graphite pencils on 2-ply Strathmore Bristol paper.

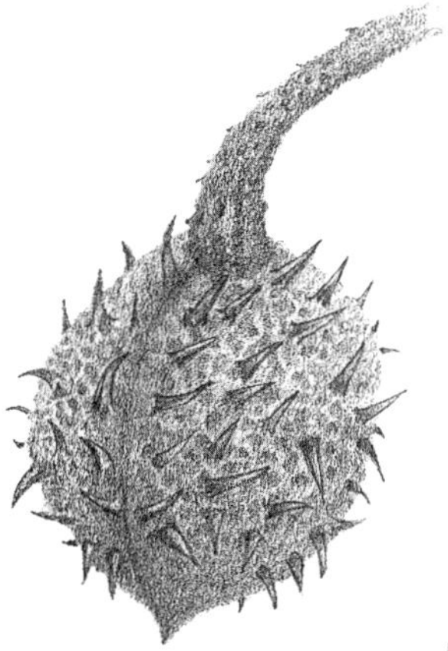

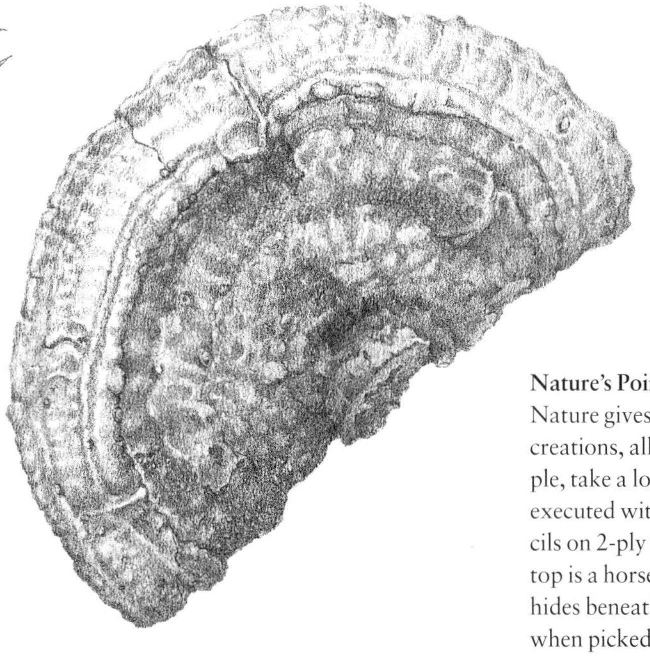

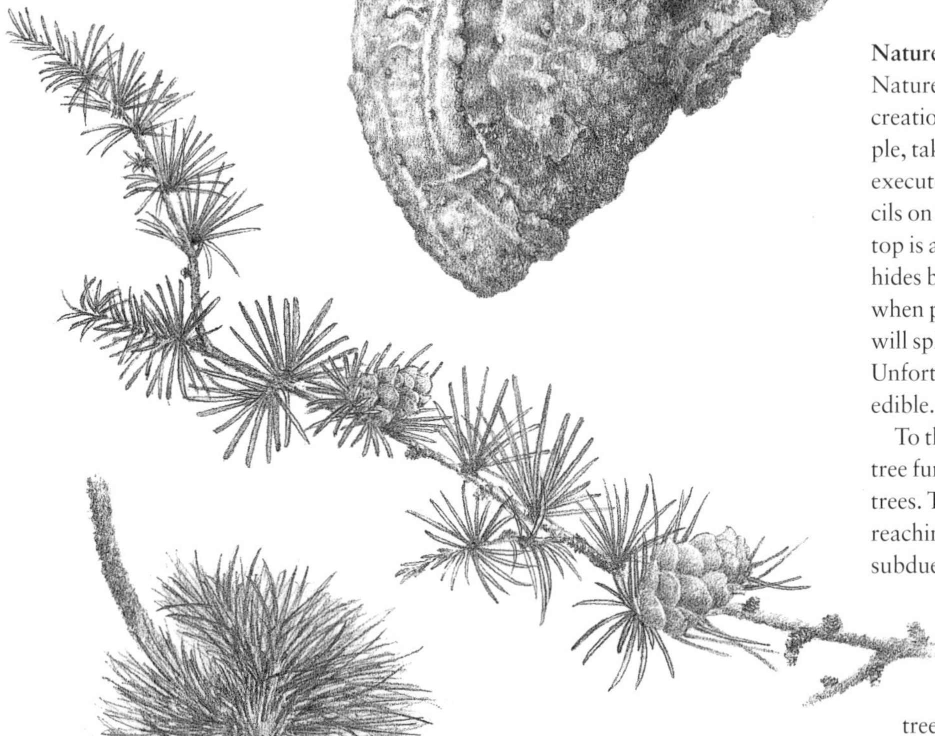

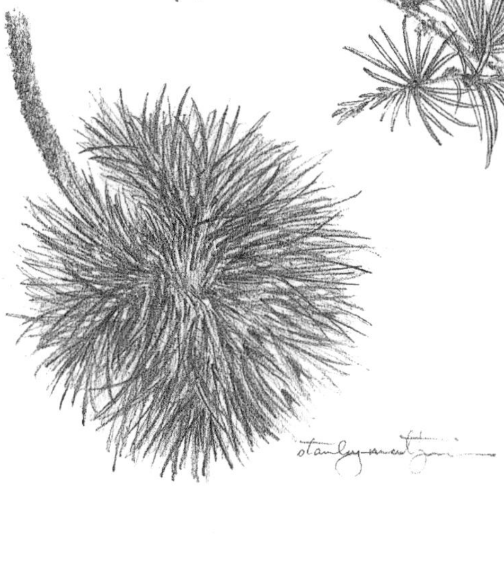

Nature's Points of Interest

Nature gives us so many interesting creations, all free for our use. For example, take a look at these finds here, all executed with 2B and 4B graphite pencils on 2-ply Strathmore Bristol. At the top is a horse chestnut. The nut itself hides beneath this prickly husk which, when picked and set aside for a while, will split apart to reveal the fruit (nut). Unfortunately, the horse chestnut is not edible.

To the right of the horse chestnut is a tree fungus that grows on unhealthy trees. These fungi are quite interesting, reaching many sizes with a palette of subdued stripes of brown. You can even draw pictures on the reverse side of the fungus!

The pine branch is from the decorative American larch tree. Its needles form clusters and it has small cones that are very appealing to wreath makers during the holiday season.

And at the bottom of the page, reminiscent of a porcupine, is a Chinese chestnut husk. Like the horse chestnut, the nut hides under the husk, but in this case it is edible.

DRAWING TREE BARK

Shagbark Hickory Bark

Illustrated to the right is probably one of the more readily recognized trees because of its scaly bark, hence the name shagbark hickory. The hickory is well known for its strength and, if you can beat the squirrels to them, you will find its nuts delicious.

White Willow Bark

Take a look at the close-up below of a white willow tree's bark, and notice the strange design of curling and twisting.

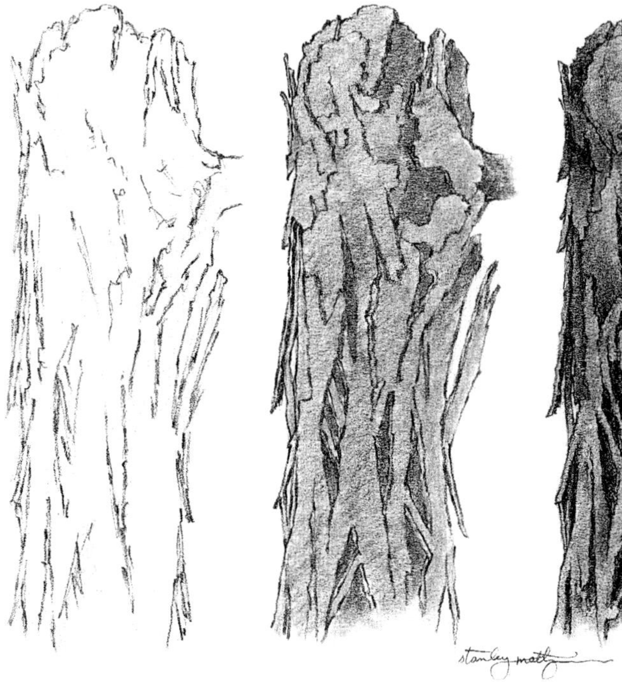

Drawing Shagbark Hickory Bark
Working from left to right, first is a light outline drawing of part of a hickory trunk with indications of the bark. The middle drawing shows the addition of an overall tone that is acquired by first rubbing with a stomp and then adding more bark characteristics and darks. The final drawing on the right illustrates how refining emphasizes the bark structure. For this set, 2B and 6B graphite pencils were used with a stomp on a sheet of 2-ply Strathmore Bristol paper.

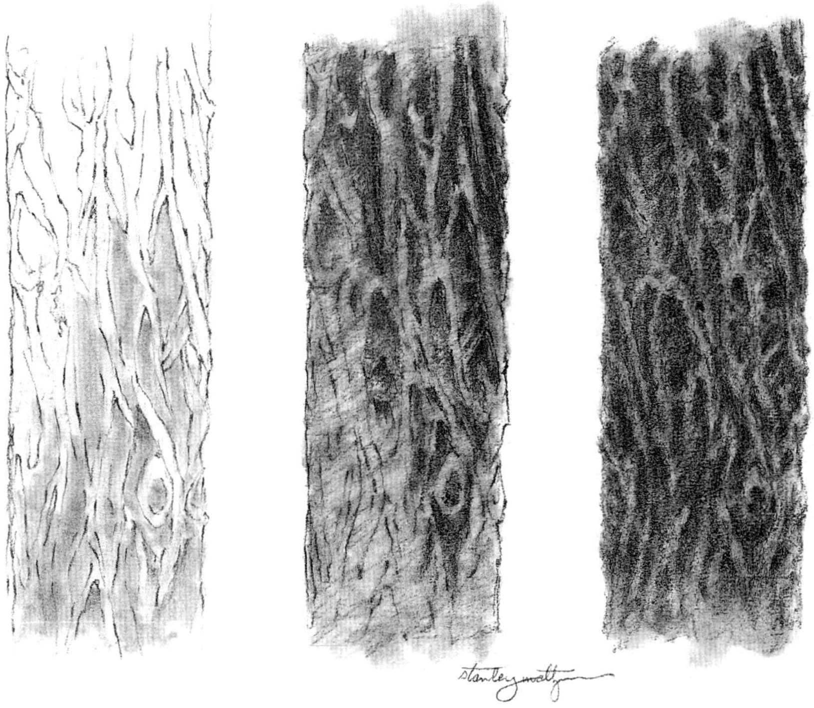

Drawing White Willow Bark
Again working from left to right, the first sketch shows a light initial drawing with toning the bark by rubbing the charcoal with a finger, tissue or stomp. In the middle sketch, notice how additional tone has been added to the overall sketch and then built with more darks. The finished drawing on the right illustrates the building up of darks by layering the charcoal until the desired values are achieved.

These sketches were completed on a sheet of 2-ply Strathmore Bristol. I started with a 2B charcoal pencil, which I stomped, and then switched over to a piece of vine charcoal. For details, I used the edge of the charcoal and then a kneaded eraser to lift out highlights.

Paper Birch Bark

The following is a great technique for acquiring silverlike grays and for experimentation. Remember there are no steadfast rules for art. You should try something different. The charcoal and wash method below works very well when rendering a birch tree like the one here.

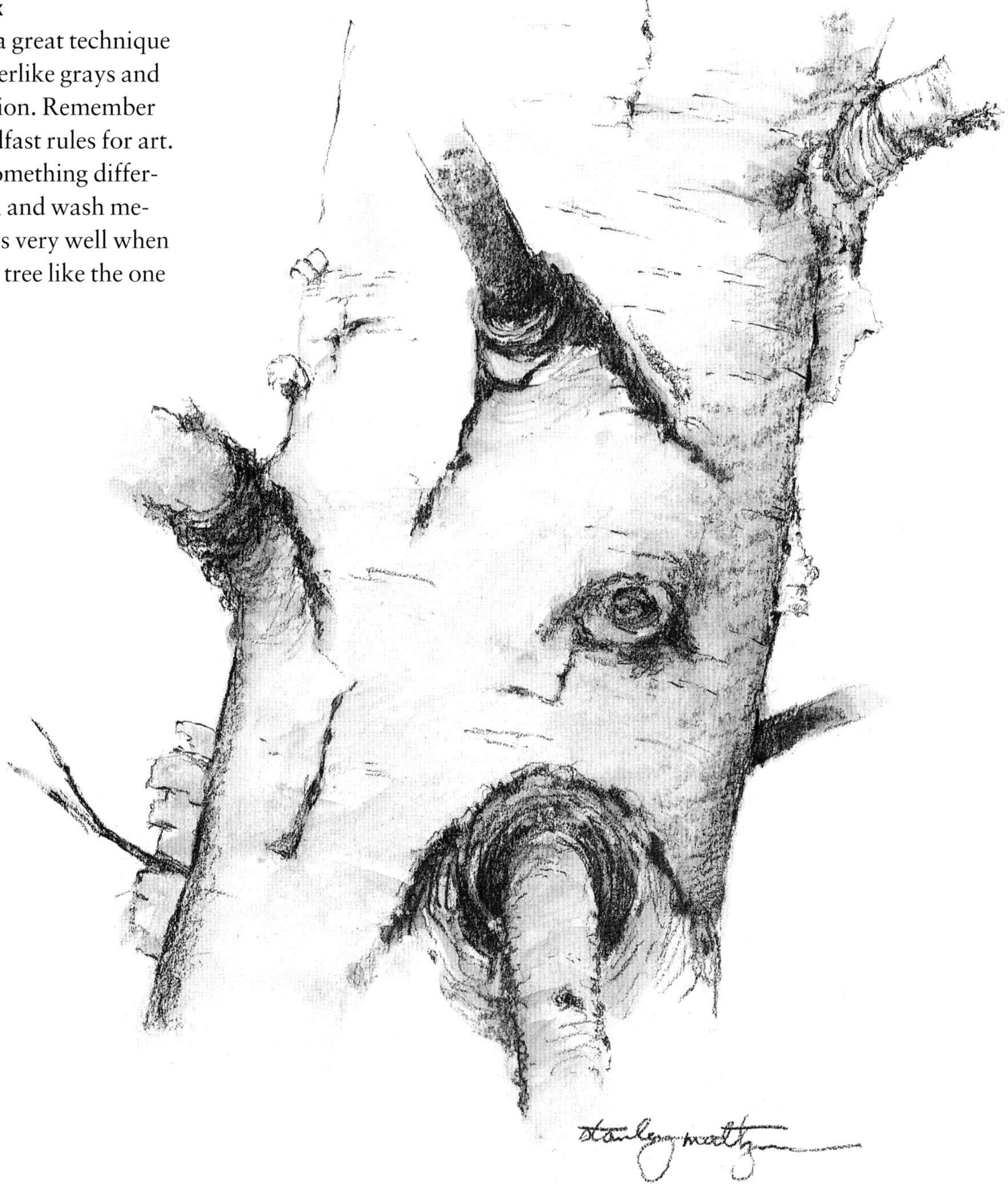

Drawing Birch Bark

Work out your drawing on a separate piece of paper. With a piece of vine charcoal start your drawing, not yet including the darkest values. Take a soft, clean brush, dip it in clean water, and brush over your charcoal drawing. This will create nice, soft grays. Clean your brush frequently, especially after going over heavy dark areas, or you will be pushing mud around.

When the wash is dry, you may return with your charcoal and rework your drawing. Be careful not to obliterate all your soft washes; leave some showing. When satisfied with your efforts, treat your work like any charcoal drawing using a couple of light coats of your workable matte fixative.

This work was done using a piece of medium vine charcoal, a soft brush and water on a piece of 2-ply Strathmore Bristol, which is heavy enough to take the washes of water.

Sweet Gum Bark

Here is the bark of a sweet gum tree, which in the fall can rival any tree with its beautiful colors. It also has tiny balls on the end of its long stems. As a youngster, I would paint these balls silver and gold to use as Christmas decorations.

White Oak Bark

Below is the bark of a magnificent giant, a mature white oak. Seek one out and make several sketches. Discover the beauty of these trees. I strongly recommend that before you start your drawing, sit back and spend a little time studying the bark and how the pattern flows. You should find this pause extremely beneficial to your understanding and to helping you capture the design on paper.

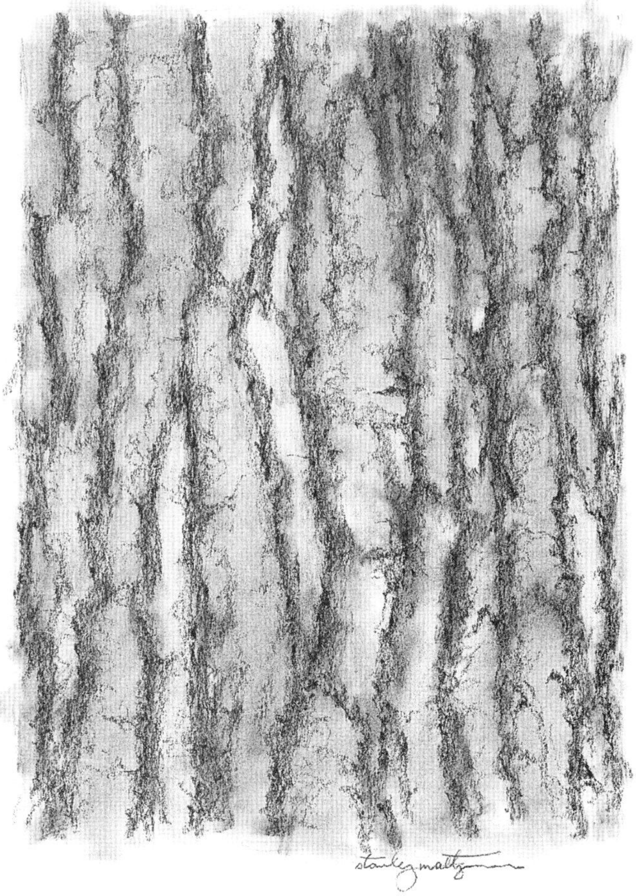

Drawing Sweet Gum Bark

With vine charcoal, make your drawing, including the ridges of the bark. Then with a soft brush dipped in water and wiped gently on a rag, so as not to make puddles, create a nice uneven gray tone. Once dry, return with your charcoal and add more detail. Using your stomp with varying degrees of pressure will create a nice variety of tones. Work the ridges of the bark with the charcoal. Lastly, using the flat of the charcoal, drag it lightly along the ridges to add texture. Using the edge of the charcoal to create fine lines, create deeper ridges here and there.

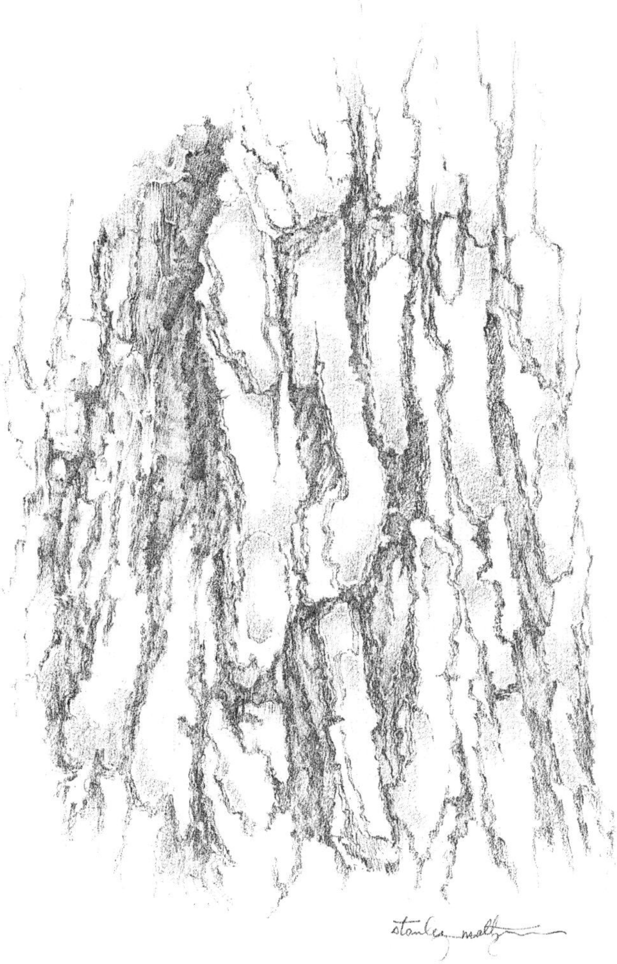

Drawing White Oak Bark

Work out your pattern on a separate sheet of paper, then transfer it to your finished paper. Starting in the middle, begin to outline the bark patterns, emphasizing their contours. Work downward first and then move to the sides.

Start with a sharp pencil point. Remember to work lightly. As the point wears down, the lead will become chisel shaped. This will give you a nice flat surface, enabling you to put down wide strokes of tone. Use the outside edge when you need a fine line for details. Keep emphasizing your shapes, adding tone and values, and repeating until you have created as much of the bark as you want for your study. This drawing was executed with 2B and 4B graphite pencils on 2-ply Strathmore Bristol.

Locust Tree Bark

This bark, with a wonderful abstract pattern, is from a very old locust tree. The moss and lichen growing on it add to the excitement and the challenge. The locust tree has a very distinct pattern that should be a big help to beginners. Remember that you do not need to complete the drawing in one day. When working on intricate drawings like this, it is best to work for a few hours and then shift to something else. A fresh eye the next day will make it much easier to pick up shapes you were missing the previous day.

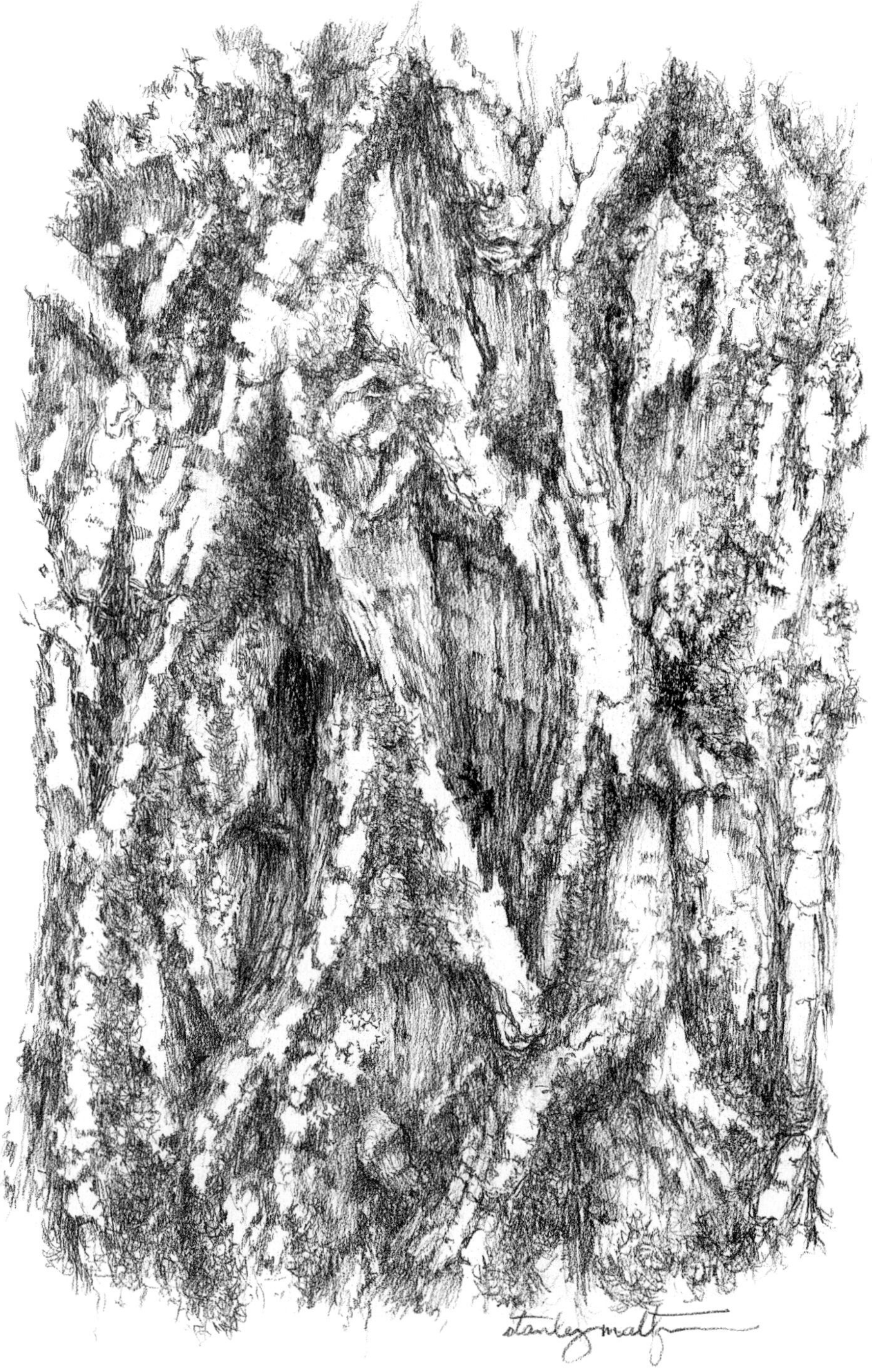

Drawing Locust Tree Bark

Work out the general pattern on separate paper, and then transfer the design to your good paper, proceeding lightly as usual. After developing your pattern, start to create your light values and begin picking up the various nuances, such as the moss, lichen, lumps and bumps. It is entirely up to you how far you want to carry the piece. Remember, pick out the obvious, shade lightly, add more characteristics and shade some more. By keeping to this kind of repetition your bark will soon be completed. This particular piece was done on 2-ply Strathmore Bristol with B, BB and BBB Wolff's carbon pencils. Wolff's carbon is richer and finer than charcoal.

KNOTHOLES

Knotholes on a tree usually indicate an area where a limb or bough once grew. In healing, a collarlike growth appears around the wound, creating yet another design for you to work with. If the wound does not heal properly, decay will form a cavity allowing all types of insects to move in. Then comes the beginning of the end of a masterpiece.

You do not need to go far to find a tree with a knothole. Most likely the first tree you look at will have lost a limb or two at one time or another. The best place to look for knotholes is in old trees. They have been through the battles; they are survivors and, therefore, will offer great shapes in addition to knots — all material for your sketchbook.

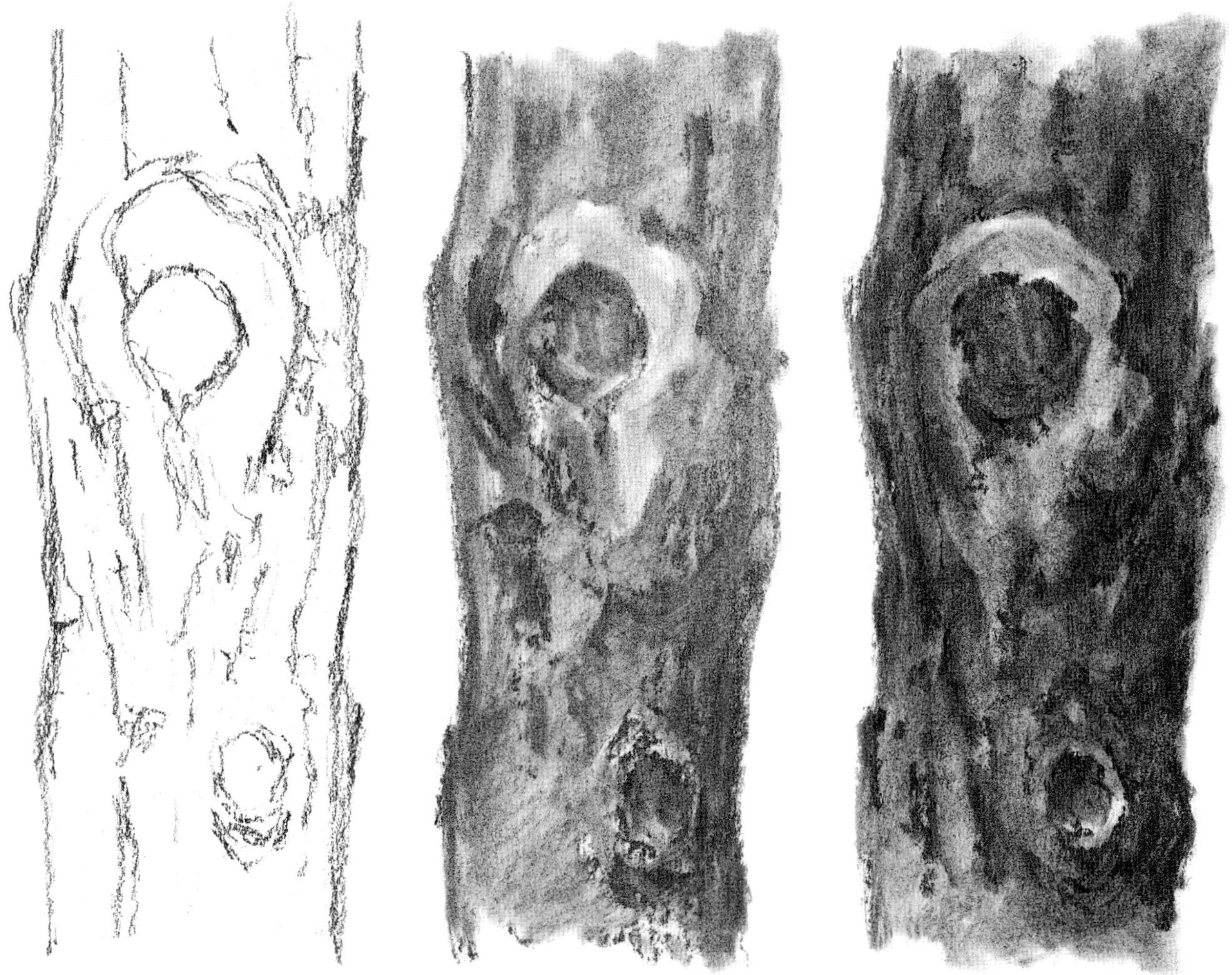

Drawing Knotholes
Here's one approach to drawing knotholes. Start with a soft piece of vine charcoal and sketch the contour of the trunk with two holes, as shown in the lefthand drawing. Then, as shown in the middle, put down some charcoal and with a soft brush and water push the charcoal around. In this case, you do not have to be too careful as a rough look works well when indicating bark. Something to be aware of is the flow of bark around the knots. Finally, add some darker details, as shown on the right.

Take a look at these variously shaped knotholes. I found them all within a few feet of each other at Olana, the magnificent Moor-inspired home in upstate New York, which Frederic Church built. Church's estate, now a historic site, has a sweeping view of the Hudson River and hundreds of trees he planted to enhance the landscape.

The left drawing is of an old knot. You can tell by the way the collar has started cracking and the inside hole is beginning to decay. But it is still an interesting shape.

The second knot on the right is not quite so old, but has a nice shape with a cavity that is going to make some bird happy when winter comes. Notice how the bark forms in harmony with the knothole, an important fact to notice and include in your drawing.

The final drawing on the bottom illustrates the loss of two large limbs and a smaller one. Notice that you can tell the direction they were growing by the shading of the holes.

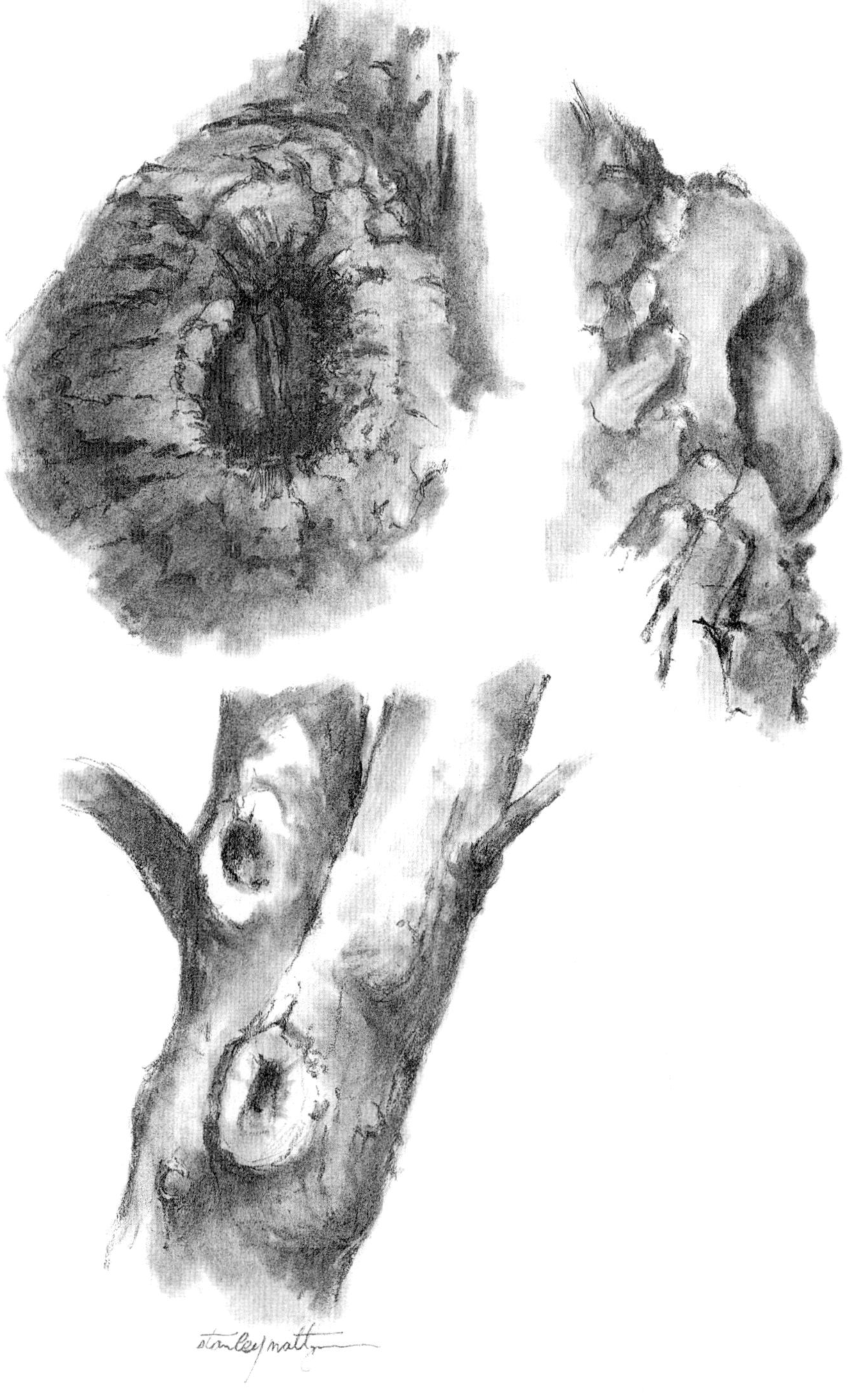

A Variety of Knotholes

All these sketches were done quickly to show you the versatility of charcoal. It can be used for fine detail as well as for sketchy drawings. With these I used soft fine charcoal and a stomp, tissue or finger — whatever was convenient at the given moment.

As you draw knotholes, take notice of the way the bark curves around the swelling of the collars. The flow is an important characteristic. Finally, if you feel the drawing needs it, take your kneaded eraser and add a highlight or two to the collars. Spray a couple of light coats of fixative and you are finished.

LIVING FOLIAGE

The proper presentation of foliage is very important to the character of the tree you are drawing. Some trees, like maples, will have heavy foliage; birches or aspens will have less. The idea is to portray the foliage so that it looks like it belongs to your tree.

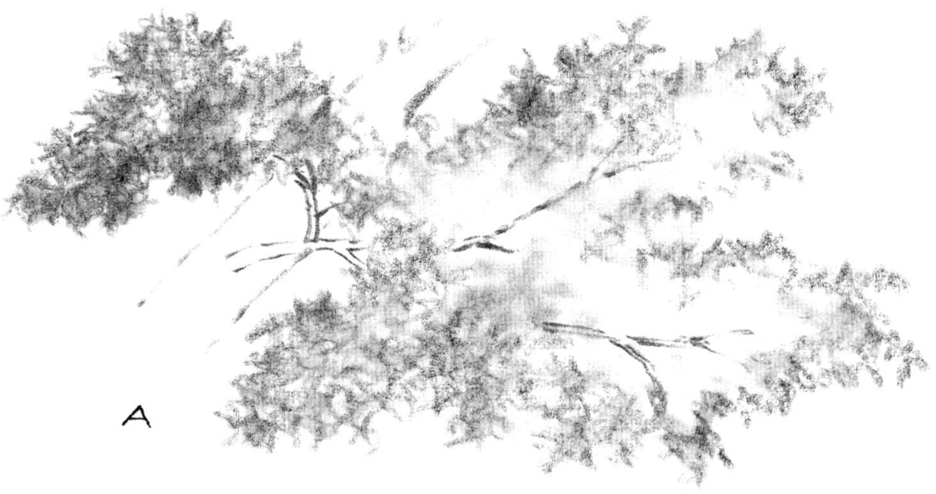

A

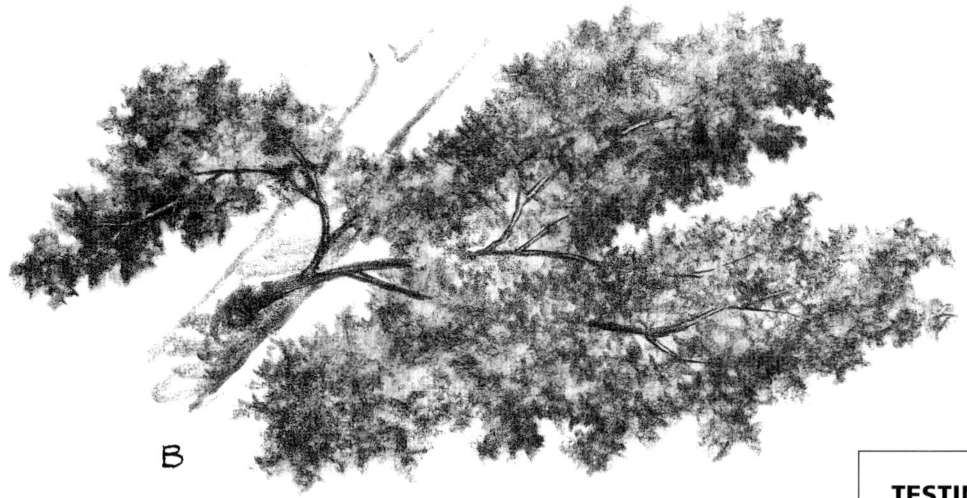

B

Make Your Foliage Look Real

To make your foliage look as if it belongs on your tree, start with a preliminary outline that shows only a suggestion of foliage, as shown in sketch A. It is important to place your branches properly so they look like they are going to hold up your leaves. If you're not sure, take a piece of tracing paper and draw the individual branches on it. You can then move them around over your final working surface until you are satisfied with the positioning. Only then should you add the branches to your actual drawing.

The next step is to start darkening the foliage, as shown in sketch B. Do not sketch every individual leaf. The idea is to create the illusion that you have drawn every leaf. As you apply the darks, curve an edge every so often. This will give the appearance that you drew every leaf. Leave some edges lighter than others. Remember which direction the light is coming from and allow some light to shine through. Do not make a solid mass of leaves.

TESTING YOUR VALUES

Here's a method for testing values for a specific area.

1. With a piece of tracing paper, trace the area in question.
2. Using a piece of paper covered with the value in question, place the tracing paper on top and cut the shape out.
3. Place the cutout value in position over the drawing.

This will help to give you an idea whether or not it is the right value for the space.

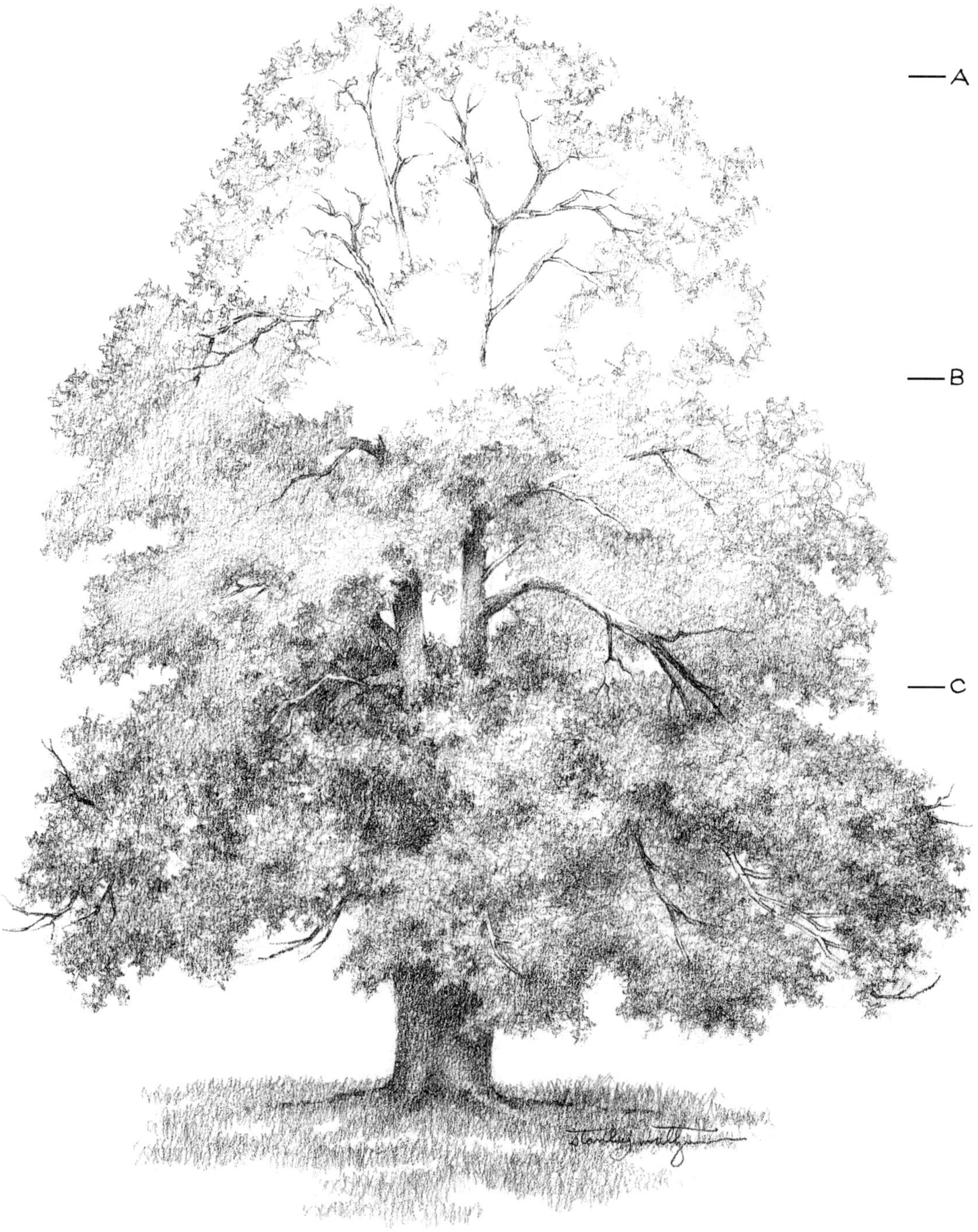

Foliage on the Whole Tree

To draw an entire tree in leaf (we'll use an oak for this example), start by lightly sketching the shape, as shown in A. If you don't want to work directly on your good sheet of paper, use a sheet of tracing paper to work out your idea.

Once you're satisfied with your design, transfer it to your good paper and continue building the outline. When the outline is complete, begin shading, indicating your light, middle and dark values, as shown in B. Do not punch up the real darks until you are satisfied that they are what you want and are where you want them, because once placed, you'll have trouble removing them.

Letter C shows the finished rendering of this stately tree. Note the downward direction of the lower limbs. Against the darks work your light limbs, and against the lights add darker branches. Every so often make the edges of the foliage irregular to create the illusion of a tree full of leaves.

INDIVIDUAL LEAVES

Here are a few select leaf drawings. The large group of leaves is from a walnut tree. This type of grouping is called a compound pinnate leaf, a type resembling feathers. There are many other trees with this particular formation, such as hickory, locust and ash. You do not have to become too technical, but it does make your work more interesting when you know something about your subject matter.

The large single leaf is from a sugar maple, and for all practical purposes it looks very authentic because the shape is interesting and represents good design. If you so desire, you can carry this drawing to a higher degree of perfection, botanically speaking.

Finally, here's a drawing of a leaf from a paper birch, broken down into steps so that you can see one approach to drawing leaves. Start with your light outline sketch of the leaf and its main features, as in A. When you are satisfied, tighten your drawing and add a middle-value tone over the whole leaf as shown above the white spaces in B. Lastly, overpaint with shapes simulating a veinlike pattern, as shown in C. Again, this should merely give the illusion of a leaf with its many veins. Remember, you are creating a piece of art that resembles a botanically accurate leaf but is not.

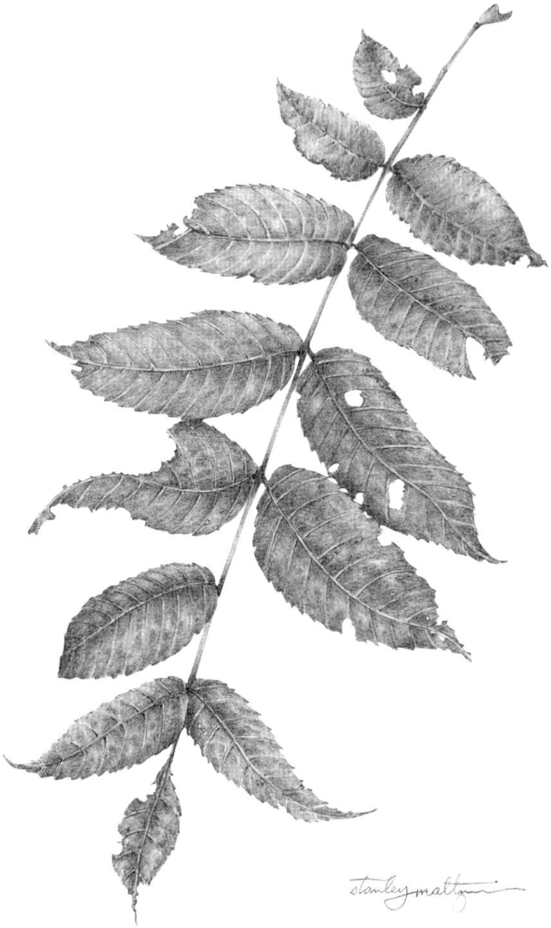

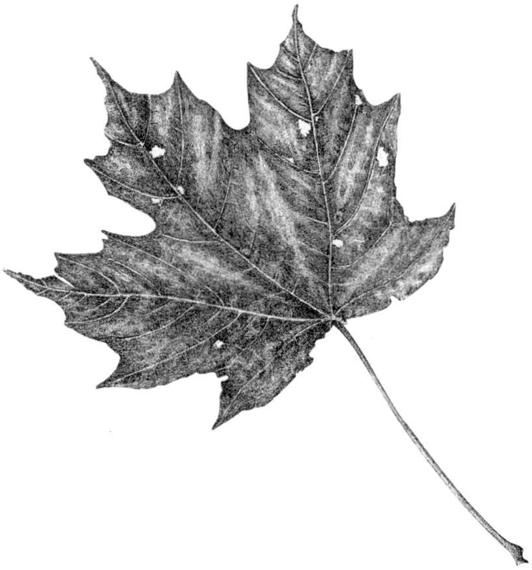

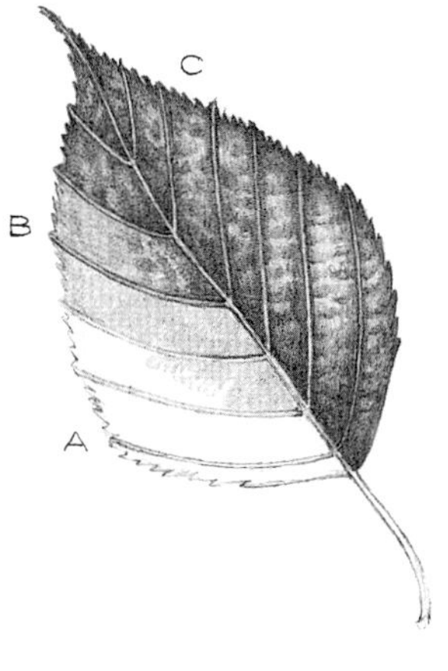

Individual Leaves
All three of these drawings were made using HB and 2B graphite pencils on Rives BFK paper, a soft surface that helps you create the veins of the leaf as you work over the general tone. You can also pull out shapes with your kneaded eraser, but do not erase over your established tones, and be wary of overworking your drawing.

DEAD LEAVES

Usually toward the end of August the leaves on many trees will start to turn brown and fall to the ground. You might even find a whole sprig of leaves. As these leaves lose their green color, they turn into interesting shades of brown and curl into many shapes. Insects might also add more interest to the picture by leaving holes in the leaves. These shapes are lying all over the ground just waiting tobe added to your sketchbook.

Though you can work with any type of old leaves, it's best to use those from the prior year, after nature has had a chance to sculpt them into interesting shapes. Start with a light sketch, then begin to build. As you work, look for the oddities, such as cracks, holes, ragged edges or pock marks.

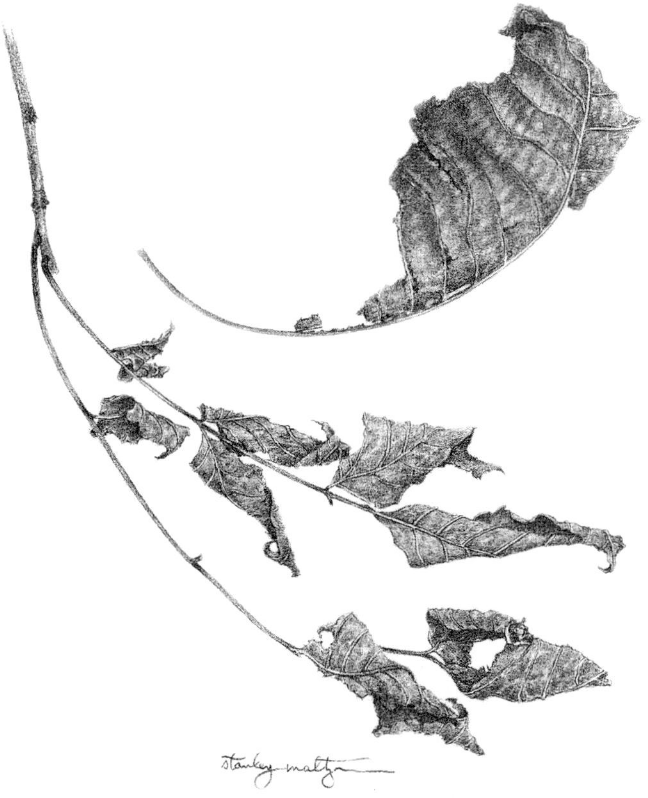

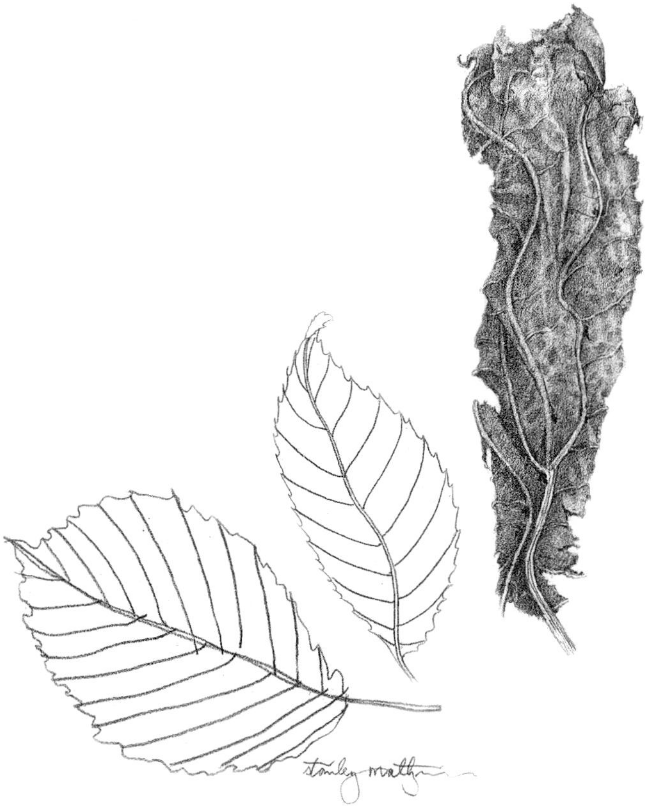

Drawing Dead Leaves
Above are some leaf studies made with Wolff's carbon pencils: HB to lay in the initial drawing, BB to do the shading. A stomp was then used for modeling, and a kneaded eraser to lift out, adding some more shapes. Finally, I returned with the pencils to emphasize different points of interest.

The paper used was Rives BFK, a soft paper that does not allow too much stomping or erasing, but takes enough to make it interesting. The softness will make you plan a little more before working the sheet, but it is certainly worth the effort.

Work Your Eye
The two outline drawings here are called contour drawings (the smaller one is a hickory leaf, while the larger is an elm leaf). A contour drawing is nothing more than a line drawing, and it is a great exercise to help sharpen your eye and memory. When creating contour drawings, the trick is to never let your eyes leave the object you are drawing in an outline. In short, never look at the paper! Your first few attempts will no doubt be off the mark, but you'll find that after a couple of tries, your drawing will get closer to what you see.

The finished drawing, created with 2B and 4B graphite pencils on Strathmore 400 Series paper, is of wild grape leaves, and it was only after I started working that I noticed there were two leaves wrapped around each other. A contour drawing would be a great way to work out the basic intricacies of this composition.

LICHEN

No matter where you walk, sooner or later you will notice lichen, either on trees or rocks. Lichen grow in clusters in some great colors: brilliant greens, yellows and grays, just to name a few. It is a compound plant produced by a fungus growing together with algae (that's as technical as you'll need to get for our purposes). What you see here is a piece of a plum tree that I kept just so I could watch the lichen grow and eventually use for this book.

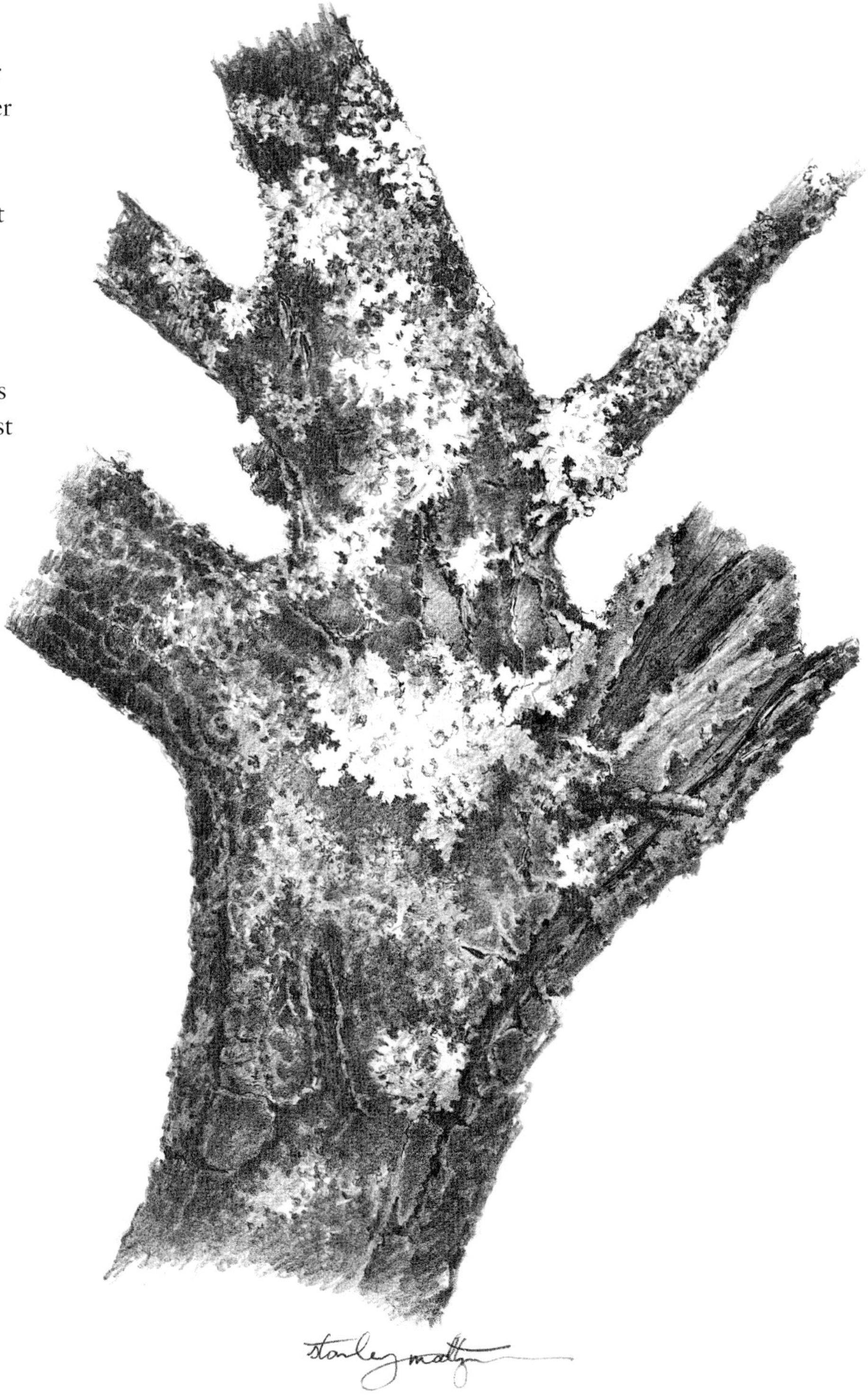

Be Familiar With Your Tools
This drawing was executed with only one pencil, a 2B Venus graphite pencil, on Rives BFK paper. Notice the value range to the left, which shows you exactly what can be accomplished with that one pencil. Learn what your pencils can and cannot do. Start light and gradually increase pressure until you reach full intensity. A few minutes will provide you with a little extra knowledge that will help you make better drawings.

FUNGUS

These two illustrations show two different types of fungi; both are members of the bracket fungus family. The first example is most often found on deciduous stumps and trees that are dying or are already dead, though I have also found this type of cluster on conifers. I found this specimen in the woods, and I kept it growing by wetting it down every other day until I was ready to bring it into the studio to study and draw. The coloring and growth shapes are very interesting and should definitely be on your list for future drawings.

The second example is another type of bracket fungus that, as near as I can determine, can be found on living and dead birch trees. This particular specimen was growing on one of my paper birches, so I decided to make a study out of it.

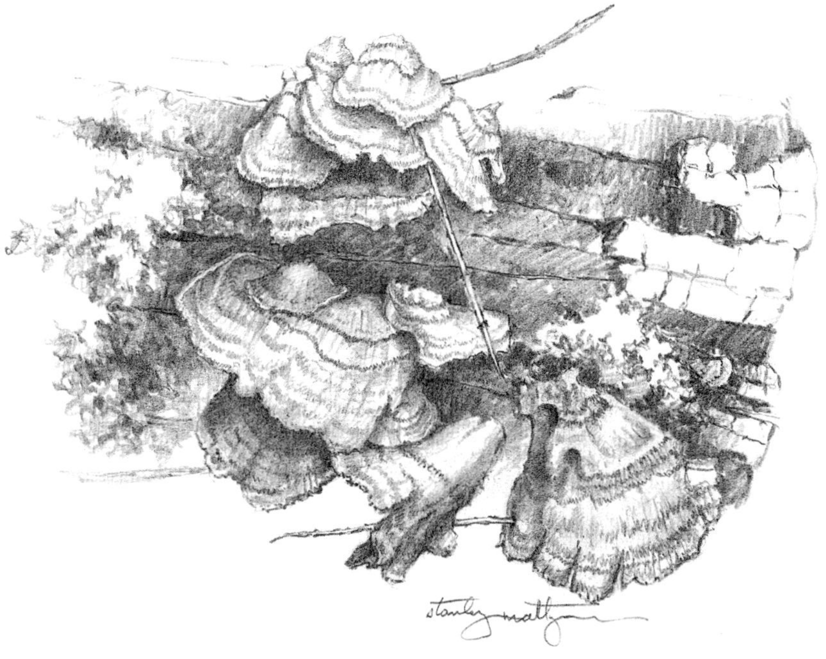

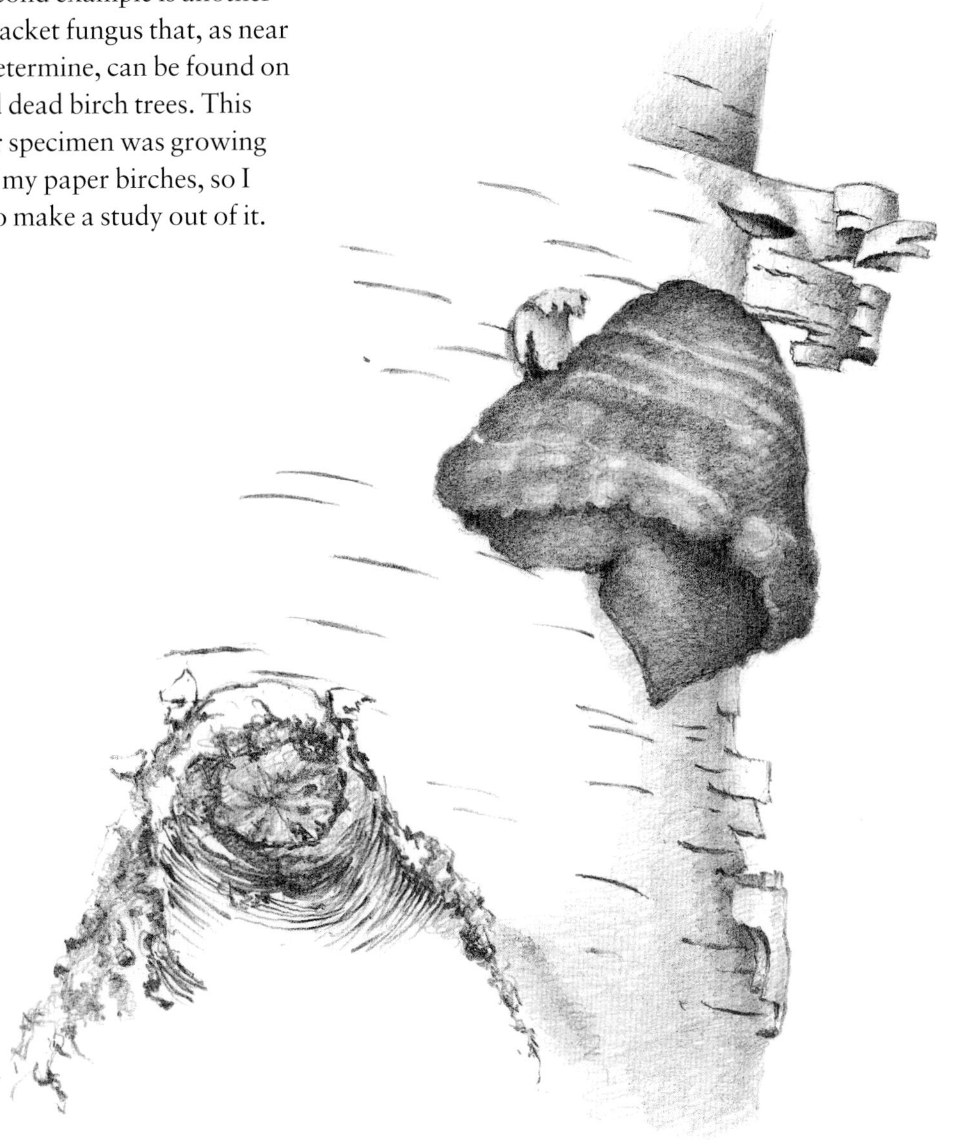

SPIDERWEBS

During your walks in a garden or woods, you're sure to run into more than your share of spiderwebs. Different species of spiders make their own style of webs that suit their various purposes, mainly to trap and acquire food. The one seen here is known as an orb web, and is probably one of the most recognizable. It is quite intricate and one of the more beautiful ones you will see. The builder uses twigs, branches or just about anything to anchor its web. Then within this frame it spins a beautiful design. If the web gets damaged while catching prey, it is easily repaired. A marvelous feat of nature, the orb web becomes even more beautiful when covered with morning dewdrops, as illustrated here.

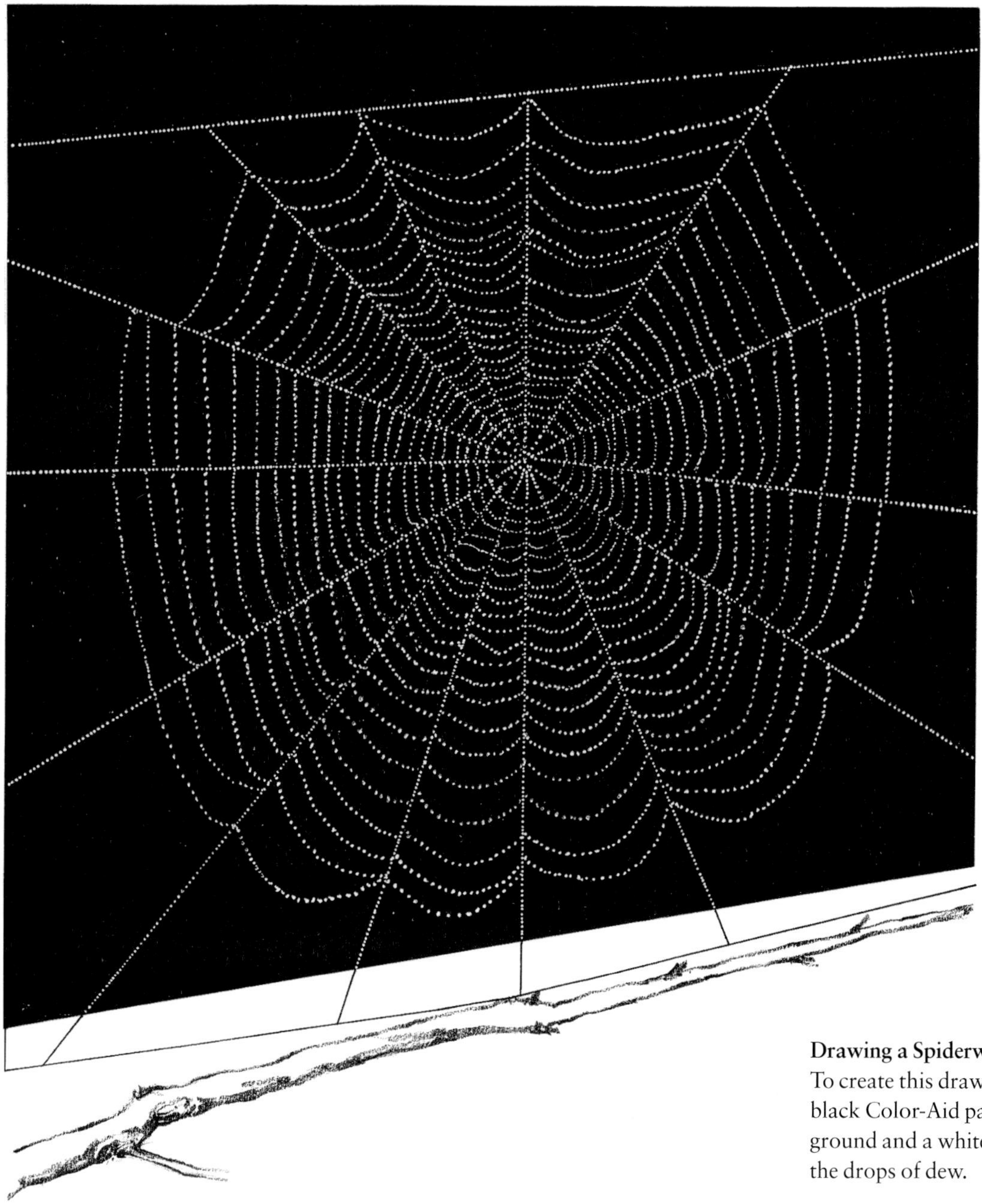

Drawing a Spiderweb
To create this drawing, use a piece of black Color-Aid paper for the background and a white Pentel pen to create the drops of dew.

MUSHROOMS

You'll notice many types of mushrooms when you go for walks in the woods. You can even find them popping up on your lawn, but mostly you will spot them growing on rotting wood.

They are very interesting to observe. The colors and shapes make them such worthwhile subjects, so spend some time sketching or painting them. Under no circumstances, however, should you pick any to eat unless you are an expert or you have someone with you who is. Mushrooms are very beautiful, but many are extremely poisonous. So observe, draw or paint them, but do not handle or eat them!

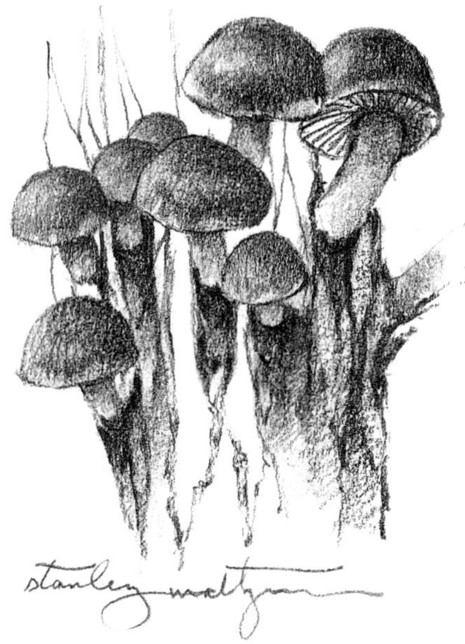

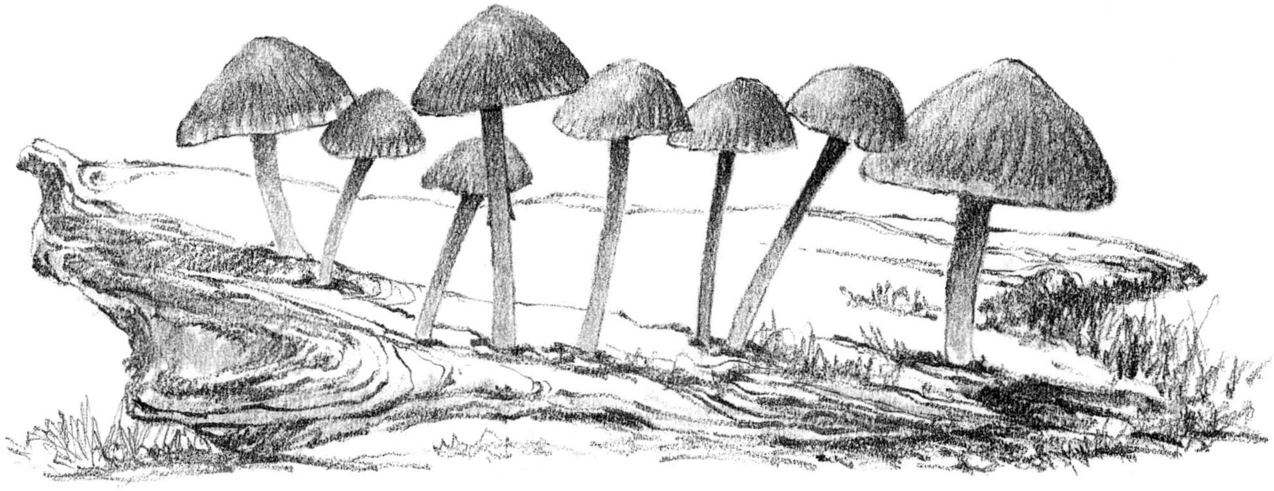

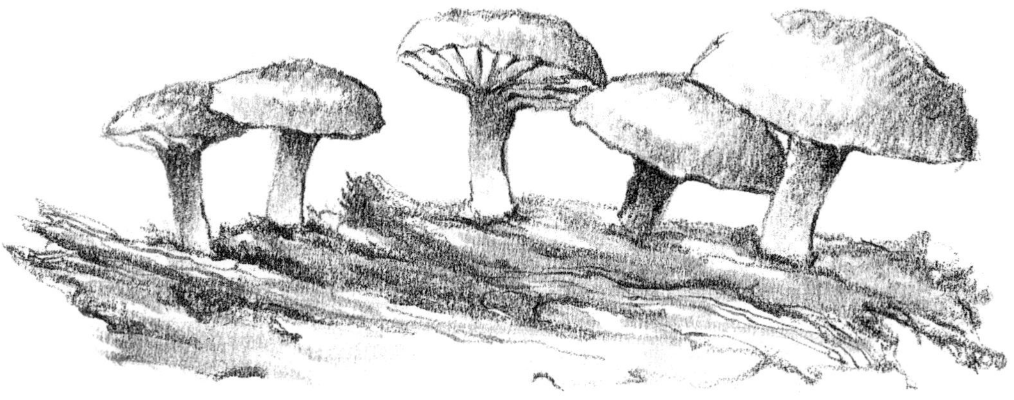

FOREST DEBRIS

What falls to the ground in a wooded area is a far cry from literally being debris. Nature, unlike many people, makes use of everything that lands on her carpet, the forest floor. Falling leaves will cover pieces of bark or needles, keeping things damp and hastening the appearance of all kinds of growth. This in turn causes decay, which makes a wonderful base for new life in the forest.

Seeds flying through the air, birds dropping seeds, squirrels burying nuts that soon get covered by more debris. With the help of dampness and some sun, the forest debris is building again.

On these two pages are trees that have fallen to the ground for one reason or another. Leaves and debris pile up, helping with the decomposing. What was once a living plant is now giving back vitality to the woods so that new growth can start again from a rich forest floor — a wonderful cycle of life. Forest debris also makes interesting material for you to work from.

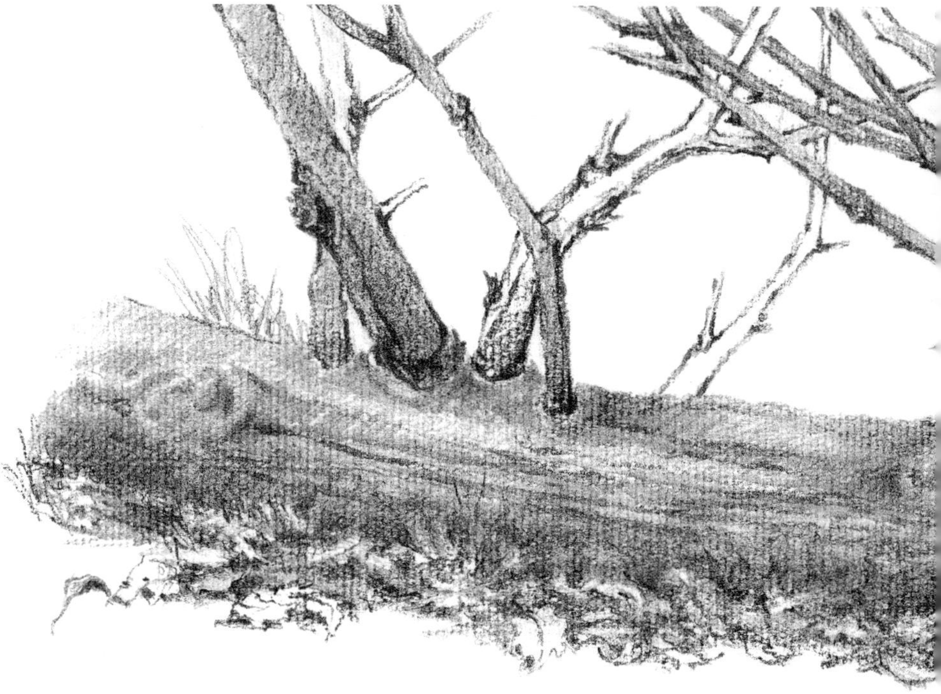

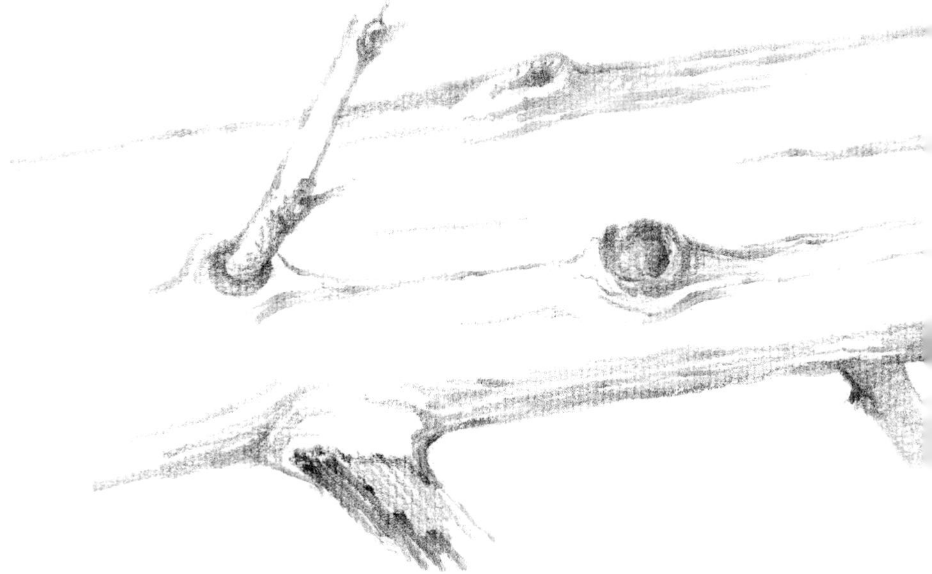

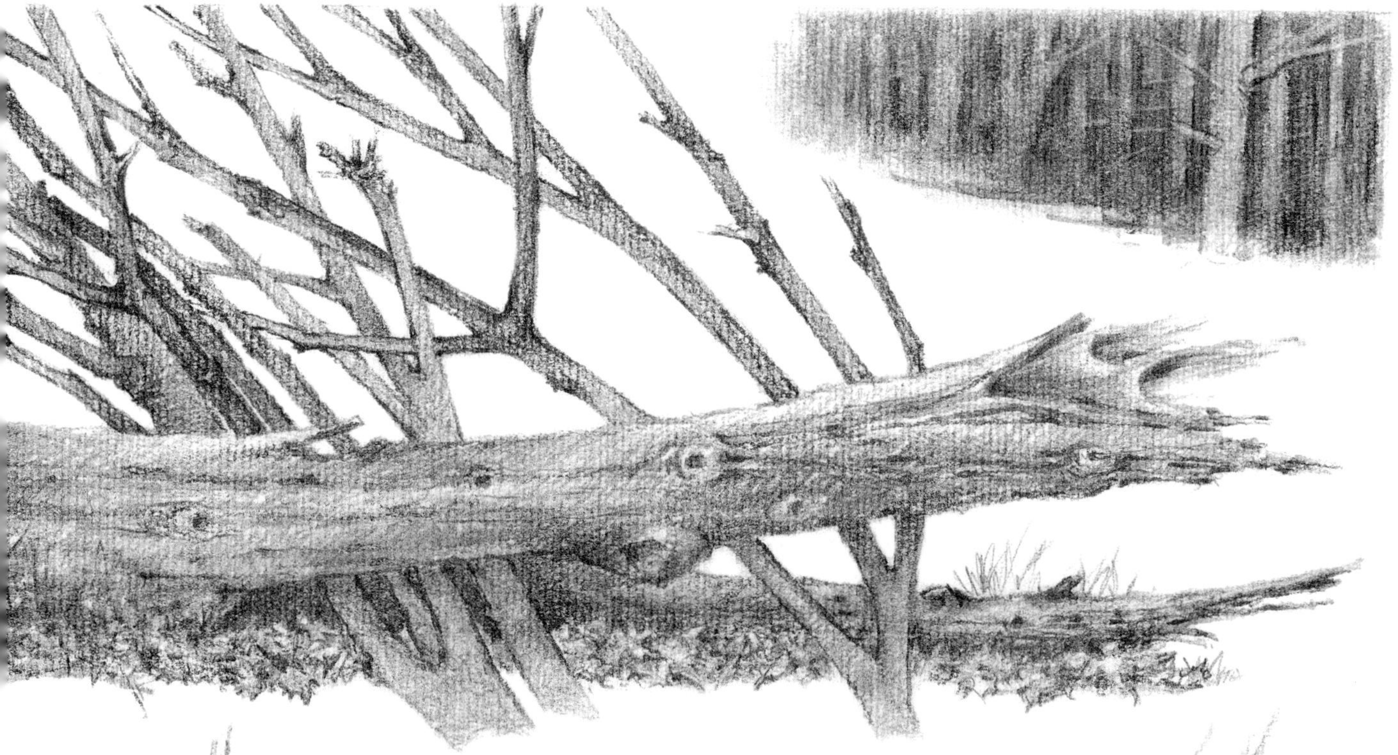

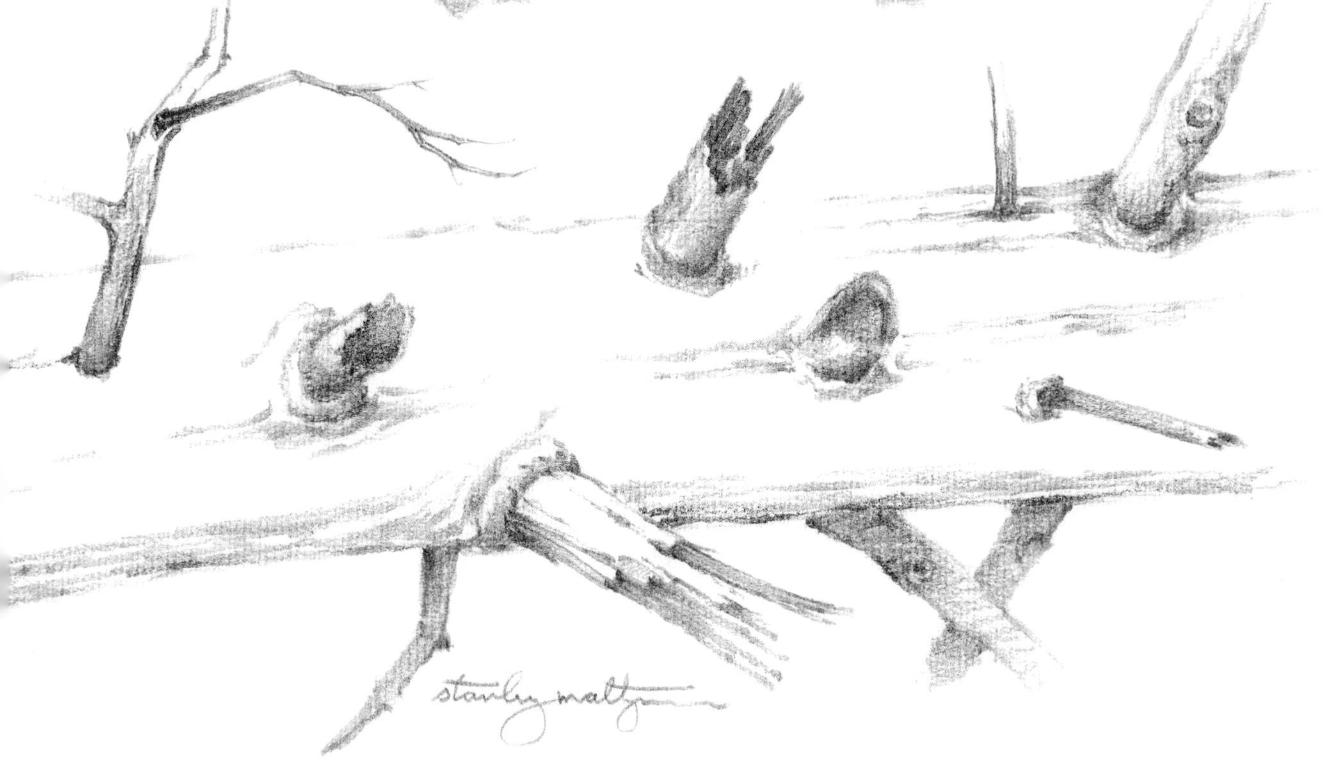

These two drawings were made on an Arches Ingres paper (a laid paper) using HB, 2B, 4B and 6B graphite pencils.

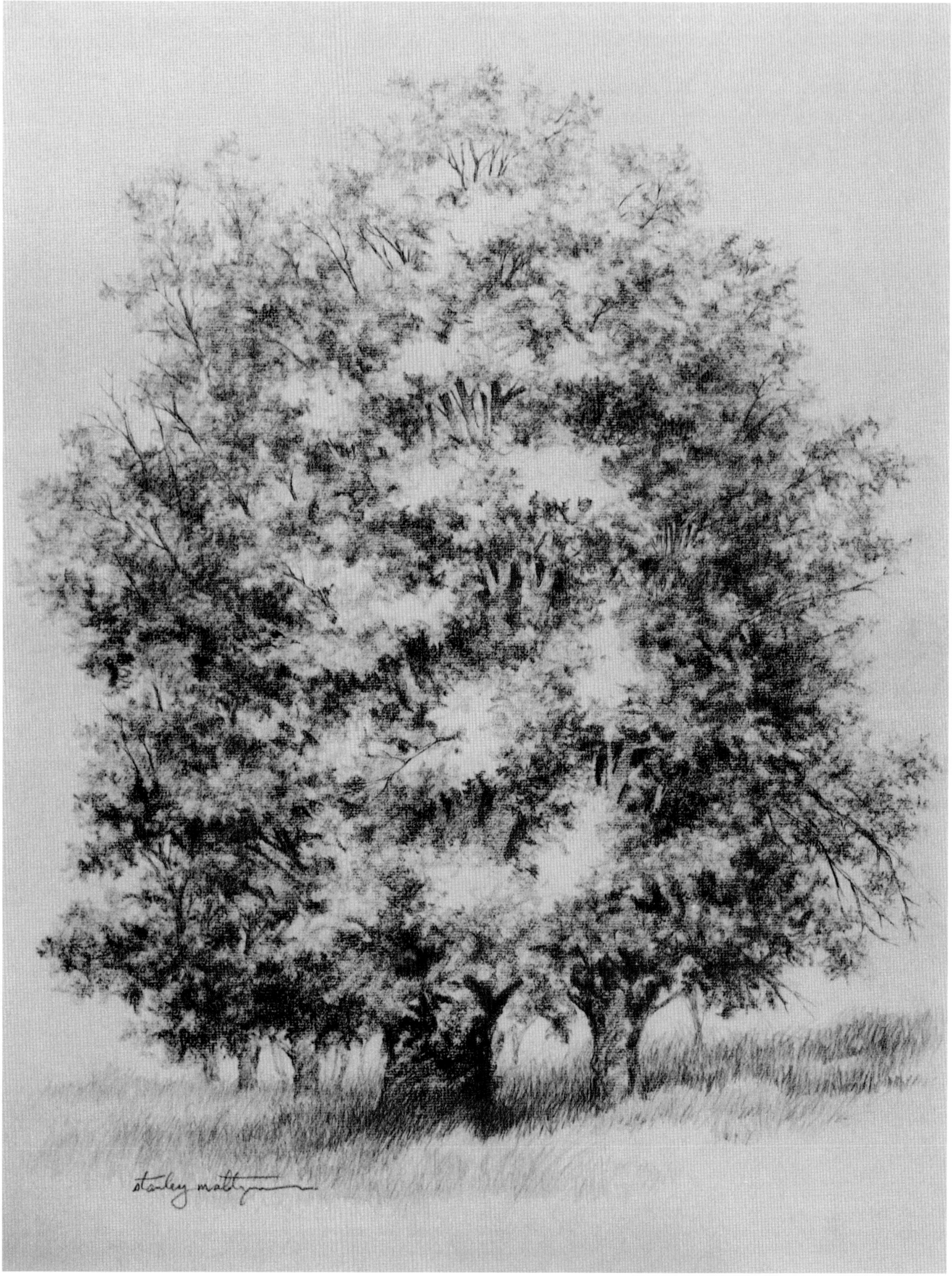

Family of Maples, 18 ½" x 24" (47cm x 61cm), charcoal on German Ingres earth-colored paper.

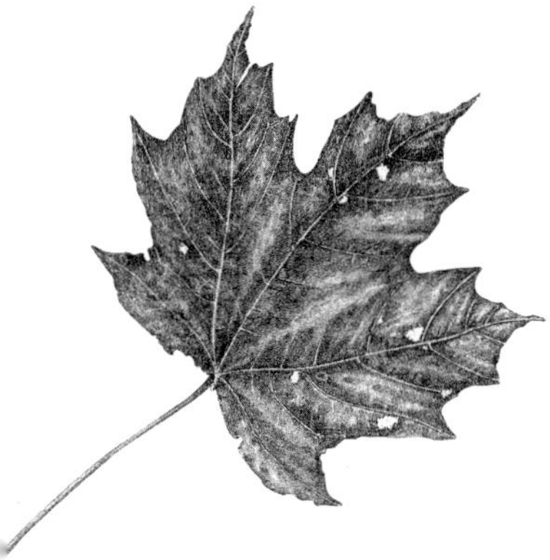

CHAPTER SIX

Enhancing Compositions With Trees

Quite often you gaze at the horizon, and at first it looks interesting, but the longer you look, the more you feel that something is missing. There are nice clouds, some mountains, a tree line, even some fence posts, but it needs some excitement. I have found that adding a tree or a group of trees to a picture will more often than not turn a so-so picture into a much more exciting one.

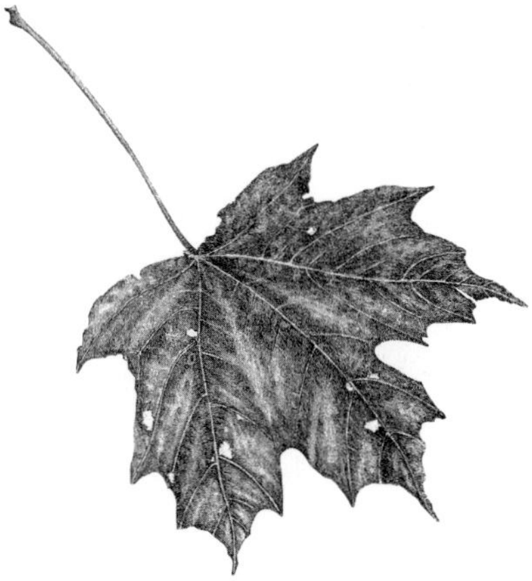

USE TREES TO ADD INTEREST

The addition of some trees to the foreground of a composition can dramatically change the complexion of the landscape into a more interesting sight. Trees both with and without foliage will do wonders to bring drama and excitement into your work. Do not be afraid to experiment. Try little sketches of your ideas to help you reach a happy solution.

Compare the two drawings on this page. The first, though well rendered, is boring and lifeless. The second example works much better because it has a compatible foreground, middle ground and background, and by adding trees to the foreground, you create interesting perspective.

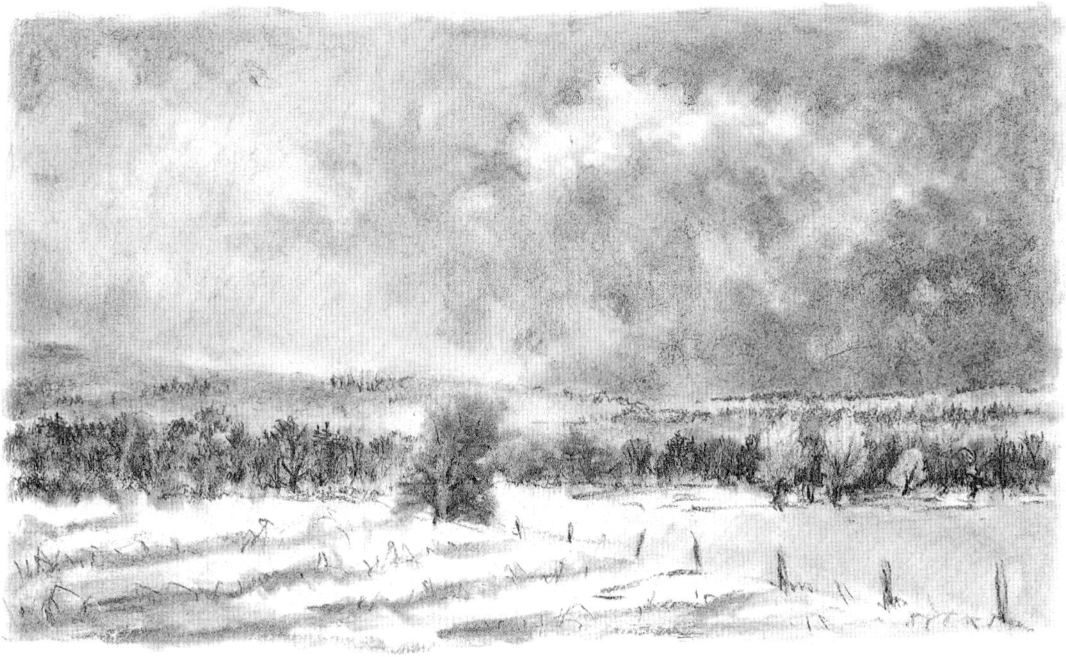

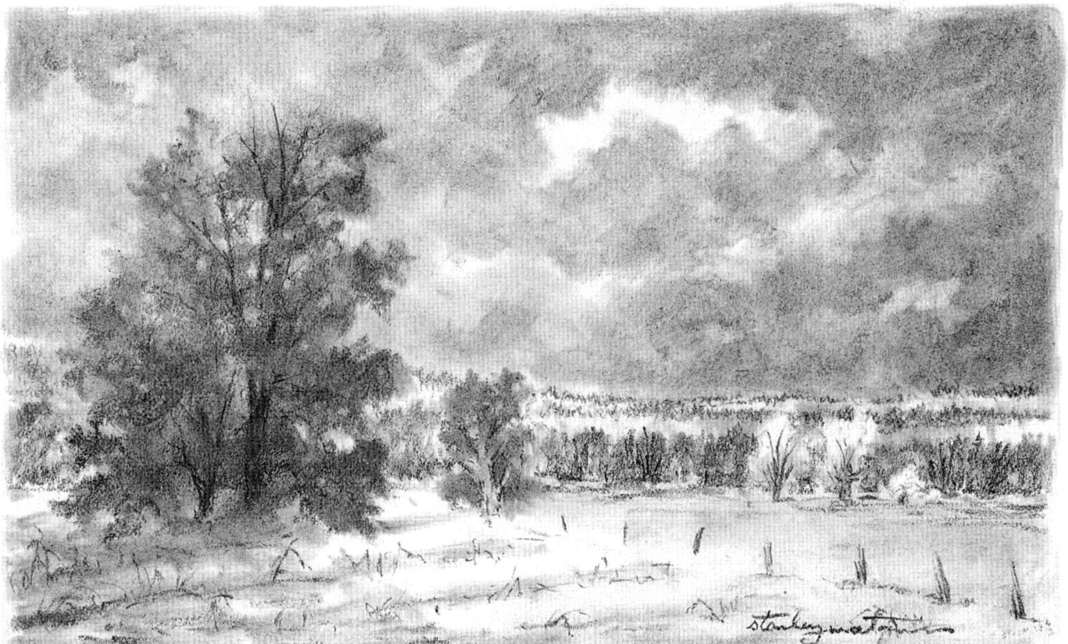

PERSPECTIVE

Take a look at this drawing of a wooded path running through the trees. Notice the white horizon line? This is an imaginary line that exists in every scene and is the place where your eyes meet the horizon. This horizon line is all relative. All people have their own horizon line based on whether they are sitting or standing and on their height, but usually it lies straight ahead. The letters VP mark the vanishing point — the spot on the horizon line where objects or lines converge until they no longer exist.If you follow the footpath with your eyes, you'll see that the futher it travels along, the smaller it becomes until it finally disappears at the vanishing point.

Notice the large tree on the left. At the base you can see more of the root system because you are looking down and it is below the horizon line. But with the second tree, less of the root system is visible because the tree is closer to the horizon line and the root system is higher in your line of vision. The same pertains to the two broken saplings. The one on the left is below the horizon so you see inside the top. The one on the right is above the horizon line so all you see is the silhouette of the top.

The bottom drawing illustrates a line of white pines in the background and a high horizon line. Distance (perspective) is created by the placement of the foreground trees with no tops or bottoms, which further enhances the appearance of distant pines.

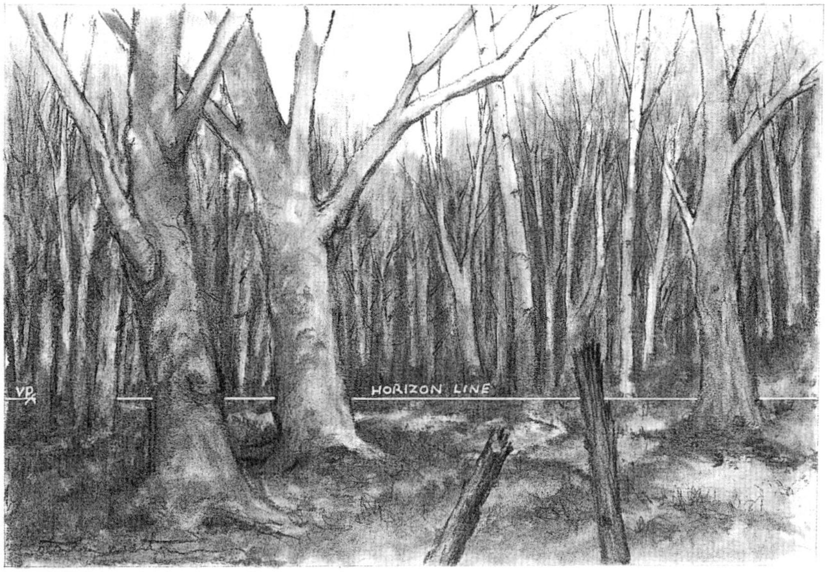

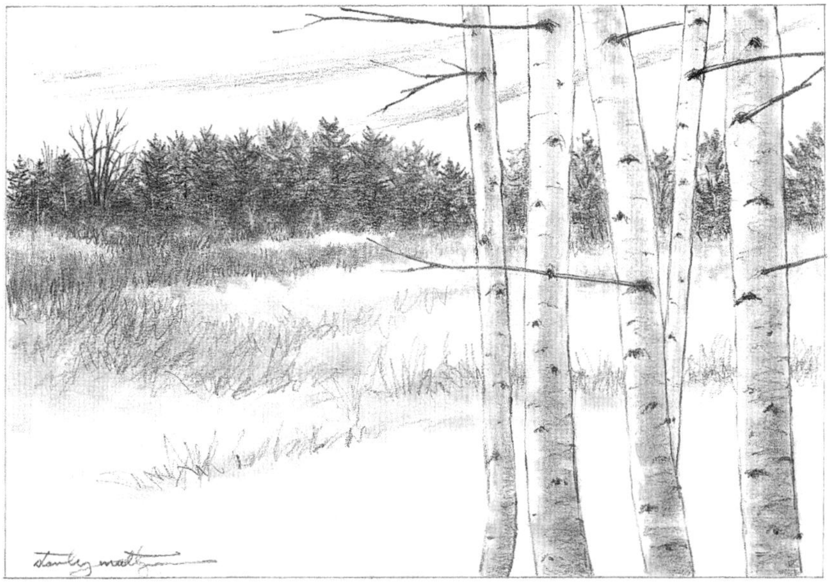

In this illustration we see a group of trees, perhaps the beginning or edge of a forest. If they were all in a straight line they would become boring, but by angling them we begin to create interest. In this composition, the horizon line runs from left to right, starting at the bottom of the distant mountains to where they slope into the large trees. Because you are below the horizon line, the base of the trees (the trunks) are visible. Your vanishing point is at the left. The large trees angle toward that imaginary vanishing point. And by making the trees irregular on the top and bottom, they are attractive to the viewer. So as you look at this picture, your eyes will be drawn to the small mountains because the angle of the mountains leads your eyes there. They can then return along the bottom of the tree line up to the top and down again to the vanishing point. Even if you look to the sky you will be directed back to the trees. The horizon line, vanishing point and perspective all work to make a believable picture.

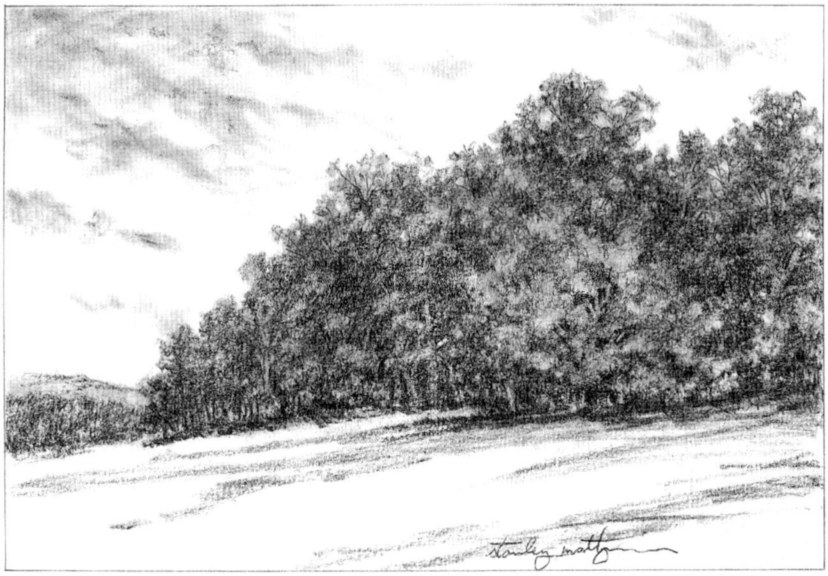

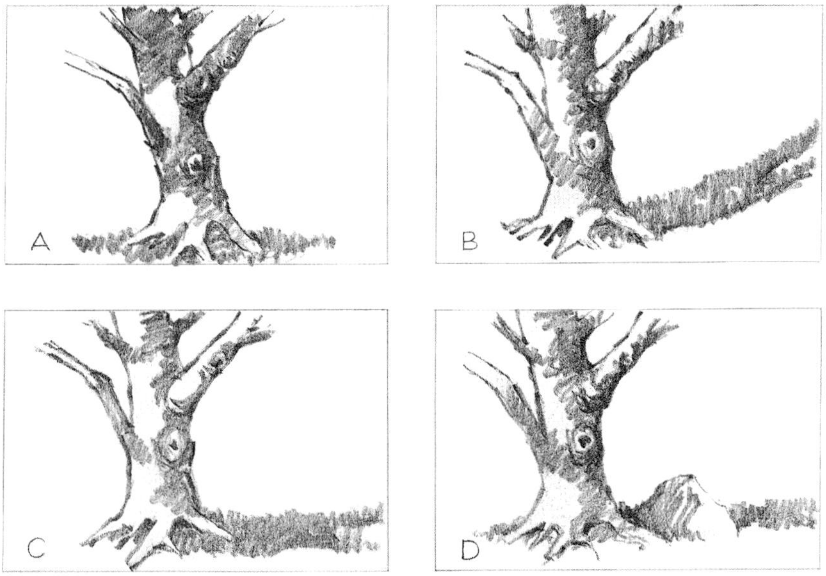

Create More Perspective With Shadows
Next time you are outdoors, watch how shadows create added perspective. Diagram A shows a shadow around a tree trunk with most of the tree in shadow. This means the sun is directly overhead. In Diagram B, you can tell the sun has moved to the left because the shadows are primarily on the right. You also can tell that there is a hill because of the direction of the shadows. Diagram C again shows the sun on the left, with shadows on the right, but now the terrain is level. Diagram D also shows the sun in the same position, but with a boulder beside the tree. The shadow follows the contour of the rock and then continues on the other side, as if there was no rock in its path.

COMPOSITION

Once you have found an area that you wish to develop into a picture, you need to start thinking visually. Decide on either a vertical or horizontal format. Make some rough sketches of what you want your drawing to look like. Decide on your values, and try various combinations of foreground, middle ground and background. And be aware of design pitfalls, such as equal spacing, centering, repetition and monotony.

Equal Spacing

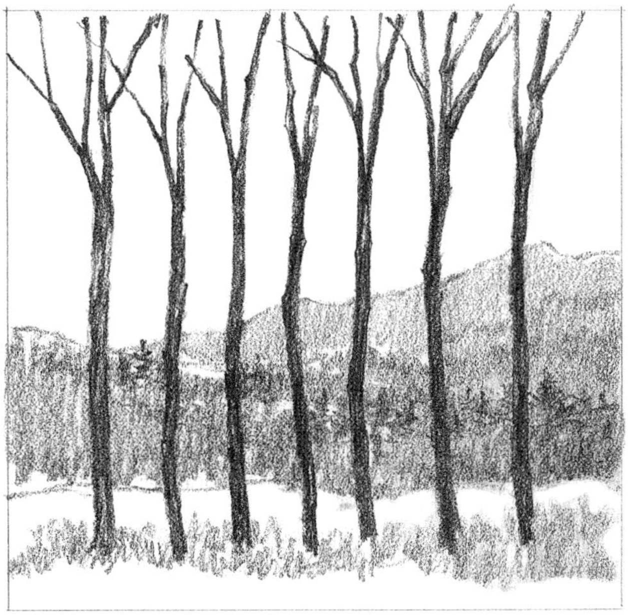

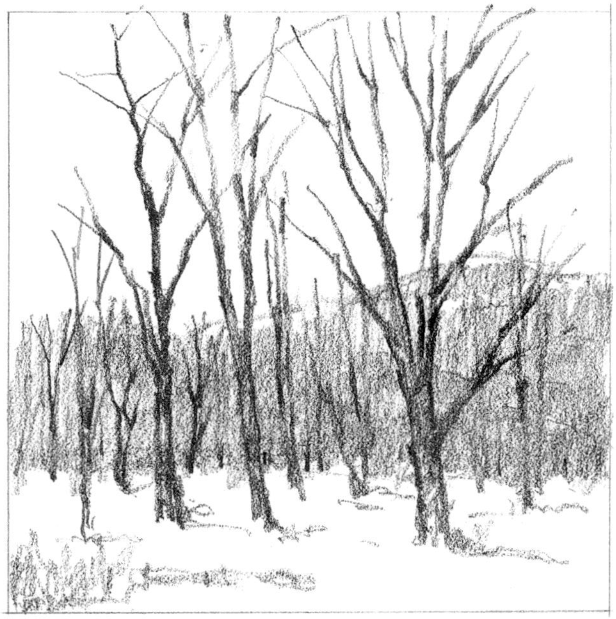

Don't
This illustration shows the type of layout you should avoid. The trees are practically all the same. The thickness of the trunks, spacing between trees and the formation of the branches are all too similar. This type of design usually leads to an uninteresting composition, definitely not the kind of work you want to produce. Be aware of formula traps — just because something works well in one picture doesn't mean it is worth repeating over and over. Keep an open mind when creating your compositions. Make many small sketches. There are no rules that you must adhere to. Have fun and look and strive for the unusual.

Do
This drawing shows the same area, but with more thought and reaching for a better composition. The background of mountains is almost the same, but it has become a more pleasant picture to look at because of the varied shapes and sizes of the trees, and also because of the positioning of the trees — some up close, some in the center and still others in the background. All contribute to making a drab picture more exciting.

Centering

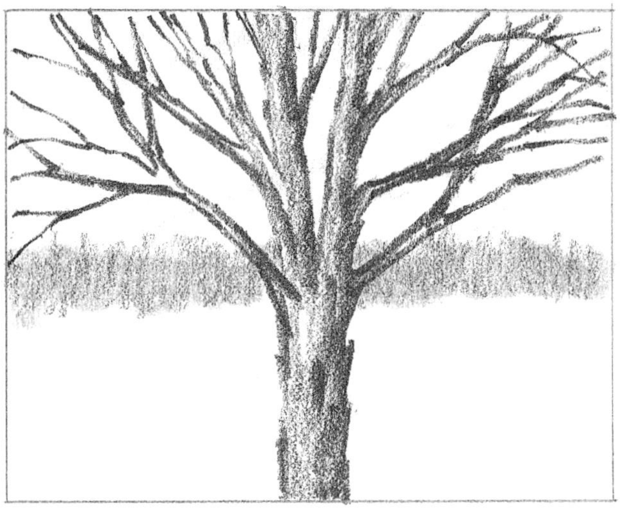

Don't

The center should be one of the least likely locations to use for your focal point. All of the objects are placed in a way that generates the least amount of enthusiasm. Here the maple tree is vertically dead center and the background is centered horizontally. And because everything is equally balanced, the picture does not hold the viewer's interest for any length of time. There is no energy or stimulation, nor anything to make the viewer linger to enjoy that nice maple.

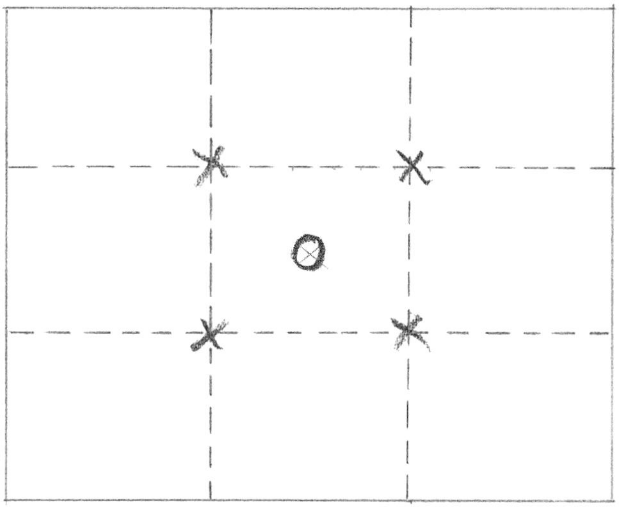

Don't

This diagram may remind you of a tic-tac-toe game. The circle is dead center and is the area you want to stay away from. You do not need to divide your paper into thirds, but any location away from the center, be it lower, higher or off to one side, will help you create a more successful center of interest.

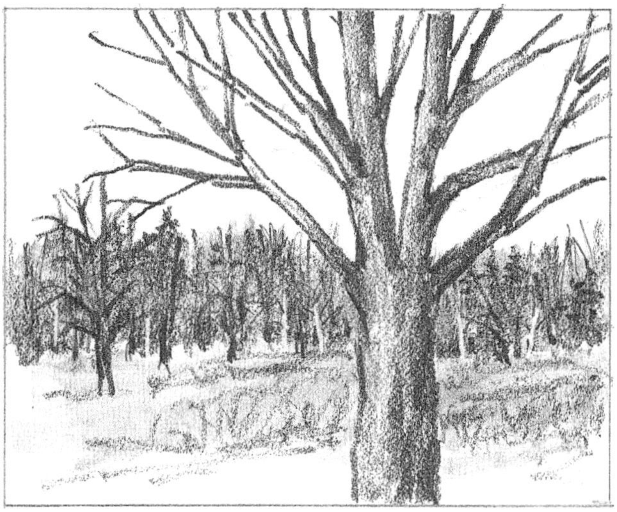

Do

Here is an example of how you can design a picture with more interest by simply lowering the background so that it is off center and moving the maple tree to the right. If desired, you could easily elaborate on this sketch, but the thing to remember is: Odd designs stir the imagination more than objects which are equal and even.

Repetition

Don't

This charcoal sketch shows two sentries guarding the edges of the drawing, standing straight as rulers, with their arms raised. By creating these two hard-edged verticals, more interest is drawn to the edges of the picture than to the picture itself. They become overpowering and will suffocate your nice sketch. You must do some planning with your small studies beforehand so as not to crowd a nice drawing.

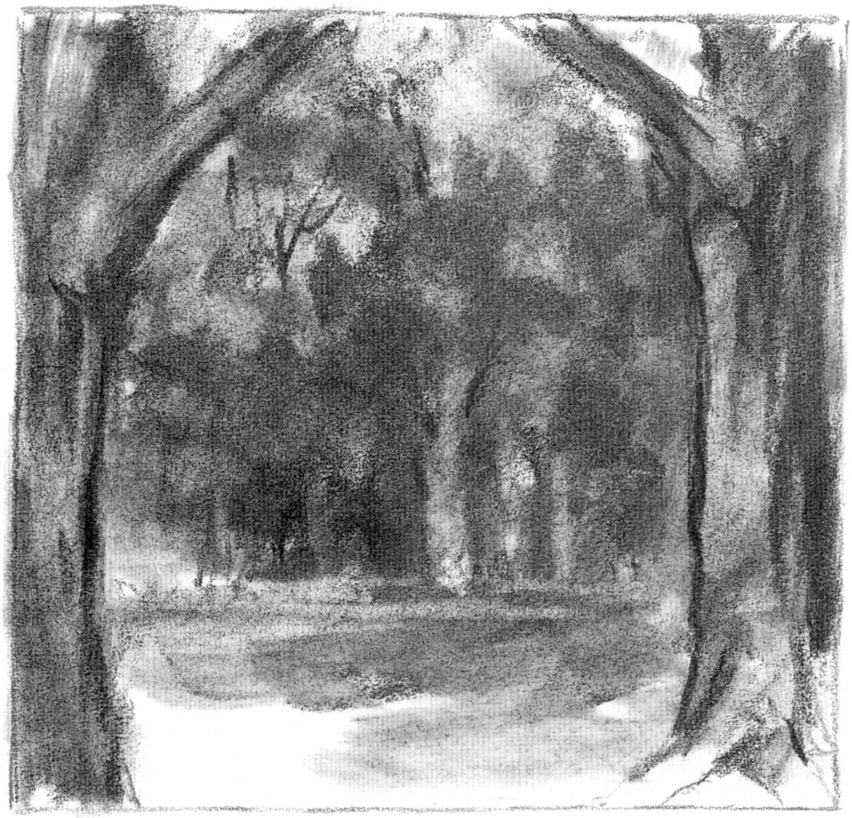

Do

In this drawing, the two large trees are moved away from the edges. The larger tree on the right slants into the interior of the woods; the tree on the left also slants, with the bough at the top returning the viewer's eyes back into the forest. Now you can see how much more interest and attention is derived from moving the trees away from the edges. The introduction of the sun's rays filtering through the forest also helps to make a more pleasing drawing.

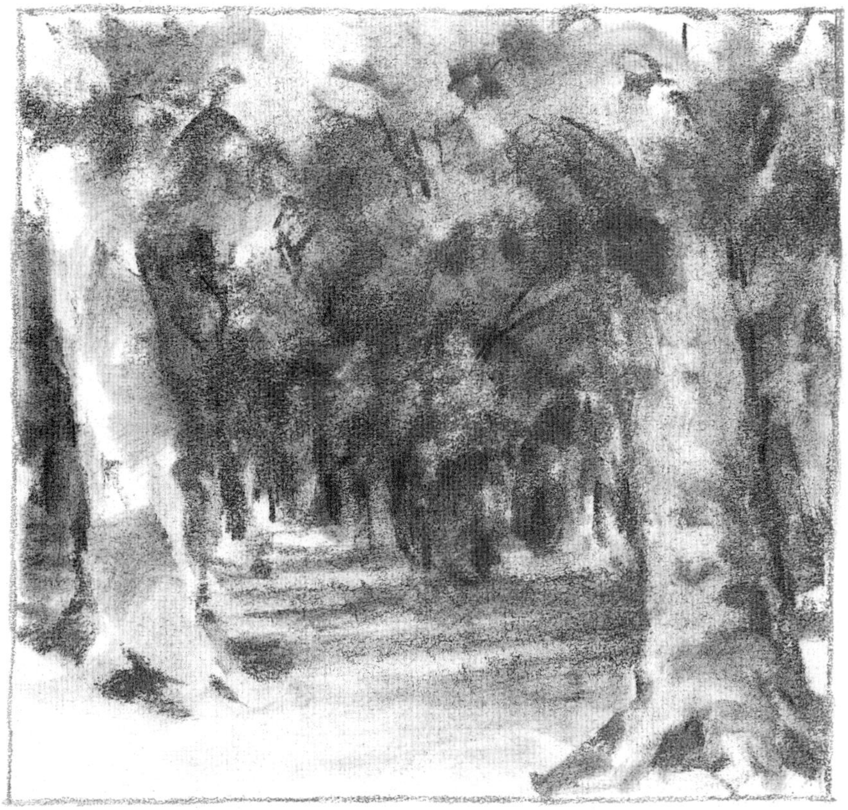

Monotony

Don't

This type of drawing leads to monotony for the viewer because the trees are of one species and height, have approximately the same amount of foliage, and are lined up looking like they belong in a larger picture. Though a great illustration of how to plant a wind screen, it's not interesting as a picture.

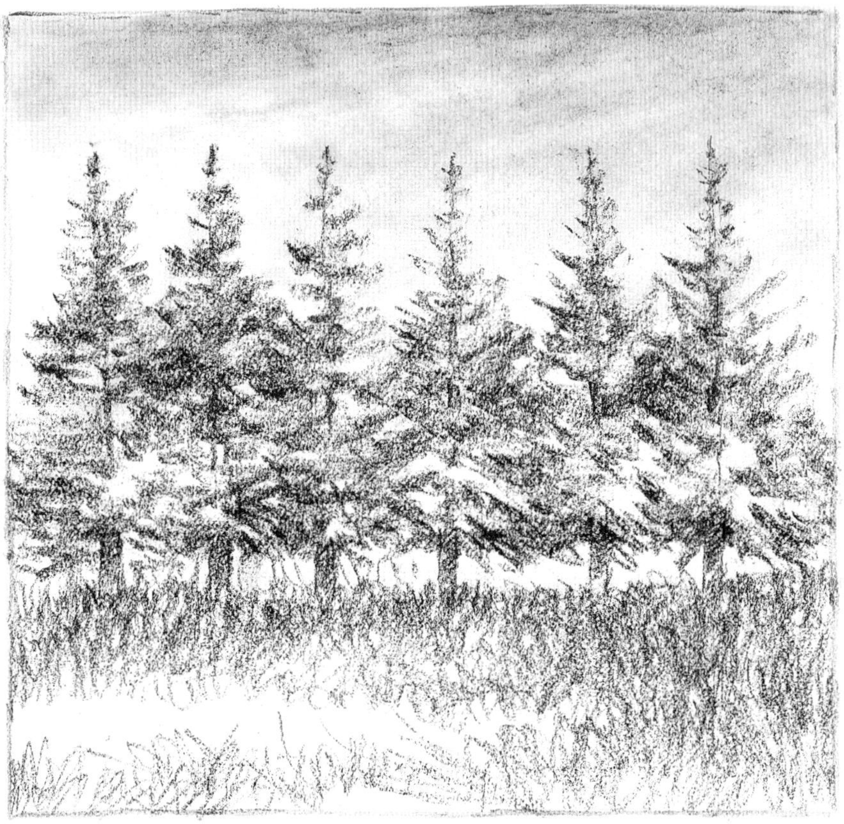

Do

This drawing is a much more interesting and pleasant use of pine trees. By eliminating some large trees and leaving unequal space between the trees, you immediately start to create interest. Make them different heights to automatically create an eye trail that will take the viewer into the picture. The horizon line was raised and mountains of trees were introduced. Depth is created by gradually showing less detail and using a less intense black as the trees recede into the background. The foreground is left quite simple, showing weeds, tall grass and whatever has been blown over by winter storms. With a little thought, the same trees could be repositioned to create even more interesting compositions.

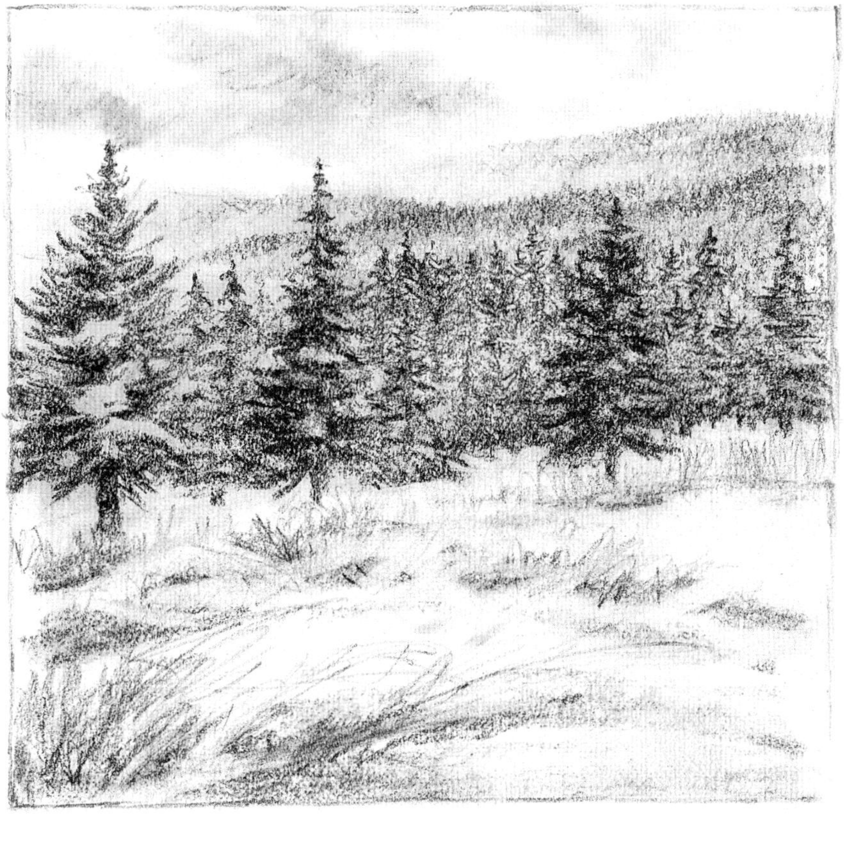

CREATE DRAMA BY LIMITING THE SCENE

Because the expanse of area in front of you can become overwhelming, a viewfinder can help eliminate a lot of distraction and serve to concentrate the view.

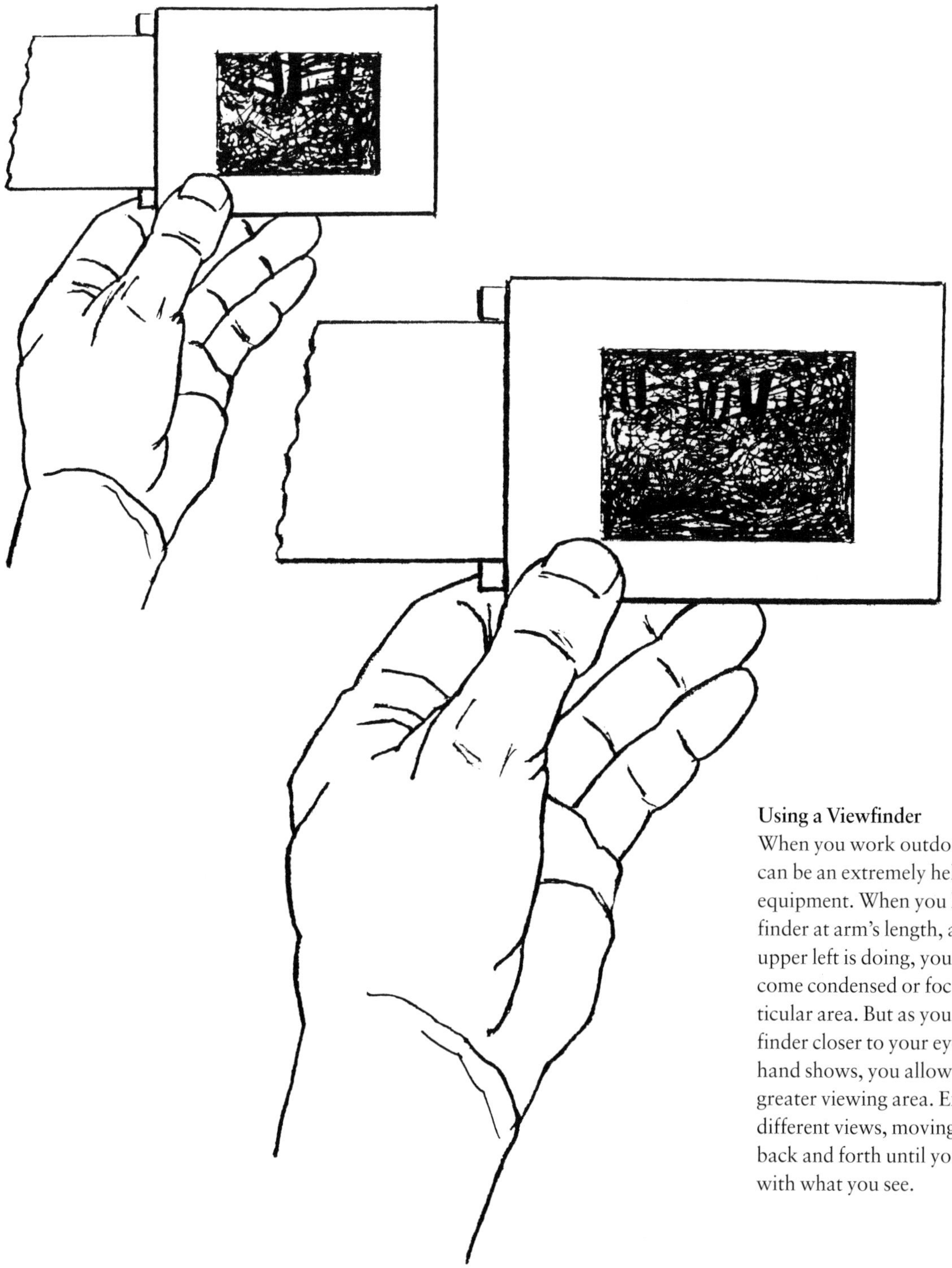

Using a Viewfinder
When you work outdoors, a viewfinder can be an extremely helpful piece of equipment. When you hold the viewfinder at arm's length, as the hand to the upper left is doing, your view will become condensed or focused to one particular area. But as you bring the viewfinder closer to your eyes, as the other hand shows, you allow yourself a greater viewing area. Experiment with different views, moving the viewfinder back and forth until you are satisfied with what you see.

DRAWING A DRAMATIC COMPOSITION STEP BY STEP

Now we're going to put into practice what we have learned about getting more interest and action from a scene by moving closer and selecting just a part rather than the whole. Follow this study of the center of a group of large white pines, and notice how moving in close increases the drama of the composition.

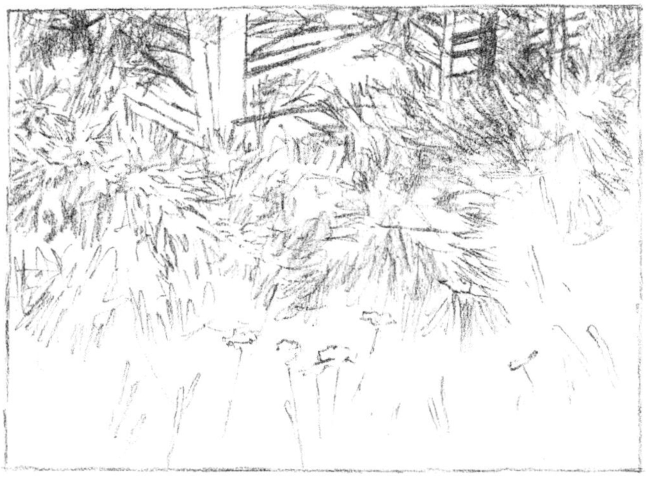

Step 1
After doing several studies, make a preliminary sketch of the center of a group of large white pines. By silhouetting the wood against the sky and showing some branches up close, an unusual and interesting picture is created.

Step 2
The drawing begins to take on more definition by adding darks and showing the pine needles in perspective. Continue adding more darks as you progress. Remember that it is important to work over the entire drawing so that your picture has a continuous flow.

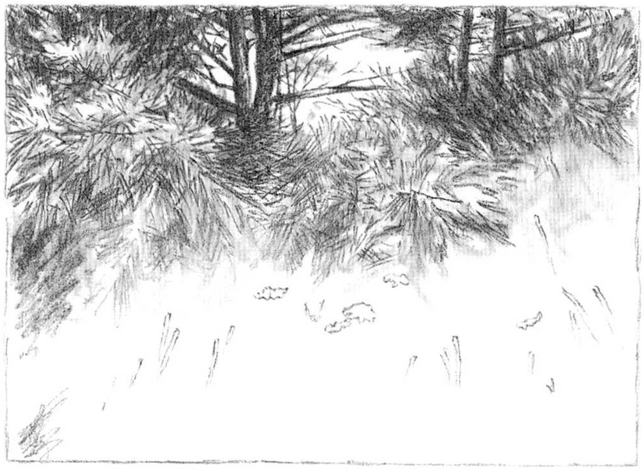

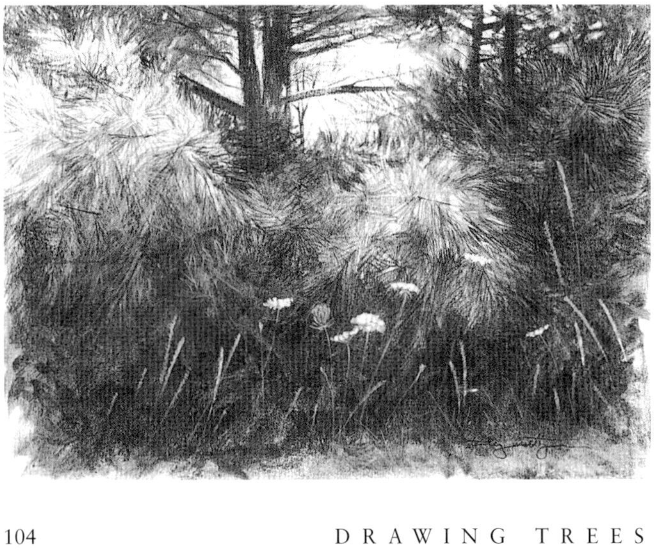

Step 3
Finally, to bring out the silhouette of pines against the white sky, push the blacks to a maximum. The pine branches with needles both in the light and dark create still more intrigue. By adding some Queen Anne's lace and weeds in the foreground, the feeling of being out in a field is created.

Evening Pines, 8 ½" x 11" (22cm x 28cm), vine and 4B charcoal pencil on Arches laid paper.

NEGATIVE AND POSITIVE SPACE

Negative space is all the area or areas surrounding the object or objects in your picture. The shapes should be varied and planned with considerable thought on your part so as to be as interesting as the positive areas. These negative shapes often take the shapes of interesting abstract designs. The harmony between negative and positive shapes helps to create better pictures.

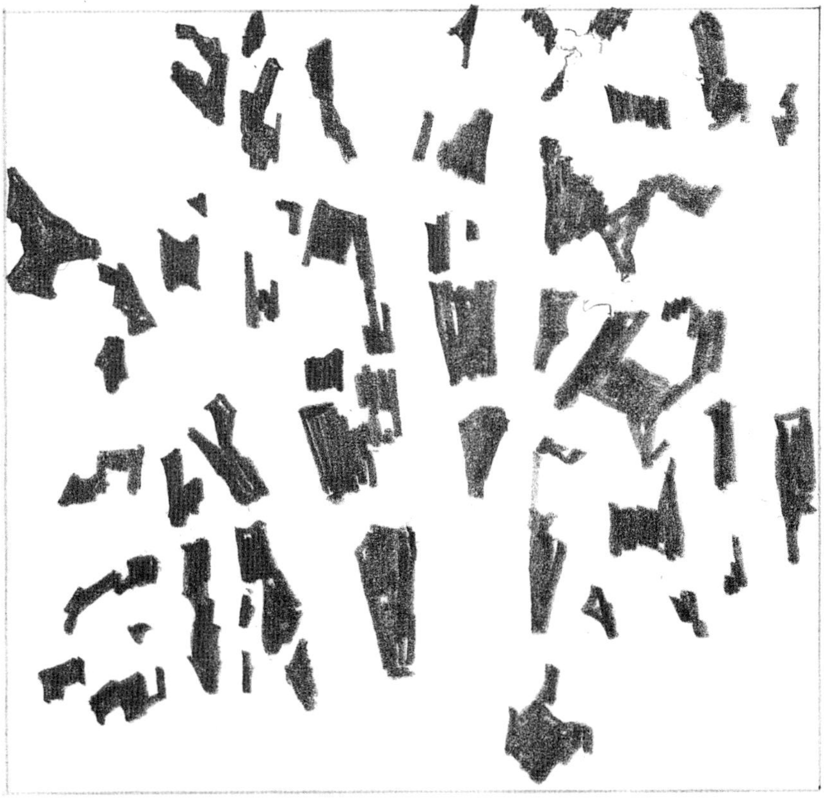

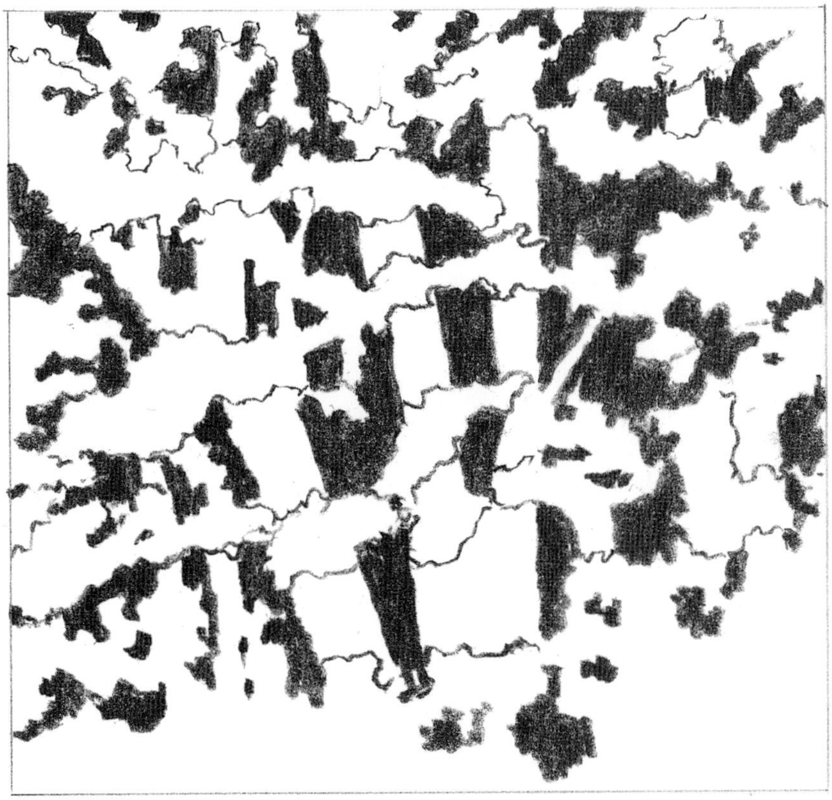

Use Negative Space to Form Foliage Patterns
These two drawings illustrate combining positive and negative shapes to form foliage shapes. By using this method, you can immediately see whether they are going to be boring or will create interest. If the shapes are not stimulating, now is the time to do something about it. Make some shapes larger, others smaller. Change the flow of the positive shapes. Remember, vary the shapes. The negatives and positives must blend together. The bottoms of these illustrations show how, once blended, harmony and a nice variation of positive and negative spacing are created. It is not difficult, and time spent analyzing your work will make for better pictures in the future.

The Final Outcome

This drawing illustrates the results of previous planning with negative and positive shapes. Satisfied with the shapes you have developed, move on to the next stage. Here you see a finished drawing, whereas before you only had black and white shapes. Now add your grays: light, medium and dark gray. Together with black and white you have a whole range of tones to work with. With the help of the grays, you will soon lose the hard edges from before and that is fine. What you did prior to the grays was create a layout which helped you to design the finished drawing. You still have positive and negative shapes, but the hard edges are gone. They were absorbed into your rendering of your final piece.

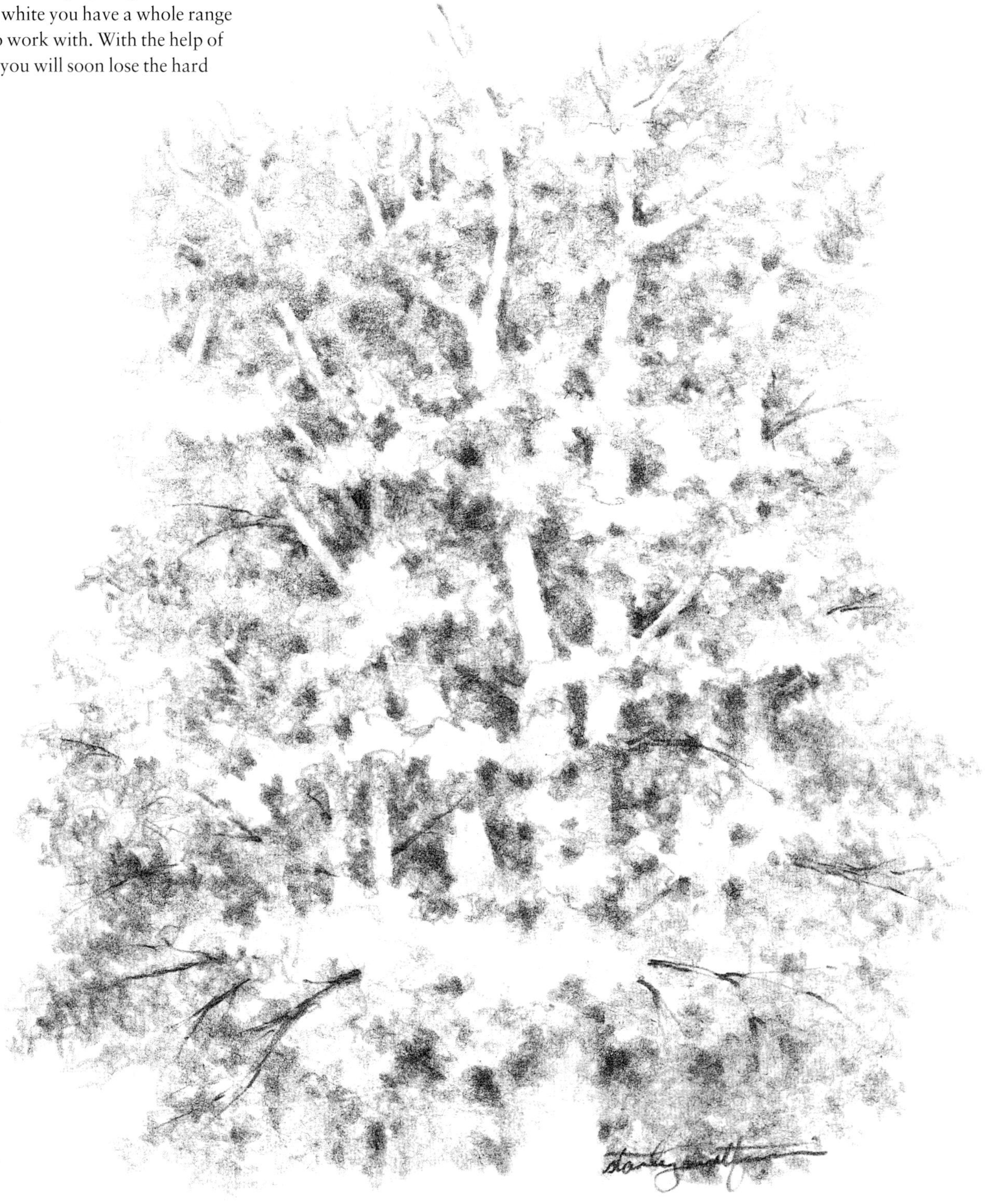

SELECTING A FORMAT

The proper format for your picture is just as important as the work you are going to put into that format. This is a problem you can solve as you make your small working sketches. The format you choose should complement your drawing. Its shape can help you to depict a mood and create excitement — that's good planning. However, once you have success with a particular shape, do not execute every picture with that same format. Experiment constantly. Always look to improve your last picture.

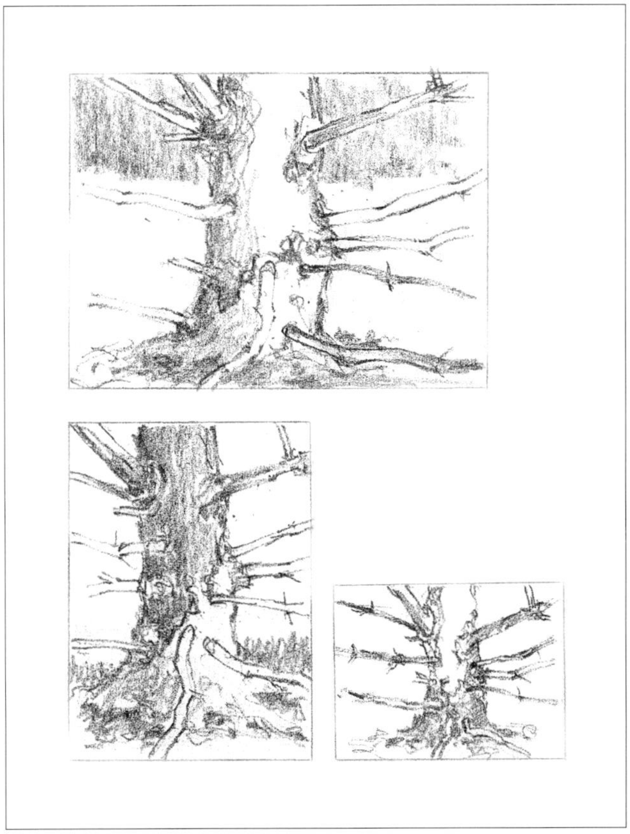

Limitless Possibilities
This illustration shows three possible formats for the same drawing.

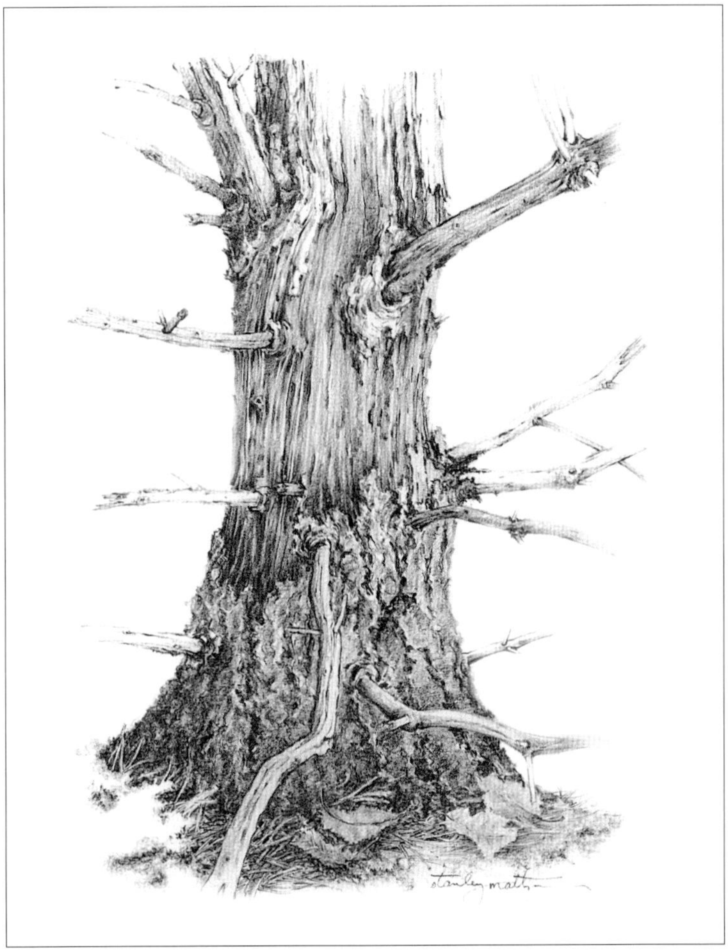

The Chosen Format
Here is my final choice for the drawing — a vertical to complement the shape of the subject. This arrangement allows you to show more of the beauty of the grain and limbs of the old timer.

The drawing was made on Rives BFK paper with a 6B graphite pencil, except for the pine needles at the base where 2B and B pencils were used.

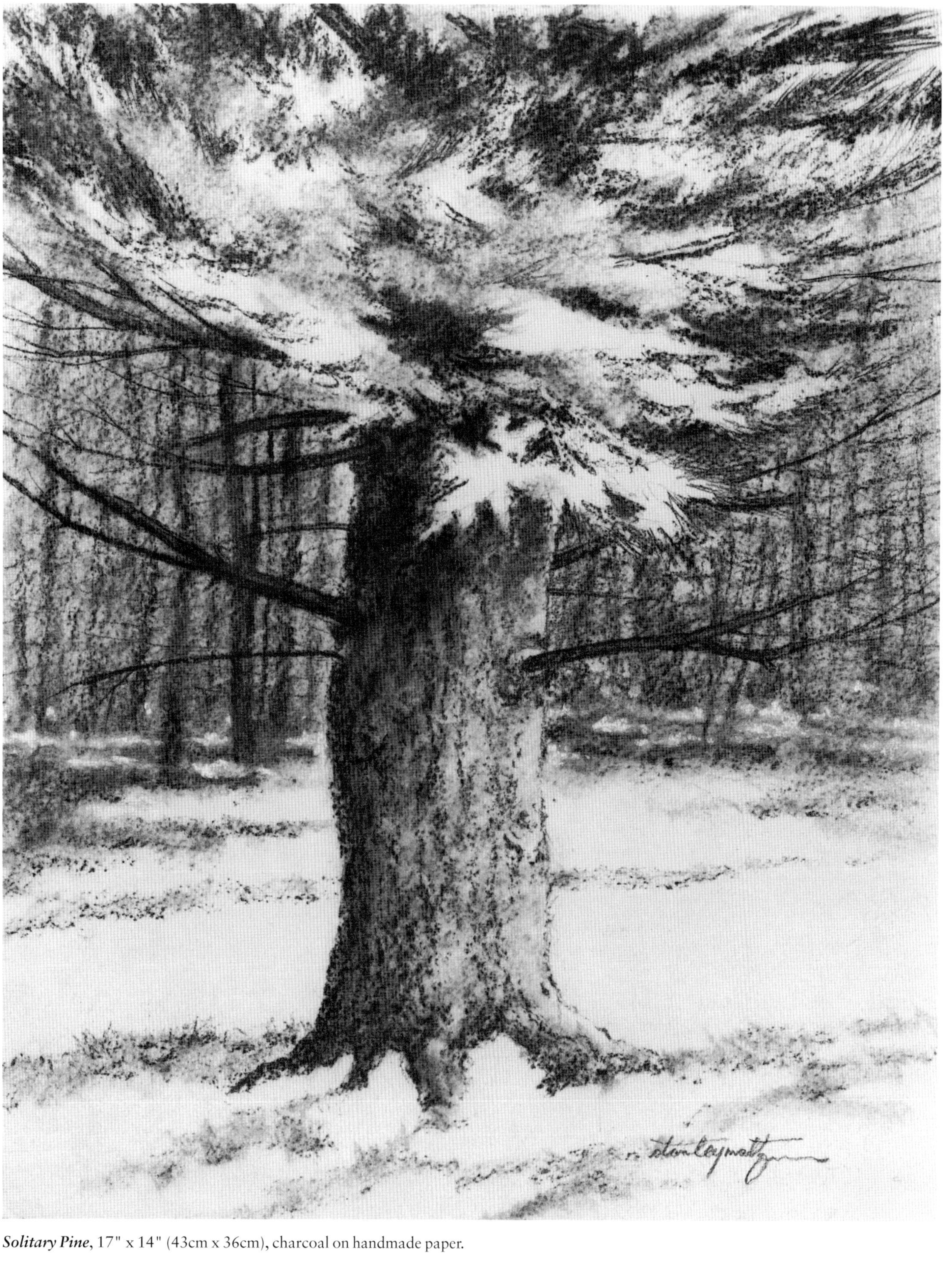

Solitary Pine, 17" x 14" (43cm x 36cm), charcoal on handmade paper.

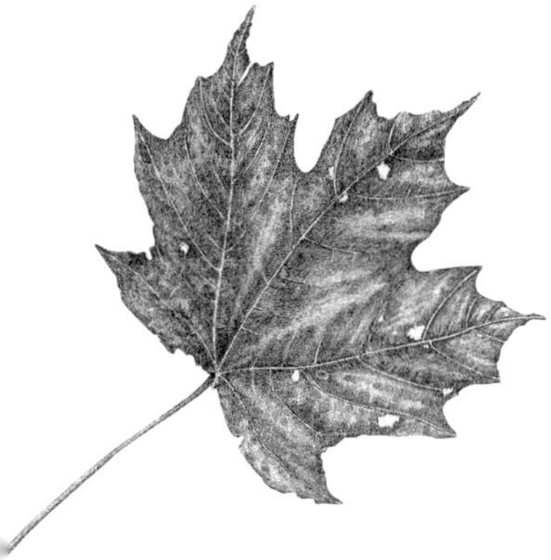

CHAPTER SEVEN

Drawing Trees in Various Mediums

Though we have been dealing with graphite and charcoal almost exclusively, now is the time to put together all you have learned and apply it to some other exciting mediums, such as watercolor, gouache, colored pencil and pastel. There are no formulas here. Rather, I want to show ways you can stimulate your own thinking, taking what you've learned and add and improve upon it.

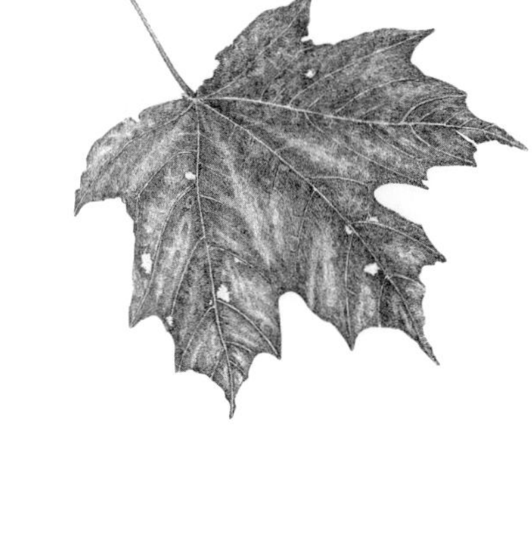

DRAWING FROM PHOTOGRAPHS

One approach to creating a successful drawing is to work from a photo. The idea here is to demonstrate that even though you are using a photo. Those are the key words: "you are using," rather than the photo using you. You can create an original piece of art that will be recognizable as that particular subject, but will have enough originality and creativity to be different and unique.

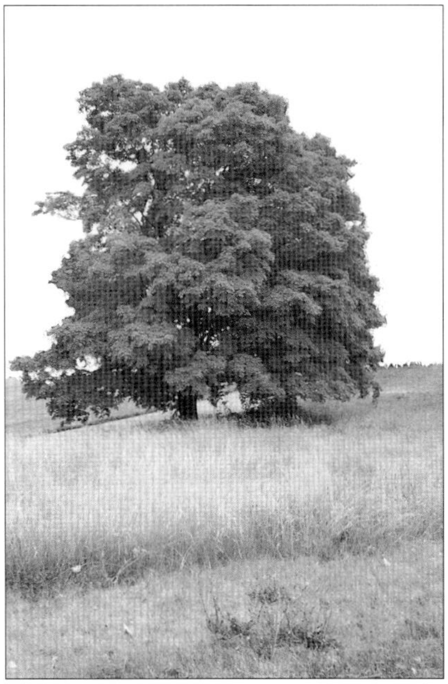

Finding the Right Photo
Here is a photo of a beautiful old maple. This is a fine example of what you will find after you get out in the field and spend some time walking around, studying the growth and characteristics of your subject.

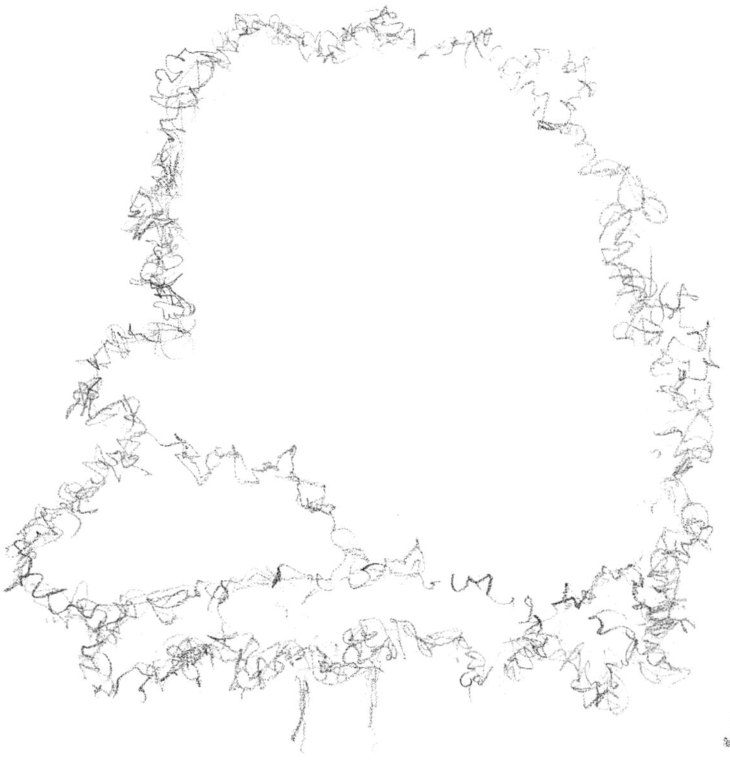

Step 1
Start with a B graphite pencil and make a loose sketch of your tree. Do not worry about making it exact. Changes will be made as you progress.

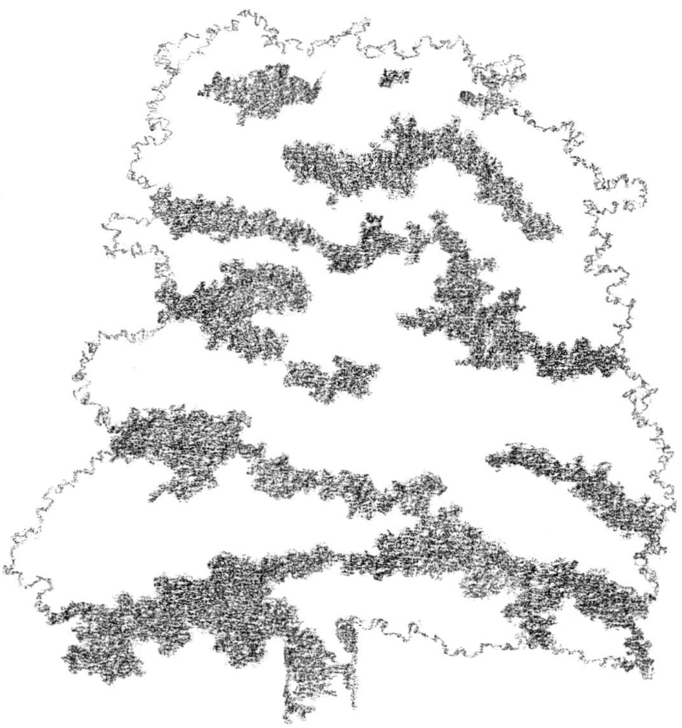

Step 2
Add the flow, or pattern, of the foliage. All trees have a pattern, and if you squint, you'll be able to pick out the flow in the form of darks and lights. Remember to keep your work light.

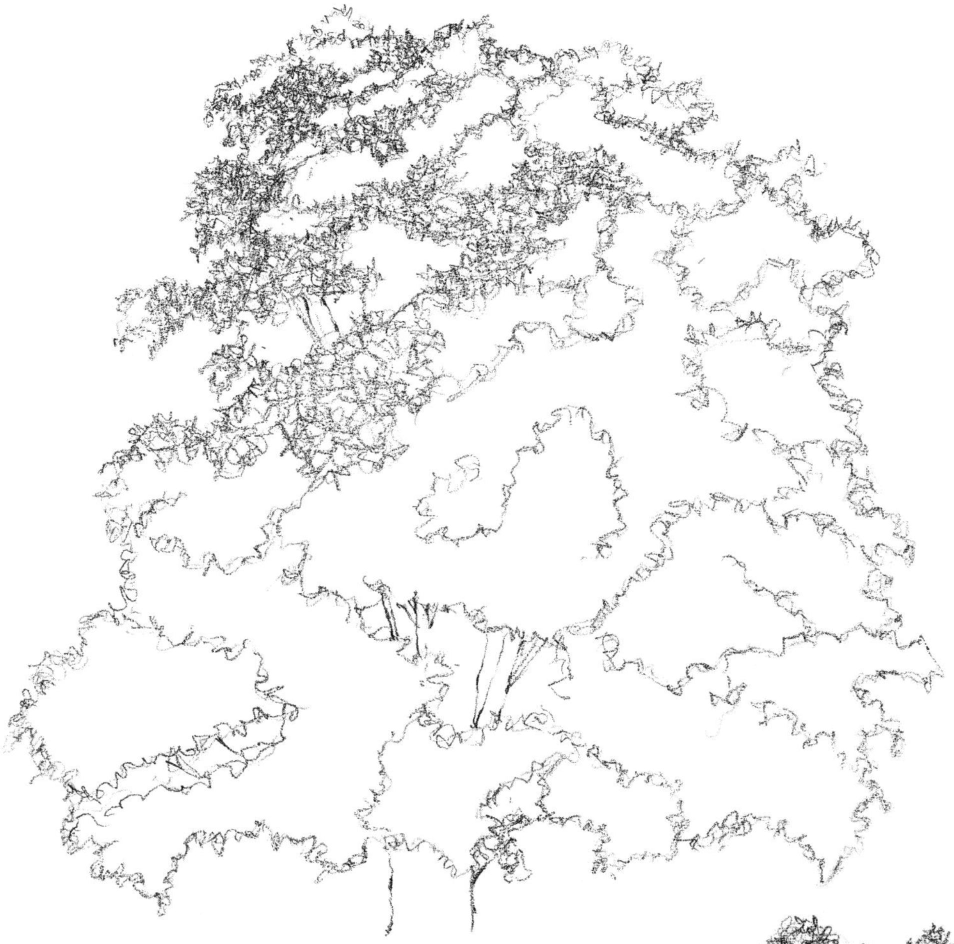

Step 3
Start to add more detail as you progress with your drawing by adding the various values (grays and darks). Do not add the darkest darks yet, as this will leave you the option to make changes, if you wish.

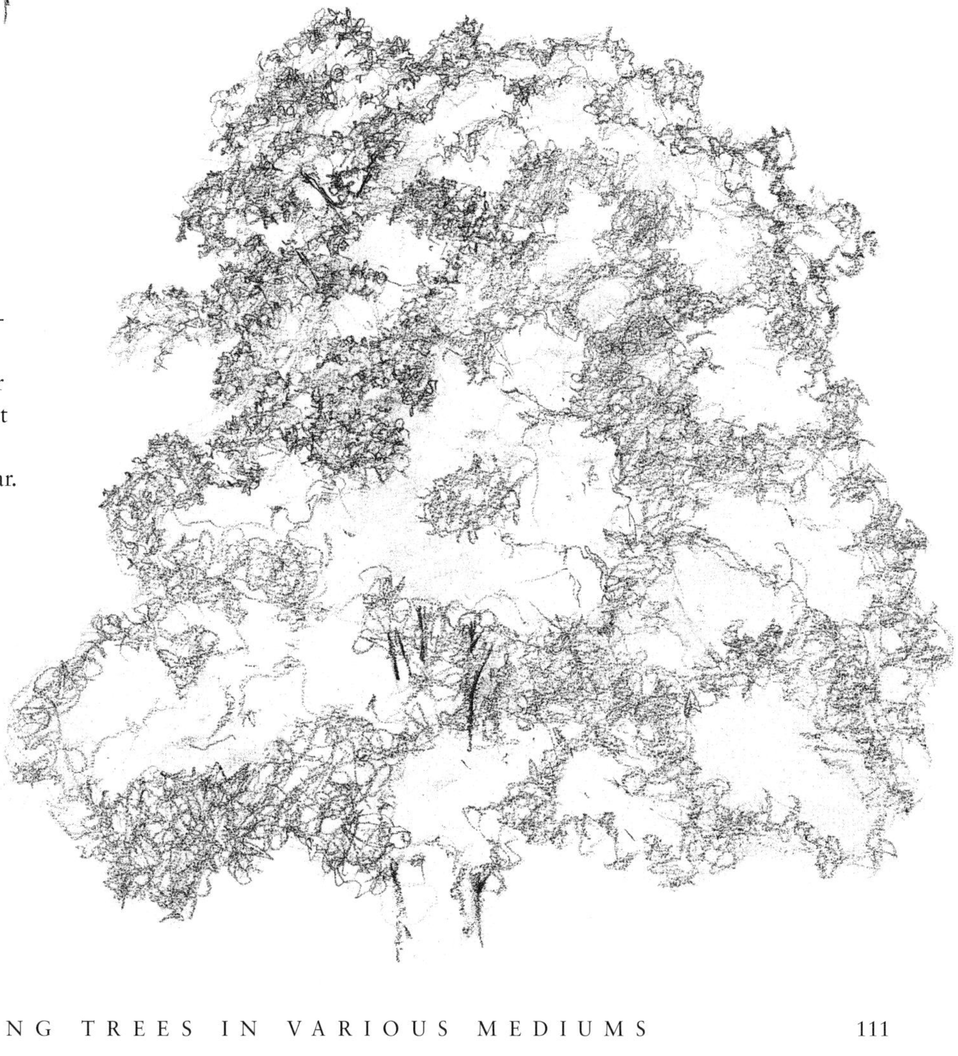

Step 4
As you continue to develop your drawing, notice how the scribbles begin to disappear as they blend into each other giving the appearance of full foliage. At this time, suggest where some of the wood (branches, twigs, etc.) will appear. Remember that less is better than an overabundance.

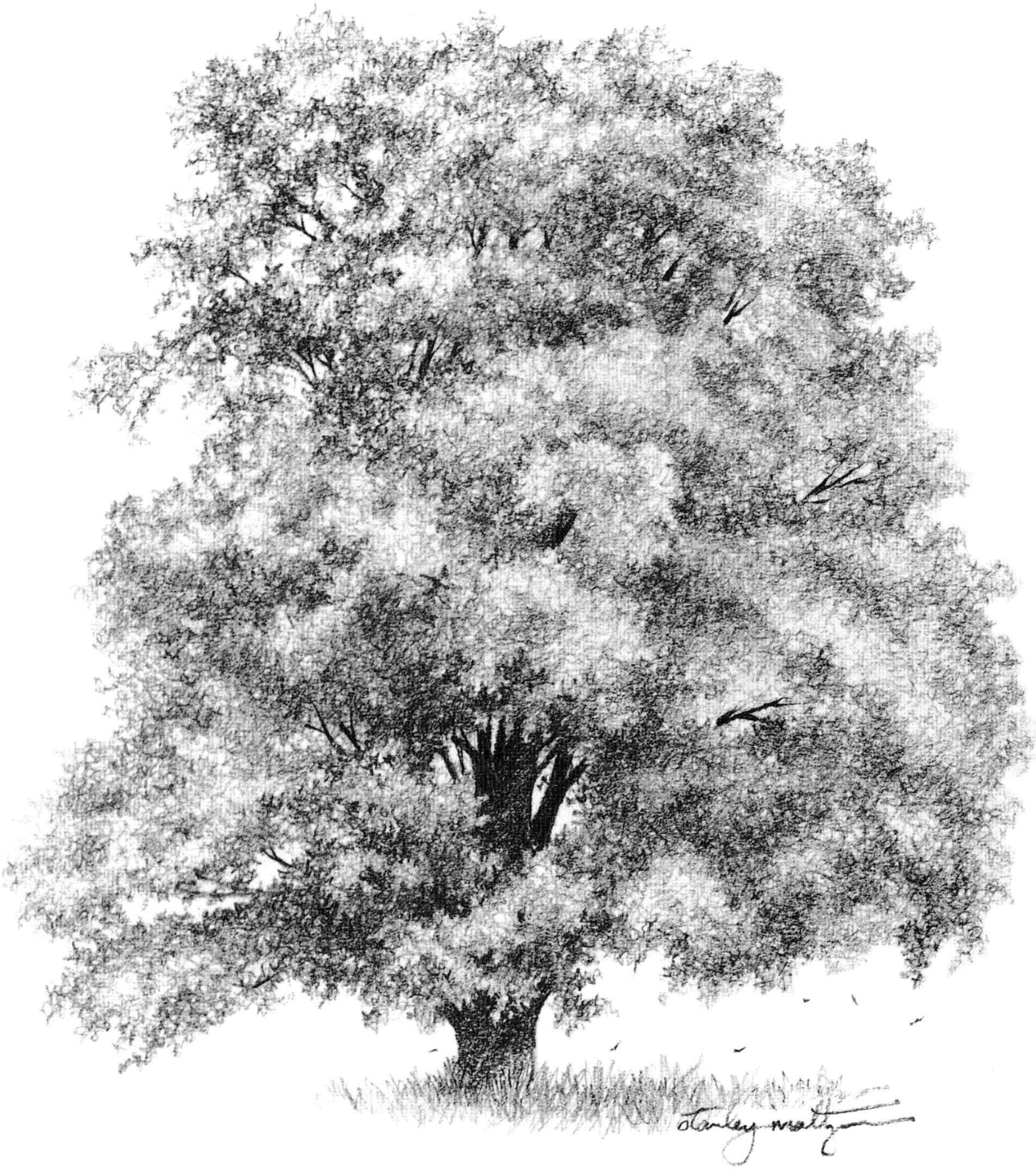

Step 5
As you continue toward completion, notice again how the scribbles have been incorporated into your finish and have disappeared. Leave a few leaves protruding from various edges so that it looks irregular. Do not make all the wood black, change the values a little, leave a few sky holes and you are finished. Even though you used a photo for reference, your thoughts, craftsmanship and efforts can't help but show this is your drawing, not a duplicate of the photo.

DRAWING WITH CHARCOAL AND WATERCOLOR

Because you will eventually cover most of this sketch with watercolor, it is not necessary to make a finished drawing. Treat your sketch as a guide, nothing more. Please note that for this demonstration, however, I made the sketches darker than normal so that you can readily see the progression. For this demonstration, I used a 2B charcoal pencil on Arches 250-lb. cold-pressed paper.

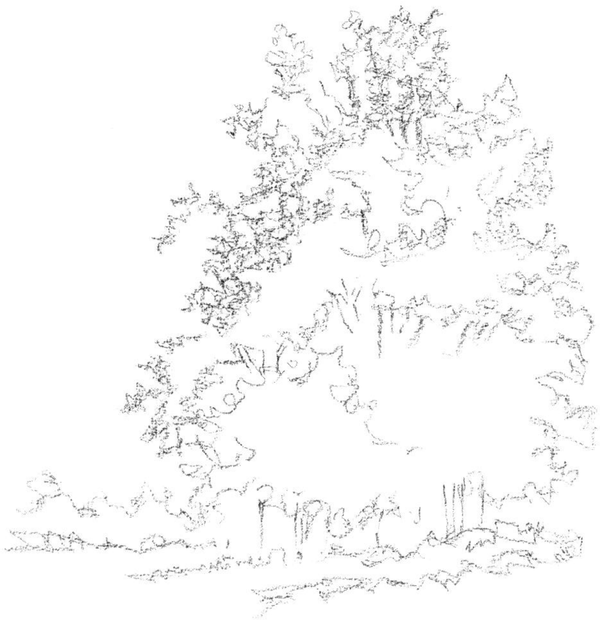

Step 1
Sketch your preliminary ouline, remembering to keep it light.

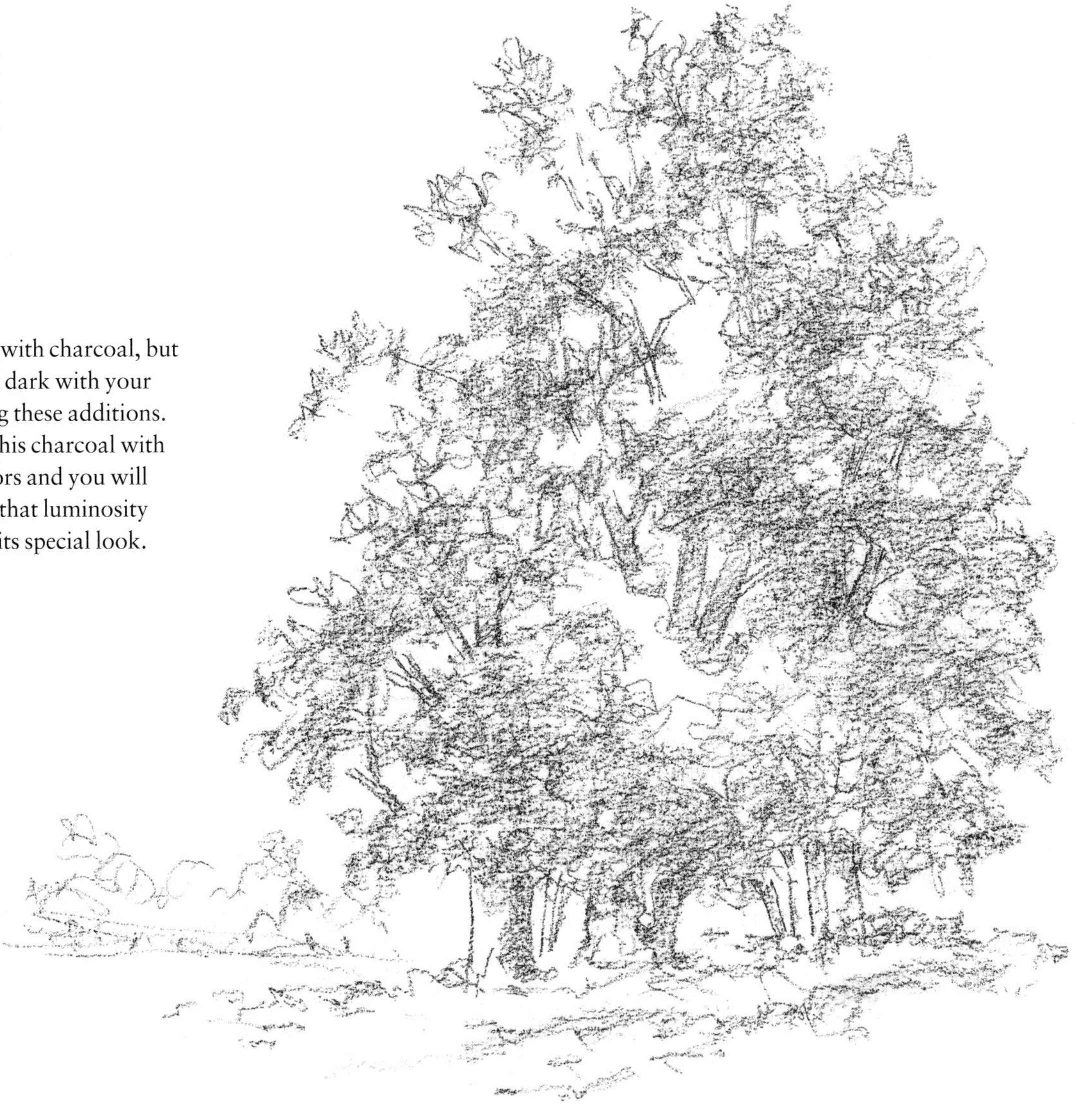

Step 2
Add more leaf shapes with charcoal, but be wary not to get too dark with your charcoal while making these additions. You will be covering this charcoal with transparent watercolors and you will want to keep some of that luminosity that gives watercolor its special look.

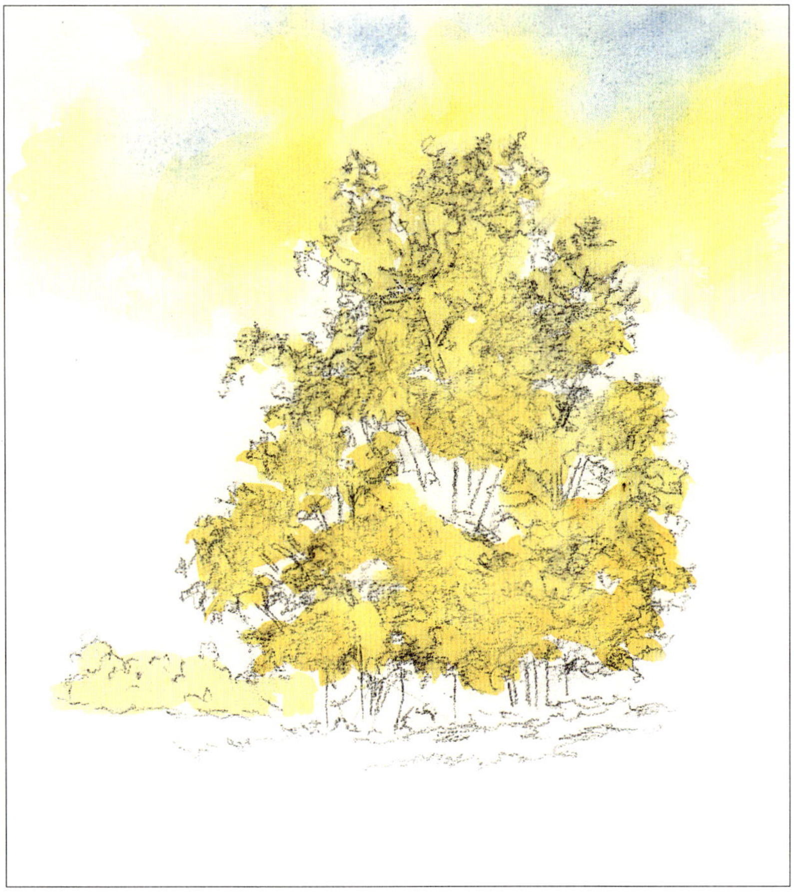

Step 3
Before applying any color, read through all the steps. Although they are shown separately, the colors should be applied in conjunction with one another and left to dry on the paper. Do not continuously go over your colors with brush and paint, as this will usually result in muddying the colors. So to start, use Winsor & Newton Gamboge Yellow on both the sky and tree. Then add a light Cobalt Blue to the sky.

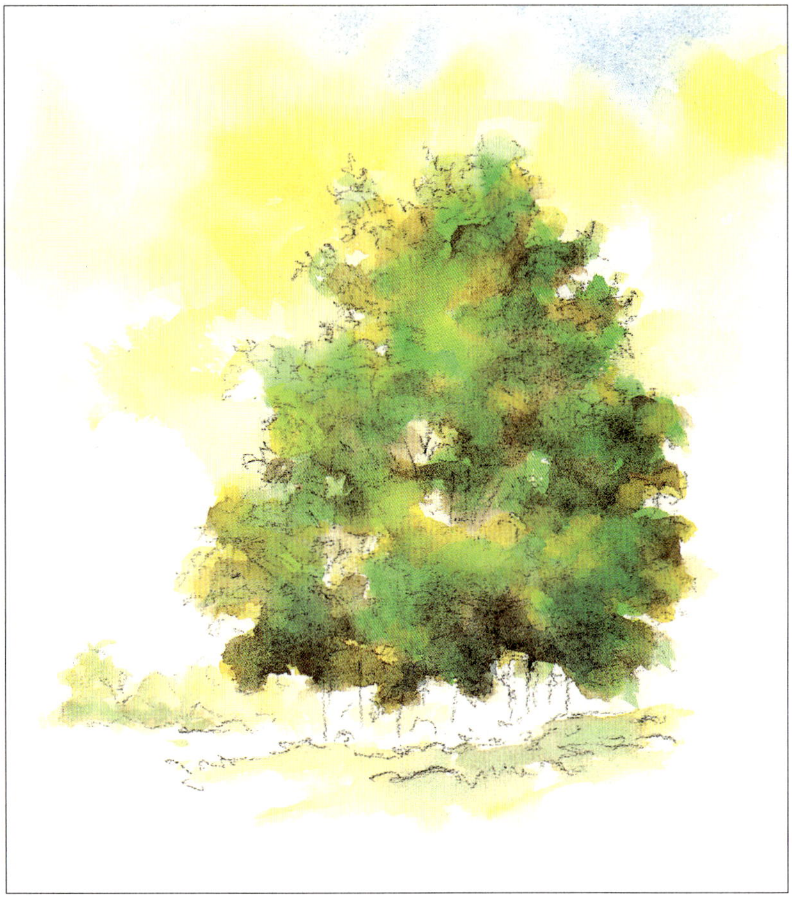

Step 4
Next, add more character to the tree group. On top of the Gamboge, add a mixture of Hooker's Green with Burnt Umber (the umber takes that hard green color away from raw Hooker's Green). Drop this mix on top of your wet Gamboge, but do not cover all of it. Let some of the light Gamboge show through. Remember, the more water you put into your paint, the lighter your mix will be in value.

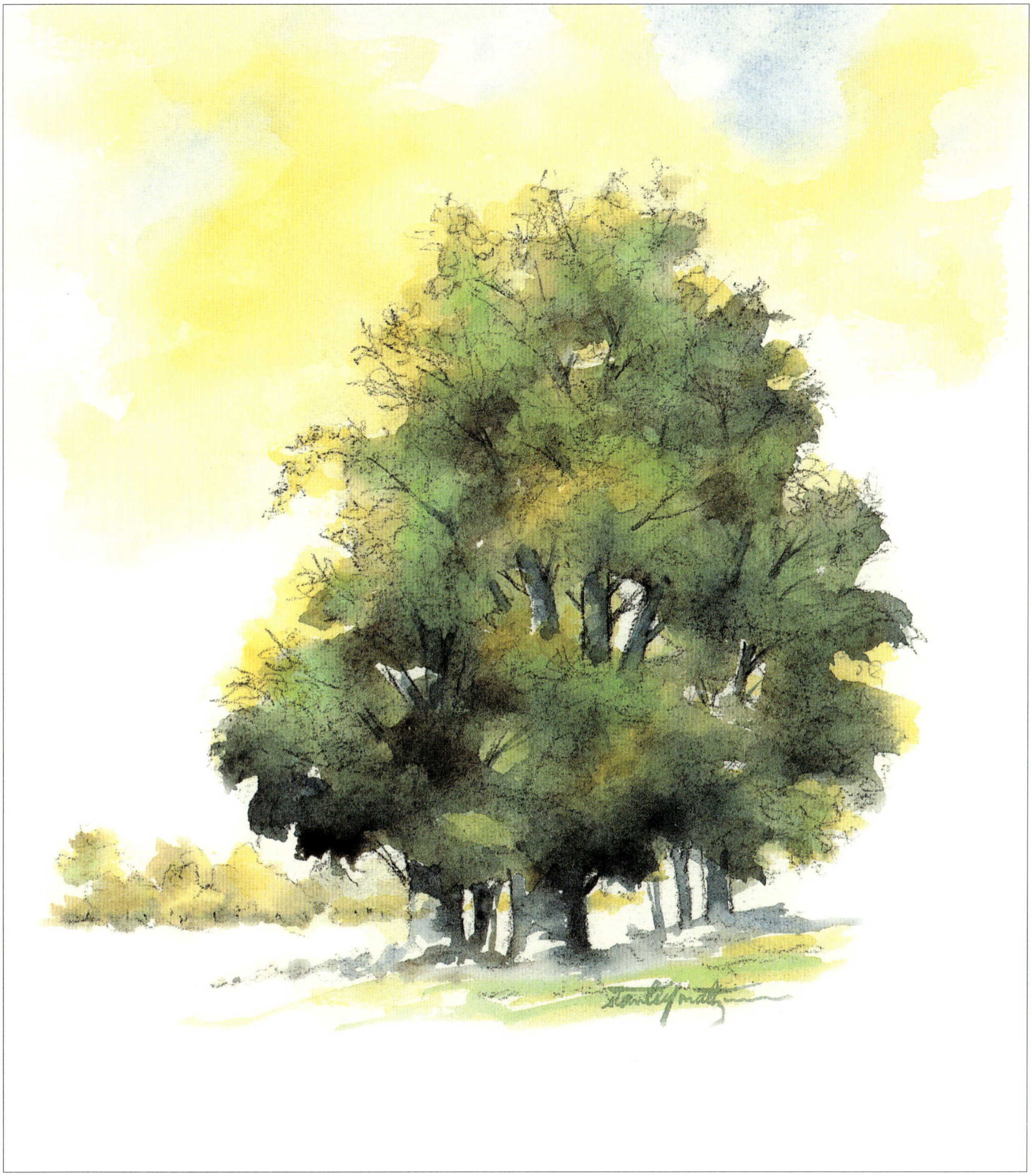

Step 5

Now add your darks, consisting of Cobalt Blue added to Payne's Gray, on top of the prior colors. When you want more darks, like the bases and trunks of trees, use Payne's Gray mixed with Cobalt Blue. Keep in mind that the tops of trees receive more light, while around the bases it is darker because the dense leaves allow less light to get through. This will add more depth and realism to your work. You can also come back with your charcoal pencil, after the paint is dry, to re-emphasize any areas that you feel were weakened by the application of washes.

DRAWING WITH CHARCOAL AND PASTEL

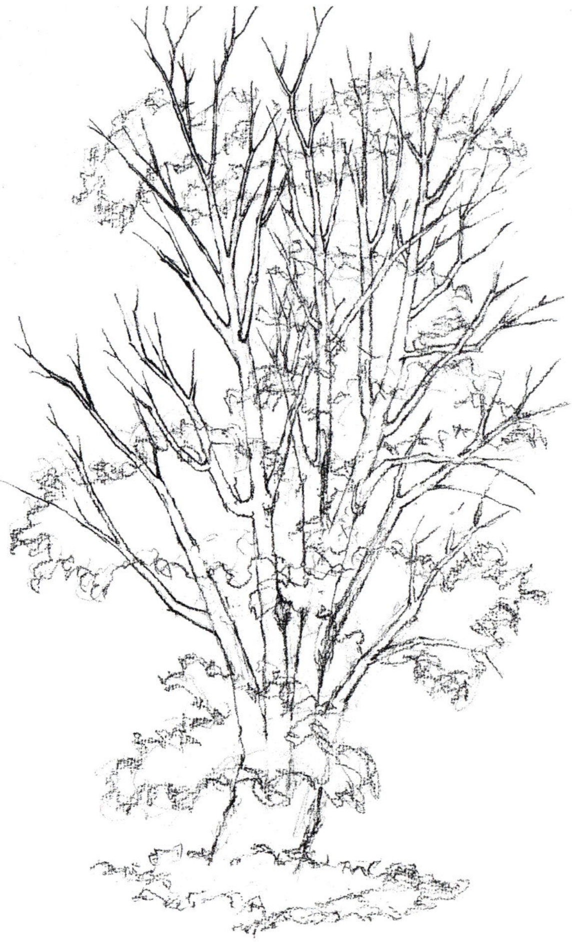

Step 1
On a sheet of Arches paper, use a 2B charcoal pencil to make a contour drawing of a tree with partial leaf coverage. Notice how I drew a slight indication of the leaves over the wood. Use this drawing as a guide. Take your time, for the more you prepare your preliminary work the easier it will be to create your finished piece.

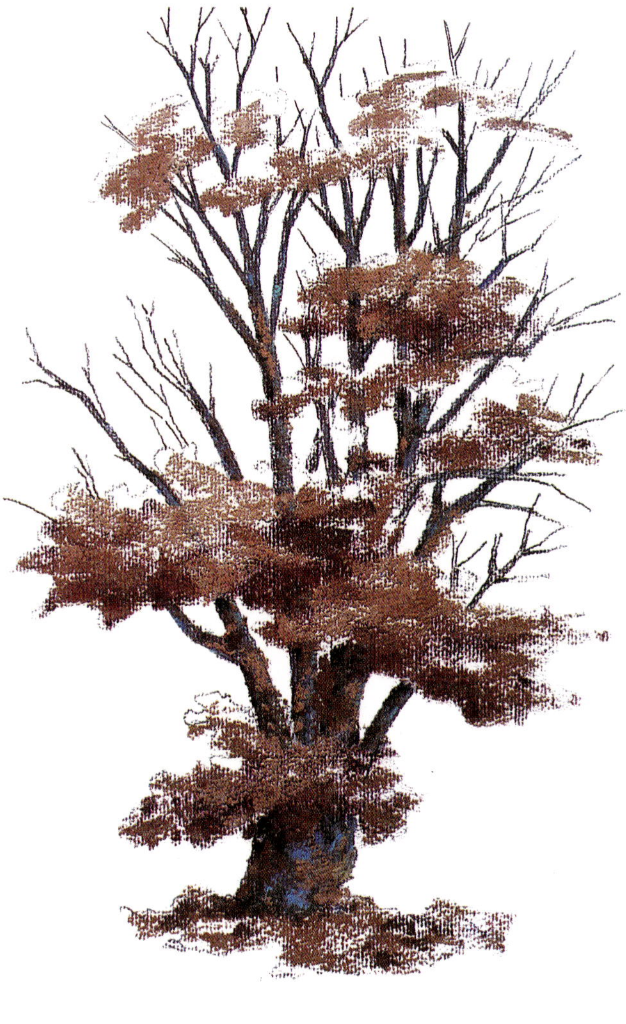

Step 2
Start adding pastel colors to your drawing (for this example, I used Winsor & Newton and Sennelier pastels). Add a light Cerulean Blue to the wood, and then some light Burnt Sienna and Burnt Umber to give it a nice woody color. Next, add the dark colors of the foliage. Lay in light Burnt Sienna on top of a deep Red Violet in a loose manner using the sides of the half-stick pastels.

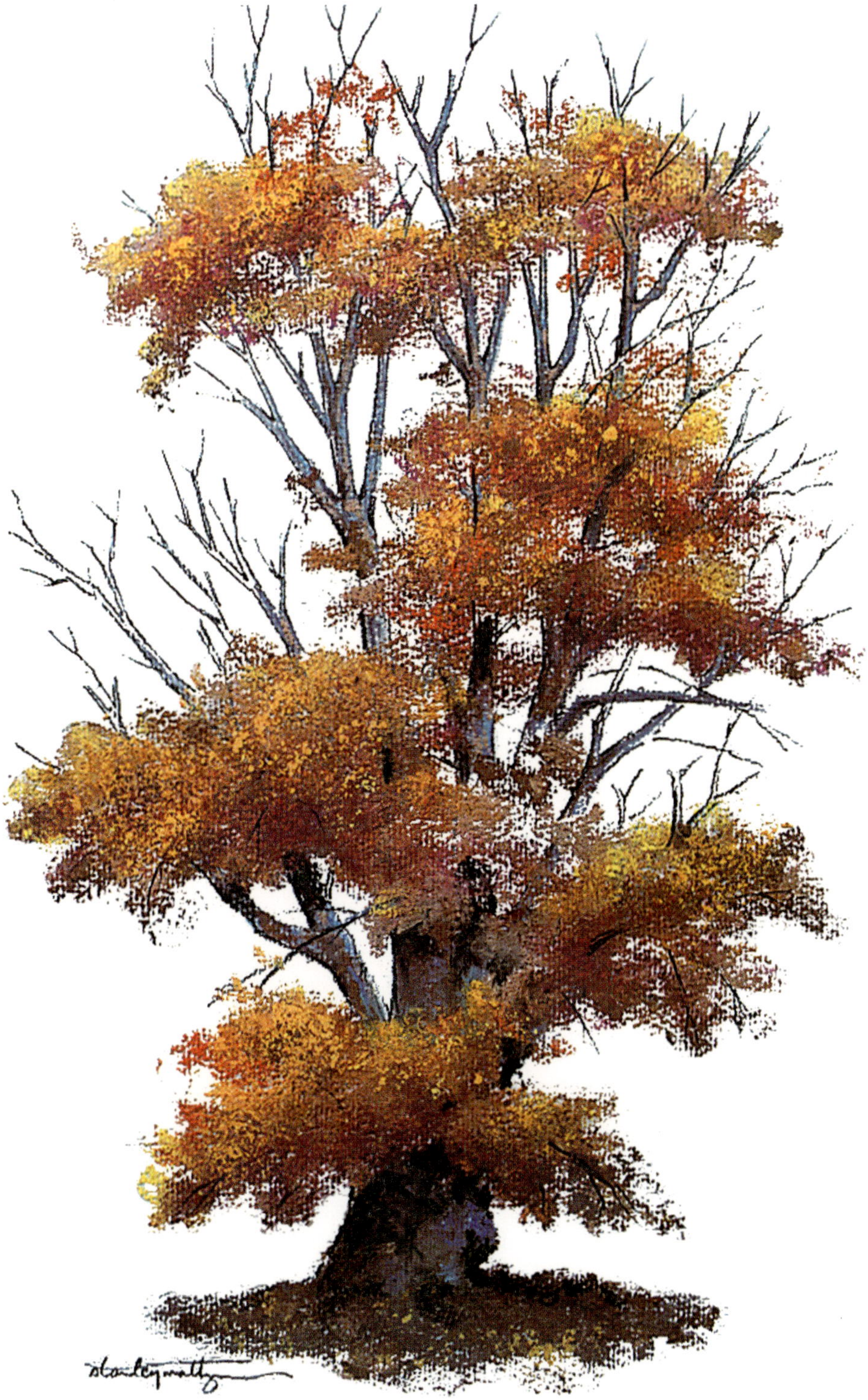

Step 3
On top of the colors already down, scumble (soften or unite these common colors) with an Orange, a Cadmium Yellow Deep and a Cadmium Yellow Light. Again, use the sides of the pastels. To create the extra sparkle on the leaves, use a razor blade to scrape the side of the pastel, thus causing dust particles to fall where you direct them. Then squash those particles with a wide palette knife to achieve this technique and interesting pattern. Then, if you wish, add more color to the trunk, boughs and branches. Remember that there are no rules, so have fun!

DRAWING WITH CHARCOAL, SANGUINE PENCILS AND PASTEL

This is a fun type of drawing that was often used by the old masters and which still looks good today, even though the masters' drawings were completed long ago.

For this demonstration, I used earth-colored German Ingres Antique paper manufactured by Hahnemuhle. This laid paper is available in other colors that can help you set a mood, or offer a second color for your drawing.

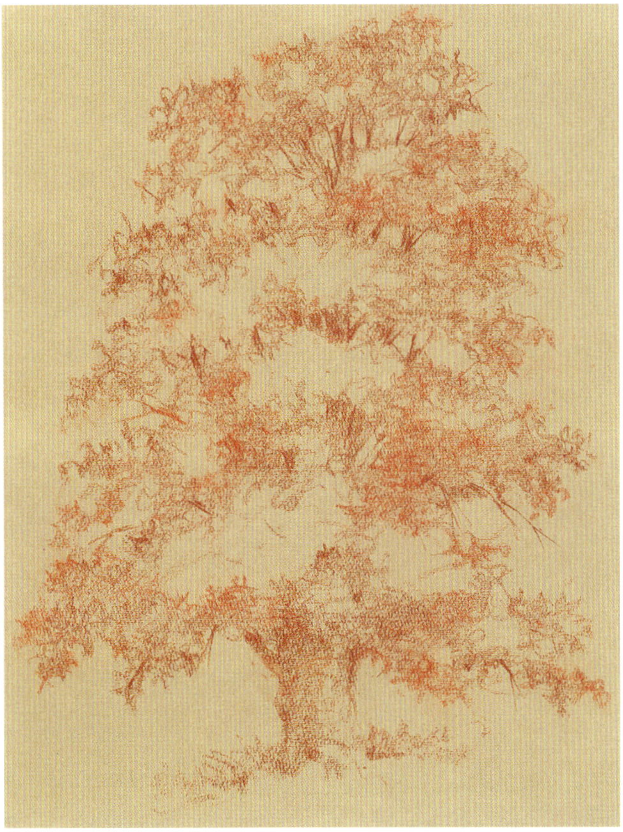

Step 1
Make your preliminary drawing using a sanguine-colored pencil or chalk. These pencils are available at your favorite art supplier and can be found in various darker or lighter shades, whatever your preference may be. I suggest that you try different pencils to determine which one appeals to you most for future drawings.

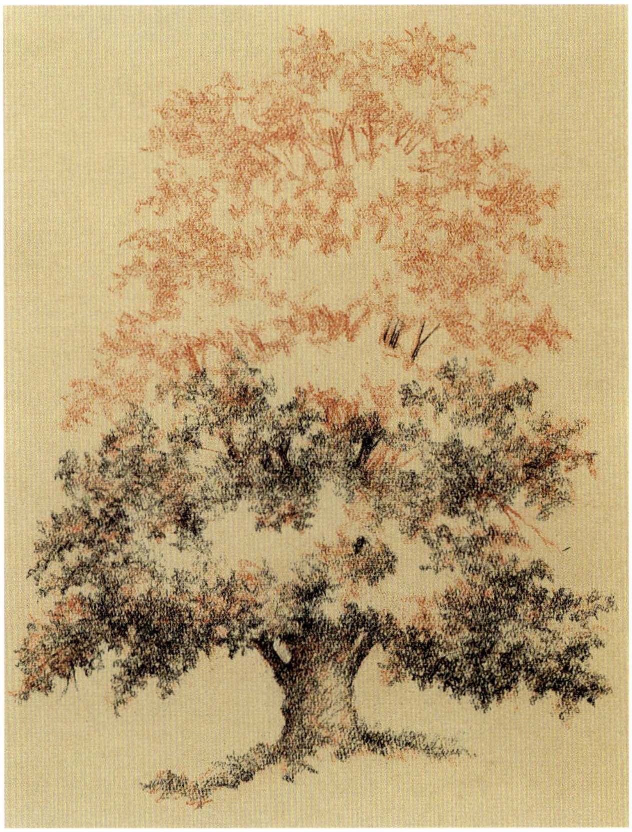

Step 2
After finishing with your sanguine pencil, switch to a 4B charcoal pencil. It does not matter where you start. In this case, I started at the bottom. Even though only a minimum of charcoal will be added, the flow of the foliage is readily visible, an important characteristic of your tree.

Step 3
Sand down the points of both the sanguine and 4B charcoal pencils to angles, and with the edges of the pencils, draw in the fine branches. Then switch back to the flat part of the pencils and add the finishing touches to the foliage. At this time, add a few spots to indicate some hanging leaves.

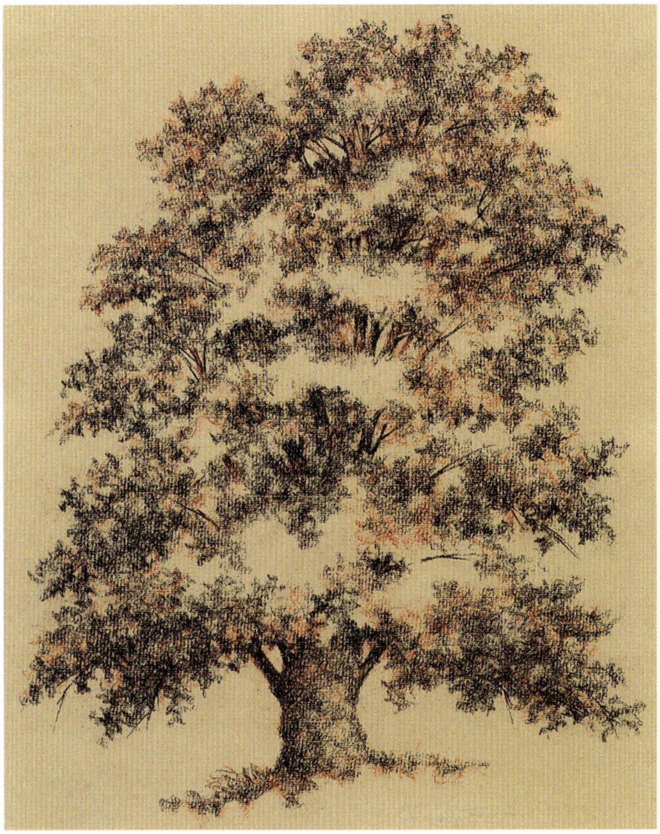

Step 4
When you are satisfied that your drawing has everything needed to show your magnificent tree, add the white highlights with a white pastel. Do not overdo this part of the drawing; keep it simple. What you should have showing in your picture is the earth-colored paper, the brick color from your sanguine pencil, the charcoal pencil and the white highlights. All of these components should be readily visible to the viewer.

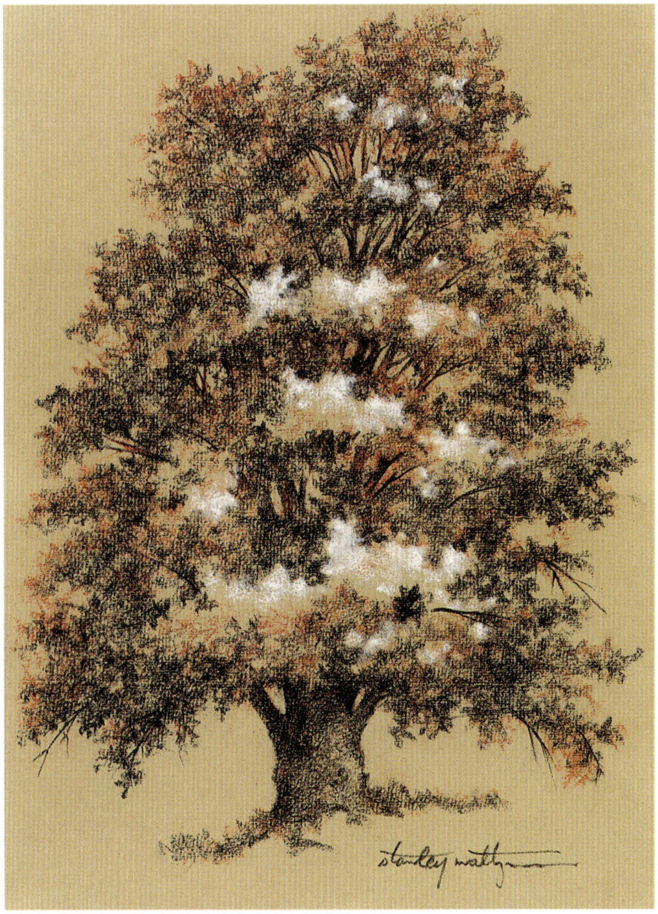

DRAWING WITH CHARCOAL AND GOUACHE

Gouache is basically an opaque water-based paint that can be used similar to watercolor, or applied with less water to retain the opaque look for which it is best noted. It can be applied in bands of color or wonderful smooth washes, or used with a fine brush to enhance details.

Gouache works best when it is not applied as an impasto, or thick application of paint. After working out your sketch, begin to apply colors. In this case the board was wet first, then paint applied, making it easier for the paints to bleed into one another.

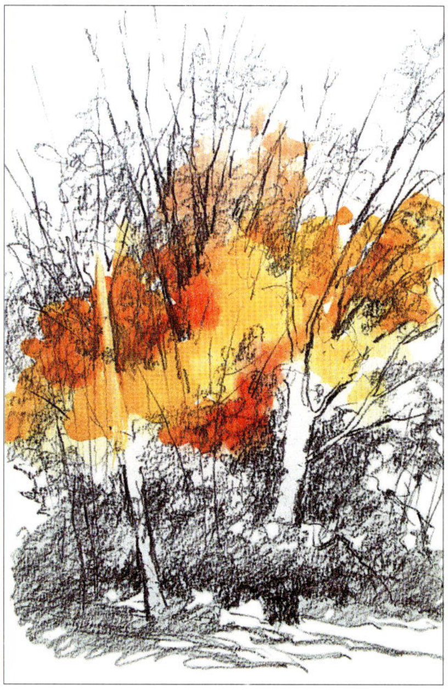

Starting Out
On a piece of 4-ply museum board, sketch your work using a 2B charcoal pencil and gouache. Again, the sketch seen here was made extra dark for you to see. Work loosely as you'll cover most of the charcoal with gouache.

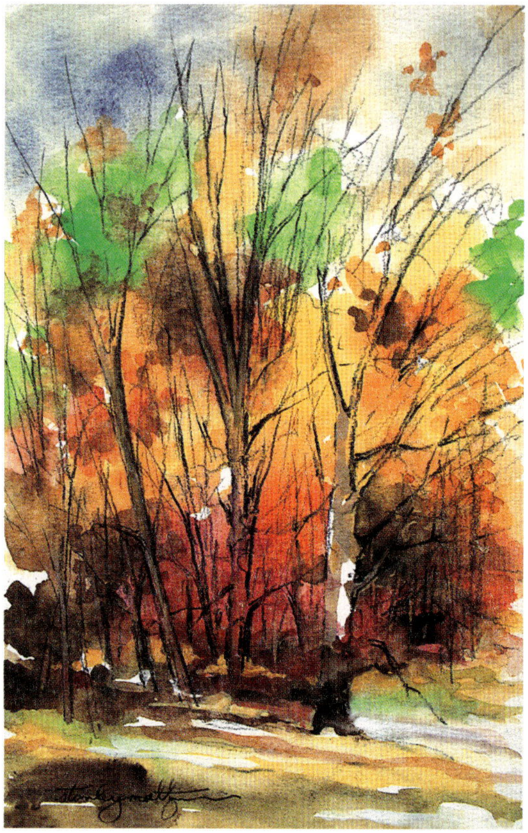

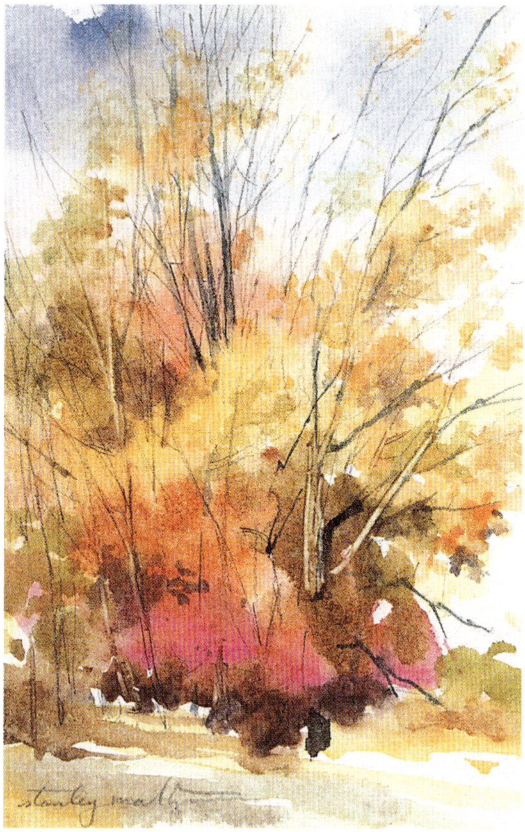

Experiment to Get a Different Look
As you proceed by adding more color, you can also wet the board, keeping the application of colors more pliable. Remember that the more water you use, the lighter and more diluted the color will be. If you feel that you have used too much water, you can easily add more paint. It all depends on what kind of look you want your picture to have, as shown by these two examples. Push the paint around — experiment!

THE FOUR SEASONS

This series of pictures gave me great pleasure and a wonderful feeling of accomplishment, not just because of the paintings, but because I planted this sugar maple and it seems to be happy in its surroundings.

All four pictures were worked on 4-ply museum board that has a neutral pH and is buffered to prevent the paper from turning brown. Also used were HB and 2B charcoal pencils. Besides improving the landscape with the addition of a tree, I also added some interesting subject matter to draw or paint.

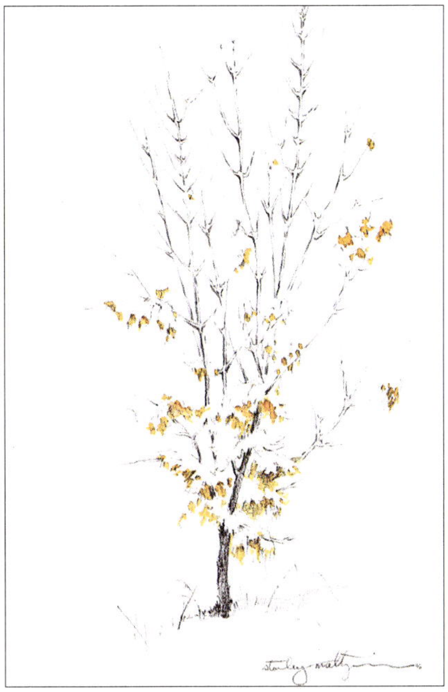

"Lady" is the name I gave to this tree years ago. One day after a snowfall I noticed the positioning of the snow on the autumn leaves. This appealed to me and thus the first of the Four Seasons paintings was created.

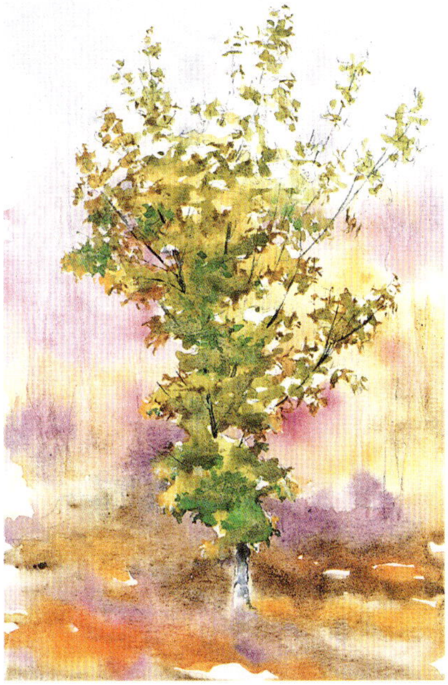

This spring scene at the end of a heavy rain gives the tree a bright feeling though the surroundings are fused and misty. You might find that your original charcoal sketch disappears as color is added over it. If you like the results, leave it alone; if not, put some of the charcoal drawing back into your picture. A Japanese calligraphy brush was used on this picture for putting the color down on the board.

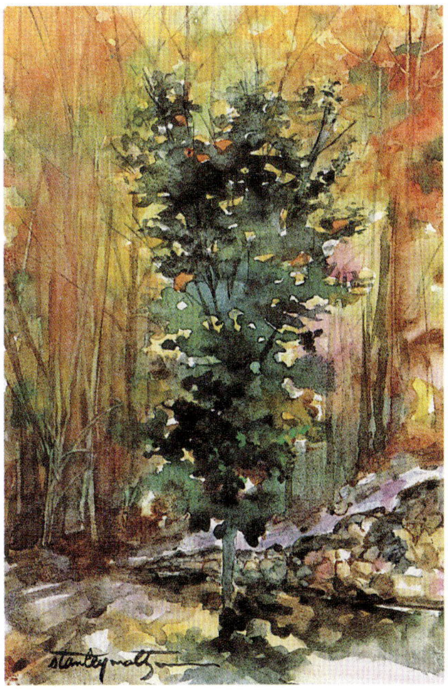

Here you see summer with full foliage and darker colors. In this case, I used backlighting to change the character. The wood pile was included with its plastic cover, and background trees were made a bit more prominent.

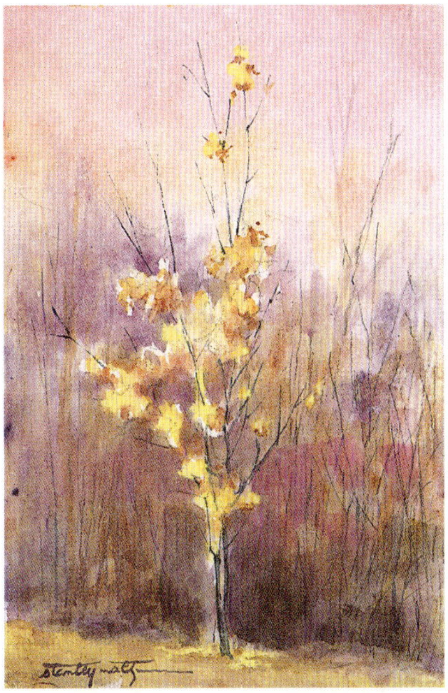

Autumn completes the four seasons. Gusty winds have taken most of the leaves, leaving a certain delicacy to the tree. Background colors are darker, bringing out the color of the autumn leaves.

THE FOREST

The type of drawing shown here on these two pages, where the artwork does not touch the edges of the paper, is called a *vignette*.

For this particular series, I selected a sheet of yellow Ingres paper manufactured by Hahnemuhle, an old German paper manufacturer. It's a laid paper, meaning that when the paper was produced the wet pulp was placed on a screen that, when dried, created a design of lines and dots on the paper. When a drawing is to be reduced for reproduction, this pattern enables your work to retain a sparkle by keeping the charcoal and Conté from filling in the shaded areas.

The yellow background creates the feeling of summer and is another instance where color can help create a mood. Try other color combinations to add excitement and interest in your drawings.

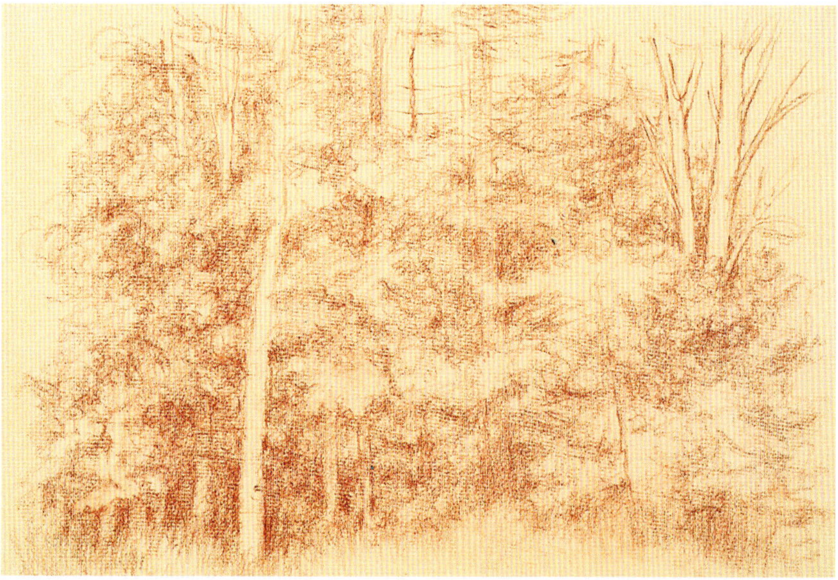

Step 1
Start your preliminary drawing by using either a Conté or Faber Castell sanguine pencil. Use whichever you like, as both brands are nice to work with.

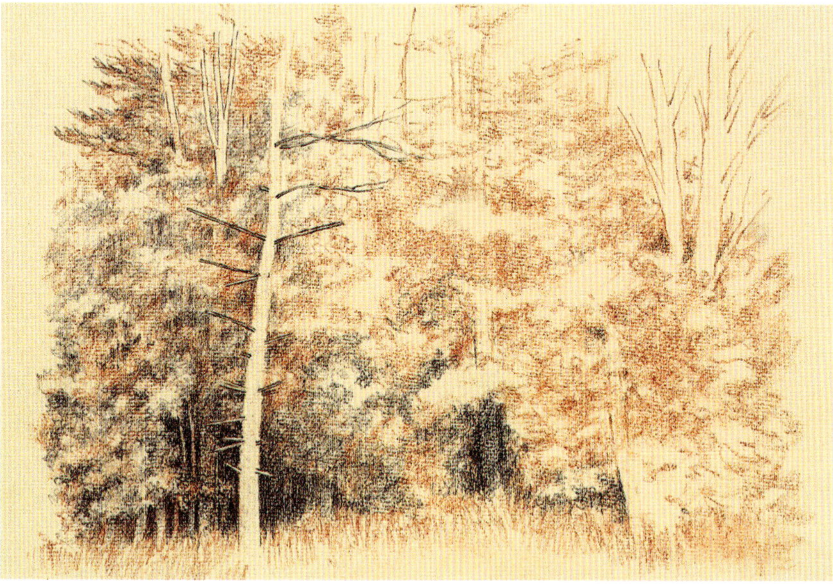

Step 2
Once you have laid in your sanguine preliminary sketch, switch to an HB, 2B or 4B charcoal pencil and start to give your trees, trunks and foliage definition. If you need darker darks, use either the 2B or 4B pencil. While you are working, remember not to cover all of your sanguine pencil. It is nice to leave some of the color showing through.

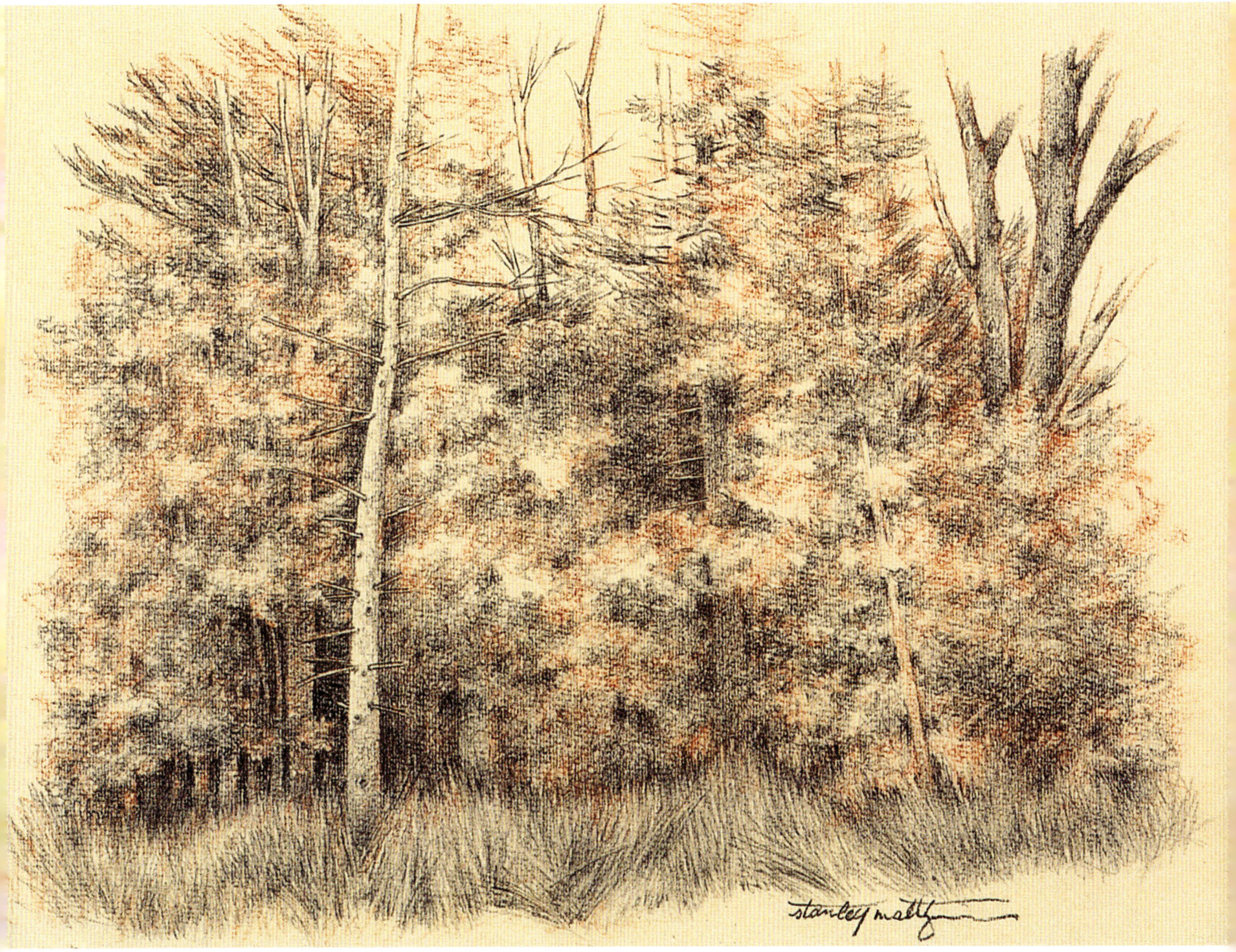

Step 3

Here is the completed drawing. The darkest colors are on the bases of the trees, with some darks scattered about for balance. If some of your fine lines (branches) disappear, cut a thin strip out of a piece of scrap paper, lay it over your filled-in area, and erase. A word of caution: Hold the paper tightly while erasing so you do not move it and create a smudge. This should give you nice thin, clean branches.

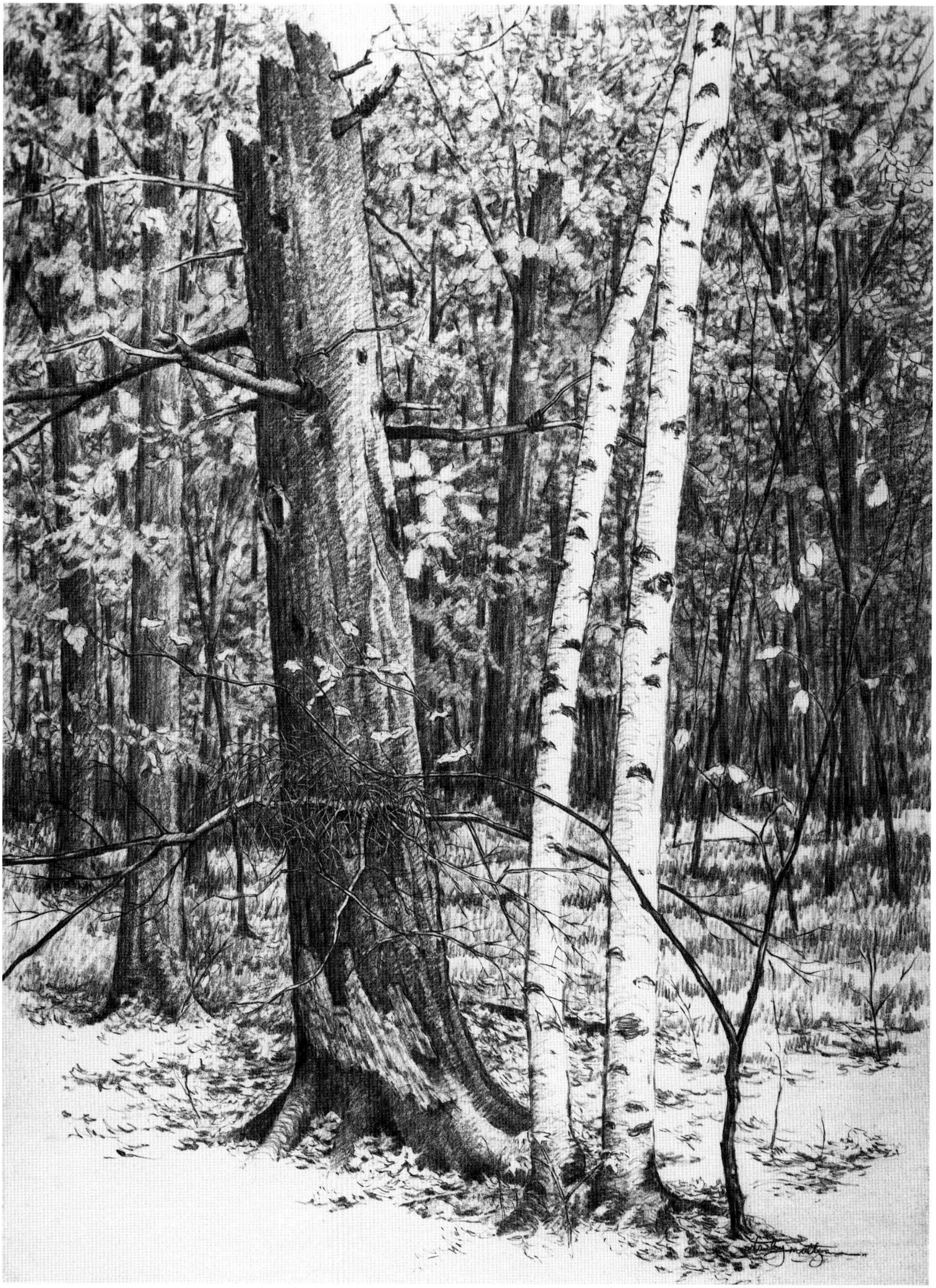

Flickering Lights, 22" x 31" (56cm x 79cm), charcoal on Japanese Misumi paper. Collection of Betsy Miller and David St. Germaine.

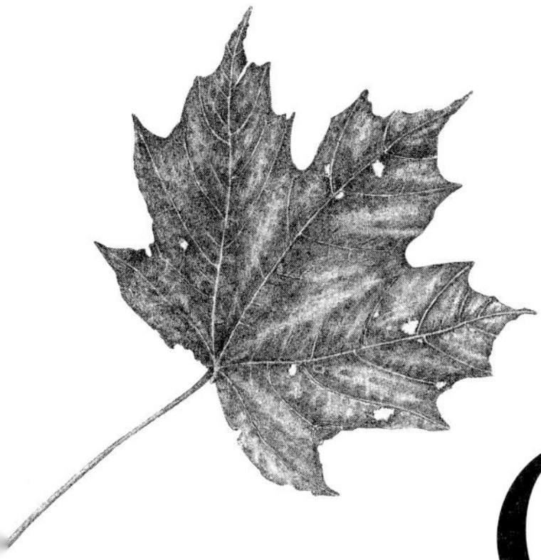

Conclusion

Once again, I have had the good fortune to walk through fields and woods with you and been able to share with you some of the many creations of nature, in this case the wonders of trees. I hope you are now aware of their eloquence, their strength and beauty, and the inspiration they can evoke whether the branches are full of leaves or they are leafless, baring their anatomy. In any season, they are waiting for you to capture them on beautiful papers in the various mediums of your choice. Experiment, discover and enjoy the wonders of the drawing medium.

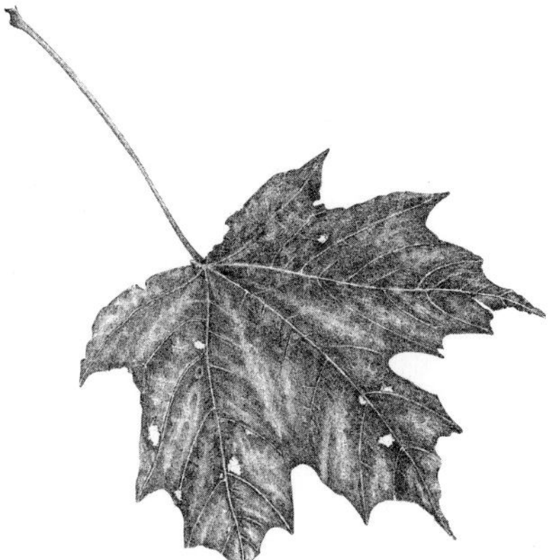

INDEX